INTRODUCTION

Suffolk's geological history has been well documented but its link with the development of the nation's fertiliser industry has received little coverage. Although the county has had few mineral resources of industrial importance there were several of interest to 19th century agriculturalists. This account looks at the exploitation of a fossil deposit found at the base of the Red Crag on the southeast Suffolk coast. It became an important raw material in the manufacture of the world's first artificial fertiliser and stimulated enormous geological interest in the area.

Few visitors to Felixstowe, Ipswich or the quiet, rural settlements on the Deben and Orwell estuaries, or even many of the residents, know of this area's role in the development of an industry of world importance. In the second part of the nineteenth century vast fortunes were made from the digging up, washing, transporting and processing of what were called 'coprolites', thought at the time to be fossilised droppings of fish, lizards and even dinosaurs! Ipswich Museum and others across the country were given or acquired extensive collections of the fossils.

The opportunities of making money were not lost on Ipswich's city fathers. Local entrepreneurs like William Colchester, Edward Packard, Joseph Fison and Thomas, Eustace, Edward and Manning Prentice capitalised on the fossil bed. Large landowners like Lord Rendlesham and Colonel Tomline made fortunes from the business. Even small landowners and farmers profited. The coprolite labourers' wages were significantly higher than those of the agricultural labourers. The income generated from the diggings provided a valuable stimulus to the local economy. Pubs opened, cottages were built and local traders benefited. What follows is an examination of the social, religious, economic and archaeological impact that this unusual industry had on the Suffolk parishes where the fossil deposit was worked.

I have to acknowledge the research work done by Robert Markham, Walter Tye, David Short, Betty Wooton, Richard Grove, Albert Sheldrick and Audrey Kiln. I would also like to acknowledge the assistance of the staff at the following institutions:-

Ipswich County Record Office,
Ipswich Borough Council Museums and Galleries,
Cambridgeshire County Record Office,
Hertfordshire County Record Office,
The Cambridge Collection, Cambridge,
Cambridge University Library,
Cambridge Folk Museum,
Ipswich Museum,
Rothamsted Archives
Sedgwick Museum, Cambridge,
The Public Record Office, Kew,
The Valence House Museum, Dagenham,
Oxford University Museum of Natural History,
Church Commissioners' Record Office, London,
Charity Commissioners' Record Office, London.

Many others have given snippets of information and encouragement but I would like to thank especially Giles Colchester, London, Roy Colchester, Mendlesham, and Colin Maycock, Boyton, but it is to the memory of those who worked in the diggings that this book is dedicated. Whilst considerable effort has been made to credit the sources, omissions will be rectified in the next edition.

19th CENTURY BACKGROUND

In 1845 a new industry started in Felixstowe, a small Victorian watering hole on the southeast Suffolk coast. It provided a very different occupation to agricultural work or domestic service. It involved the digging up, washing and sorting of a phosphate-rich bed of coprolites, barrowing it up a 'two-way-gang-plank' from the beach and emptying it into shallow draught lighters or sailing barges to be transported to manure works in Ipswich and elsewhere. The work was locally called 'fossiling' and helped fuel an international fossil mania. Over the next fifty years this new occupation provided a valuable source of income for many hundreds of families in this area.

Great Britain's population doubled over the first half of the 19th century. Improved health care reduced the death rate. There was better midwifery; more doctors and 'lying-in hospitals' were being built for women in labour. Smallpox inoculations were introduced after 1760, dispensaries opened and there was a general agreement that fresh air was good for one and that hygiene and ventilation should be improved. There was also a better diet with increased consumption of white bread and roast meat. Another factor was the strong tradition of having large families. Having ten children in a family was not uncommon.

With the increased wealth generated by the Industrial Revolution and trade with the British colonies and other countries of the world the gap widened between rich and poor. There were strong feelings about social inequality. One remembers Charles Dickens' novels about the lives of the underclass. Crime rates in both urban and rural areas were high. The gentry's response of hard labour, capital punishment and even transportation to Australia was commonplace. But beyond the rural communities of Suffolk there were dramatic changes taking place.

The 18th and 19th centuries saw developments during the Agricultural Revolution like labour-saving farm machinery and the

Enclosure Acts. In most of the country many of the poorer sections of society were forced off the land. People were attracted by the employment opportunities in urban factories following the inventions of the Industrial Revolution. There were also jobs in retail, commerce and administration. However, in Dymond and Northeast's book, *A History of* Suffolk, they state that most of Suffolk's enclosures took place before the 18th century. Just over a hundred acts were passed between 1770 and 1880 compared to some 2,500 in the rest of England. They included parishes with areas of lighter soil close to the southeast coast. Agricultural labourers' lives were still dominated by the farming gentry. Tied to their cottages, it took a brave labourer to criticise their employer.

The ending of the Napoleonic Wars with the defeat of the French at Waterloo in 1815 brought a period of peace and prosperity to much of Great Britain, but not to Suffolk. The round Martello towers along the Suffolk coast were no longer in a state of military preparedness. The price of a hundredweight (50.8 kg.) of Suffolk wheat, a commonly used measure of prosperity, dropped almost 50% in the first half of the 19th century. It ranged between 13s. 9d and 27s. 11d. (£0.69 and £1.39) in the first decade. From 1840 and 1849 it ranged between 10s.4d and 16s. 3d. (£0.52 and £0.81). While some of the impact would have been the Corn Laws, the overall effect on agriculture was disastrous. Suffolk spent one of the highest amounts on Parish Relief.

By 1816/17, the situation was desperate: farmers who had bought land now, found that it was not worth as much as they had borrowed, while those who leased land could not pay their rents. ...and farm workers found it impossible to manage on wages reduced by a third.

(Dymond, D. and Northeast, P (1995), *A History of Suffolk*, Darwen County History Series)

In most of the country, towns and cities expanded rapidly, especially those on the coalfields and alongside the major rivers, canals and, by the second half of the century, the railways. There was also significant out-migration from many rural parishes. In rural Suffolk, however, apart from in Ipswich and the market towns, levels of prosperity did not improve. Many people in the clothing industry had to find alternative work when mechanisation of the weaving process and new factories opening in the north brought the demise of what was a lucrative business. Many of them and some soldiers from Suffolk who returned from the wars may have gone back to farming as there was a growing demand for food from the growing towns and cities.

The exodus of the more motivated, younger sections of the community to the urban areas resulted in an enormous demand for cheap accommodation and food. The back yards of typical two-up two-down Victorian terraced houses did not have the gardens to grow fruit or vegetables or the space to keep a pig, goat or chickens. Having an outside toilet was a luxury. People needed to buy food from the High Street, the market or the corner shops. Victorian entrepreneurs were quick to recognise the growing demand. Small family-run concerns dominated the food retail business. As their profits grew they opened more shops, invested in better transport and had more money to buy from the farmers. If farmers could increase production there was more money to be made.

One can probably remember from one's schooldays Jethro Tull's seed drill, Lord 'Turnip' Townshend's four-course crop rotation method, Thomas Coke's land management methods and the Earl of Leicester and other agriculturalists' attempts at crossbreeding pigs, cattle and sheep. Experiments began in an attempt to increase crop production, partly because at the beginning of the 19th century Great Britain could no longer feed herself. She was a net importer of wheat and corn.

Over several thousand years people had experimented with adding a whole range of materials to the soil. In Suffolk local minerals like chalk and sand were used to lighten heavy soils and clay was added to improve lighter soils. Even seaweed and crushed or burnt shells were added! Since at least the early-1700s Suffolk farmers had been spreading a shelly material on their soils, locally called the 'Red Crag'. It was found on the coastal marshes and heathland between the Orwell and Alde estuaries. Its phosphatic nature proved useful on the infertile sandy soils. The 1838 Ordnance Survey map of the area shows numerous crag and clay pits. For centuries the Red Crag had been used as road filling material. In the wet weather cartwheels and the hooves of horses, sheep and cattle being driven to market, left huge ruts in the roads and farm tracks, especially on sloping land. This slowed down and caused inconvenience for traffic.

THE EARLY USES OF THE FOSSILS

Walter Tye, an employee of Fisons in the 1920s, researched the origins of the fertiliser industry. It started about five miles (8 km) southeast of Ipswich. He quoted from a 1764 book by John Kirby who claimed that its origin was due to an accidental discovery by Edmund Edwards:

"In a Farmers Yard in Levington, clofe on the left as you enter from Levington into the faid Chapel Field of Stratton Hall, was dug the firft Crag of Shell that have been found ufeful for improving the land in this and other Hundreds in the neighbourhood. For though it appears from Books of Agriculture, that the like manure has long been ufeful in the Weft of England, it was not ufed here till this Difcovery was cafually made by one Edmund Edwards, about the year 1718. This man, being covering a Field with Muck out of his yard, and wanting a load of two to finifh it, carried fome of the Soil that laid near the Muck, tho' it looked to him no better than Sand; but obferving the Crop to be beft where he laid that, he was from thence encouraged to carry more of it the next year; and the success he had, encouraged others to do the like. There is no need for me to explain that Edmund Edwards' discovery was soon broadcast throughout south-east Suffolk, where the crag was found. Large quantities were very soon carried and scattered over the heaths

and sheep-walks, where the soil had always been hungry and inadequately fed."

This use of what was locally called the 'Red Crag' was noted in the mid-19th century in White's 1844 *History, Gazetteer and Directory of Suffolk*. It described the extent of the operation, its uses and some of its limitations.

"The Crag is a singular mixture of cockle and other shells, found in great masses, in most of the parishes extending from Dunwich to the Orwell and Woolverstone Park; it is both red and white, but mostly the former colour and the shells are broken as to resemble sand. ... There are pits of it to be seen in various places, from which it has been got to a depth of from 15 to 20 feet, for improving heaths; but on lands long of tillage, it is not much used, and upon light soils it has been found to make sands blow more."

OTHER ADDITIONS TO THE SOIL

Other natural remains had been found to have a marked effect on plant growth. Coal and wood ash from household fires were emptied onto the contents of the privy and cesspit to reduce the liquidity and smell. Another reason was its fertilising properties. Ash was often sieved over the garden to remove the cinders that were put back on the fire. The human manure was then shovelled into buckets and added to the rot heap to further decompose before being added to improve the soil. Even today Anglia Water provides Suffolk farmers with your treated sewage.

Animal manure had been used for thousands of years. Cow, pig, horse, sheep, goat and chicken manure is still used today but in the 18th and 19th centuries it was not available in large enough quantities to make more than a localised impact. Decomposed seaweed worked especially well but it was mostly used in coastal areas. The transport costs made it prohibitive further inland. Dried animal blood was used, even crushed and burnt animal bones. It is said that the word bonfire comes from bone fire. Soot, ground and dried fish and even rags from discarded wool and cotton clothes were tried on the fields. Maybe one can remember the rag and bone man?

There was a keen interest in the sciences during the Industrial Revolution. One field where research took place was with plants. The application of science and capital was being expended on agriculture as it had been on the manufacturing industry. Once the analytical chemists acknowledged that phosphate was a major nutrient in plant growth, the search was on to discover new supplies.

In 1828 phosphorite, a rock phosphate started being exploited in Ontario, Canada. Chemists had found its value as a fertiliser and samples were tested in Great Britain. When Alexander Von Humboldt, the Prussian naturalist and explorer, returned to Europe in 1805 after a six-year journey round South America, he published a report which included details of the coastline and the ocean current which was named after him. It also described the plants, animals and minerals he had seen. This led to the Europeans 'discovering' the use of 'huano' or guano. This was an accumulation of up to 450 feet (150 m) of phosphate-rich bird droppings that had impregnated discarded fish carcasses, feathers and skeletons of sea lions, pelicans, boobies, penguins, black skimmers, black cormorants, red-legged cormorants, Incan terns and gulls on the Chincha Islands off the coast of Peru. The locals would not excavate it because of the smell so American entrepreneurs brought indentured Chinese labour across the Pacific to work it. Shipping companies started to import it into Ipswich docks from 1838 where it was sold at up to £14 per ton. This was the most expensive fertiliser on the market but a successful advertising campaign in the pages of *The Gardeners Chronicle, Agricultural Gazette* and *The Mark Lane Express* led to its widespread usage.

In other parts of the country, particularly on the chalk downlands in the southeast of England, farmers were using a deposit of phosphatic chalk marl on their hop fields. Marling was the practice of adding the material found along the junction of the chalk and clay deposits to the fields. Reports on the varying success of these applications appeared in the *Agricultural Journal* and *Gardeners Chronicle* that entrepreneurial agriculturalists read with enthusiasm. In Norfolk the chalk, sand and gravel had been widely exploited, as had the boulder clay that underlay the greater part of the district.

Undated photograph of guano workings on Chincha Island, Peru.
The deposits were up to 80 feet (29.6 m.) thick.
(Clayton, A. (1985), *W.R. Grace & Co. The Formative years,* Jameson Books, Illinois)

CLAY, BONES AND CHINA

The London Clay in Suffolk had been worked from as early as 1639 and the London Delftware potters were reported to regard it very highly. A field of Potter's Clay in Boyton is said to have had double the calcium carbonate content normally required and was so much in demand that it was shipped to Holland and Pennsylvania (Maycock, C. (1993), 'Charity, Clay and Coprolites – The Story of a Suffolk Almshouse Foundation', Mary Warner's Charity, Boyton, p.10).

One has probably heard of bone china. Why bone? In 1797 Josiah Spode introduced the ancient Chinese idea of adding bone ash to the clay to produce a hard ivory-white, translucent porcelain. Other potters quickly followed suit. Josiah Wedgewood was manufacturing it by 1812 and so increased demand for bones.

In the 1830s Baron Von Justus Liebig, the German analytical chemist, determined that the main constituents of animal bones were carbonate of lime and phosphate of lime. He recognised that lime and nitrate were important nutrients absorbed by the root system that improved plant growth. His tests with ground bones showed that they took a long time to decompose, as they were not immediately soluble in water. In 1839 he suggested that bones could be used to produce super phosphate of lime by dissolving them in acid.

The first success in using bone dust commercially was attributed to farmers in Sheffield. They took advantage of the waste product of the Sheffield cutlers and sparked greater interest in bones. It was found that the fine dust and shavings from their carved and ground bone knife handles proved a very effective fertiliser when added to the soil. Augustus Voelcker, the analytical chemist of the Royal Agricultural Society, commented in 1862 that:

"... bone dust was almost the only artificial manure which was applied to the land. The general use to arable land is reported to have been in the neighbourhood of Sheffield, where a large quantity of fine dust was made in turning and preparing knife handles. For some time this was to be had at a small cost; but like everything else that is really good, its value increased and very soon the supply was not equal to the demand. Consequently bones were collected in the neighbourhood of Sheffield, and mills erected for crushing them into dust; and in a few years the consumption of this manure extended considerably in the counties of York, Lincoln, Nottingham and Chester. The demand for bones so rapidly increased that large quantities were and still are imported from abroad. But neither the home nor foreign supply of bones was at all adequate to meet the demand for a manure which was found to be specially useful in the growth of turnips and other green crops."

The corn mills used by the agricultural suppliers were not able to meet the demand for bone meal and this led to the setting up of bone manure works. Given that Great Britain was at the height of its empire in the 19th century there were many parts of the world from where bones could be imported. The bone trade led to the erection of bone crushing mills in Ipswich and other coastal ports. Entrepreneurs were quick to recognise the profits to be made from importing foreign supplies. They set up manure companies to provide the county's farmers with this new form of fertiliser. There were reports of thousands of mummified Egyptian cats and sun-bleached bones from the Sahara Desert finding their way into the crushing mills. Their most popular products were half-inch bones. These were burnt or crushed and added to the soil as bone meal. This was enough to prompt Liebig to comment that:

"Great Britain is like a ghoul, searching the continents for bones to feed its agriculture ... robbing all other countries of the condition of her fertility. Already in her eagerness for bones she has turned up the battlefields of Leipzig, Waterloo, and of the Crimea; already from the catacombs of Sicily she has carried away the skeletons of many successive generations."

As knowledge of the bone trade became more widespread, concerns were expressed in some quarters. Given the money to be made, it did not deter those involved in the trade. Rev. Brodie, a religious academic with an interest in geology, wrote an article in 1872 on the phosphatic materials being used in agriculture and commented that:

"... some persons have an antipathy to bone manures, under the idea that they are apt to be used by fraudulent millers and bakers, to mix with the flour. But as the former article is expensive and usually more expensive than the latter, they need not have much fear on this account. Perhaps they are not aware that the Pyramids are rifled of their contents by cunning Arabs; and Egyptian Mummies are imported into this country, and the dust largely employed, especially in Norfolk and Suffolk, as a bone-manure; so that indirectly some of us may be deriving our bread food from truculent Egyptian Pharaohs, and dark-eyed beauties of Thebes and Memphis. I cannot say what they might have thought of the matter if they had known that in future ages their dust would have been employed to improve the soil of a little far distant and then unknown island, which has since helped to people and civilize a large portion of the known world."

By 1839 the bone business was worth £250,000 per annum and about 30,000 tons were being imported annually. The agricultural press gave detailed accounts of the efficacy of these new manures. The major criticisms were that crushed bones had proved to be slow to dissolve in the soil water so it took a long time before their mineral potential could be fully absorbed by the plant roots. Bones were also expensive and the machinery for grinding them had not been perfected (Graham, J. (1839), 'A Treatise on the Use and Value of Manure', London p.6; Pusey, P. (1840), Journal of the Royal Agricultural Society (J.R.A.S.), England, p.1).

CHANGES IN RURAL LIFE

Life in the agricultural communities where these new ideas were being practised was not the quiet and peaceful rural idyll that characterised traditional images of country life. There were tremendous economic and social changes brought about in the nineteenth century. The introduction of the Enclosure Acts after 1799, many of them on the lighter soils by the coast, generated extensive parklands for the wealthy classes: Freston Park, Wherstead Park, Hollbrook Park, Rence Park and Orwell Park to name but a few. Instead of the open fields of ridge and furrow, commons and fallow fields used since medieval times, larger fields were seen, surrounded by fences, hedges or walls. Harsh trespass laws were introduced and in some estates mantraps were set to deter poachers. Many landless peasants were forced off the land when they lost the right to use the open fields. The loss of gleaning rights after harvest, the loss of the common for grazing animals and poultry, the denial of access to the newly fenced or walled in woodland reduced their 'free' catch of rabbit, pheasant, partridge, nuts and wild fruit. The reduced demand for labour meant farmers did not take on as many men and women at harvest time. The 'hiring fairs' where men and women were taken on according to the decorations they wore in their lapels, began to die out. David Ellison, the Cambridgeshire local historian, commented on the 'startling' social effects that resulted.

"The repeal of the Corn Laws and the lower prices of corn for farmers had made them all try to save costs by mechanisation and reducing their labour forces... farm labourers had often noticed the immense gulf between themselves with their £25 to £30 a year, and the rectors with £300 - £400, comfortable rectories, and often land as well as house servants."

Suffolk agriculture was in depression until the 1850s. The implementation of the new technology introduced during the 'Agricultural Revolution' had a dramatic impact on some rural villages. Ransomes of Ipswich made a fortune manufacturing agricultural equipment and the development of the steam engine allowed much more than four horse-power to be put to work in the fields. New steam-powered agricultural machinery, designed to save time and labour, was introduced by farmers who were keen to profit from the increased demand for food. These machines, like the steam traction engine, seed drill, threshing machine, elevator and deep plough, resulted in an increasing number of redundancies in farm labour. Whilst some people developed useful mechanical skills there was widespread unrest in most rural communities.

Many people were forced off the land. Agricultural labourers had been and were still entirely dependent on the farmers for their livelihood. They were often provided with a tied cottage from which they could easily be evicted at the whim of the farmer or farm bailiff. Not being seen at church for the Sunday service was a dismissible offence. Going into the public house before the farmer and farm bailiff arrived after church was unwise. Crowds waited at the door in deference. There was considerable poverty and overcrowding in crumbling 'shit and stubble' or wattle and daub thatched cottages in many rural villages.

The more motivated sections of the community, mainly young adult males and females, left the countryside to find employment in the industrial towns and cities where better paid factory, office or domestic work was available. Some were attracted by the numerous advertisements in the local press to emigrate. Hard working, temperate labourers and craftsmen were attracted by advertisements in the local press that offered employment and land in the colonies in Canada, South Africa, Australia and New Zealand. But it was another enterprise that slowed down this out-migration and very much brought this area of Suffolk into the Victorian era of industrial and economic change.

Most of the villagers were engaged as agricultural labourers on the local farms and large estates or were employed as domestics in some of the country houses of the gentry. Wealthier landowners lived in larger properties employing domestic servants and having extensive gardens whilst the majority of the villagers lived in small, cramped, thatched cottages with a small garden for growing fruit and vegetables, keeping a pig, goats and chickens.

When families got together at Easter and Christmas and for baptisms, marriages and funerals, stories of the changes in rural and urban life would have been common. With improvements in education and increases in the numbers of pamphlets, newspapers and journals, there was a growing awareness of the disparity between town and countryside. For those who were unable to leave, some manifested their dissatisfaction with the state of affairs by acts of vandalism. This period, known as 'The Swing' after the number of hangings of offenders, saw incidences of farm machinery being destroyed and haystacks, barns and fields set alight. Farmhouse windows were smashed and sometimes farms burnt down (Fowle, K. (1992), *'Coton through the Ages'*). However, the discovery of a fossil seam reduced this unrest in southeast Suffolk. As shall be seen, this dissatisfaction diminished during the coprolite years with higher wages and a variety of new jobs available.

COPROLITES

What were these 'coprolites'? When they were first discovered they were thought to be fossilised droppings. There are numerous variations of their spelling, due in part to the poor literacy of the census enumerator but also to variations in local dialect. They include coprolite, copperlight, copper light, copperlite, coupperlite, copralite, corporolite, coprelite, coproilite, coperlite, coporlite, coparlite, coprolithe and coperalite. No wonder there was confusion over their origin (analysis of the 1861–1891 census data).

The word came from the Greek 'kopros' meaning dung and 'lithos' meaning stone. Dung stone - fossilised droppings! Rev. William Buckland, the Dean of Westminster, coined it when he was the first professor of Geology and Mineralogy at the University of Oxford. In

1829 he went on a geological excursion to the Dorset coast at Lyme Regis. Maybe you have heard of Mary Anning, the woman from Lyme Regis who made a living selling fossils specimens to enthusiastic collectors. Examining the clay and sands exposed by a recent landslip he found the complete fossil remains of an ichthyosaurus. Unusually, it also included its fossilised stomach contents.

A TRUE ECCENTRIC

Liebig accompanied him on the excursion. Although he was fascinated with the finds, the Dean was obsessed. Buckland had a tabletop inlaid with slices of polished coprolites as well as making earrings out of them! It is unknown if he wore them! His dinner parties were very entertaining. A jackal stalked the hall. Guinea pigs lived in his study. A bear used to wander around the dining room behind his guests and a monkey sat on his neck or on furniture near the window. The menu often included samples from across the food chain, starting from plants and working up through the animal kingdom! The worst tastings were reportedly moles and bluebottles! Dinnertime conversations must have included a challenge to the established religious circles. Buckland had found tiny bones of baby ichthyosaurus in the coprolites. This meant that ichthyosaurus ate ichthyosaurus. They were cannibals! This contradicted the fundamental religious belief that life before Adam was one of peace and harmony. Some argued that Adam and Eve frolicked with dinosaurs in the Garden of Eden. Maybe the issue was discussed over dinner with Mr and Mrs Mantell who were the first to report 'iguanodon' remains in Sussex in 1822 and Sir Richard Owen, the anatomist who first came up with the word dinosaur to mean 'terrible lizard'. Owen was just as eccentric. On New Year's Eve 1853 he invited twenty scientists to a dinner party inside a life-size model of an iguanodon in a London park!

NEW DEVELOPMENTS

Experiments using the hard coprolites showed that, when ground to a powder, like bones they took a long time to break down and be fully absorbed by plant roots. Sir James Murray of Dublin, the Irish doctor who invented Milk of Magnesia, had successfully dissolved bones with vitriol, the then term for sulphuric acid, in as early as 1820. Tests in 1835 by Escher, a German chemist, found that the resulting mixture was soluble in water. This was confirmed during Liebig's tests on the chemical composition of bones. He found that, when dried and added to the soil, it was a super phosphate, soluble in water and far more beneficial for the plants than ordinary manures. He did some tests on Buckland's coprolites and his analysis showed that they had a high phosphate content, a mineral much needed in plant growth. In his 1840 work, *'Organic Chemistry in its Application to Agriculture & Physiology'*, he pointed out that:

"The fertility of the soil of England is diminishing in consequence of the too frequent repetition of Corn crops; but that the Fertility may be restored by applying to the land the coprolites or Beds of Fossil Guano which are known to exist in some of the Chalk and Limestone Strata."

In 1842 he was granted a patent for making the world's first compound fertiliser, a dry superphosphate made from phosphates and potash. However, as it had to be held together with lime which made it insoluble. Despite this, he went on to advocate the more general use of phosphates, pointing out to farmers and agriculturalists that *"a field in which phosphate of lime or the alkaline phosphates form no part of the soil is totally incapable of producing grain, peas or beans"* (Liebig (1843), *'Familiar Letters of Chemistry'*). Demand for phosphates began to rise.

JOHN BENNET LAWES' "DISCOVERY"

One of Liebig's students, Mr Gilbert, was friendly with John Bennet Lawes, a Hertfordshire landowner, who was experimenting with different manures on his estate in Rothamsted. It has been suggested that Lawes learned of Liebig's methods from Gilbert, as he too successfully dissolved animal bones, mineral phosphorite and Felixstowe coprolites in vitriol in the 'den' in his barn. The resulting mixture, once dried and bagged, he initially termed bisulphate but later he called it 'super phosphate of lime'. His tests showed that it was soluble and that the plant roots could rapidly absorb it. He experimented with it on plants in pots and test beds and found it to be an extremely effective manure, especially for root crops. This was the world's first artificial chemical manure! Immediately, he recognised the enormous commercial potential of such a 'discovery'. He called it 'super' and realised that its application would so dramatically increase turnip yields that it would be much in demand by the nation's farmers.

They were eager to improve supplies of winter fodder. This was because once farmers had got the harvest in and knew how much fodder was available over winter, large numbers of surplus cattle, sheep and pigs had to be slaughtered. Meat commanded higher prices over winter until the new stock was brought onto the market in spring. Any way of providing increased fodder therefore would be very popular with farmers. In 1839, despite his colleagues and his mother being appalled that a gentleman should go into trade, especially manure, he ignored both and set up 'Lawes Chemical Manure Company'.

Caricature of J.B. Lawes in *Vanity Fair* 8th July 1882

SIR JOHN B. LAWES, BART.

John Bennet Lawes (1814 – 1900) of Rothamsted, Harpenden, took out the patent of superphosphate in 1842. He sold his coprolite and fertiliser interests in 1872 for £30,000. (Courtesy of Rural History Centre, Reading University, Lawes Collection No. 60)

Accordingly, on the 23rd May 1842, Lawes was granted a patent for certain improvements of manures. Its detail was found in a document in the archive of Rothamsted Research.

1 - By means of sulphuric acid, decomposing "bones, bone ash, bone dust, apatite, phosphorite, and other phosphoritic substances" for purposes of manure.

2. - Combining for manurial purposes phosphoric acid with any particular alkali, as potash or soda or magnesia or ammonia, or any earth containing such alkalis.

3. - Making a manure by combining silica (in the state of ground flint or sand) with either potash or soda, or applying as manure crystal or glass ground to powder."

It was hardly a coincidence that, on exactly the same day, Sir James Murray took out a similar patent for the improvement of manures in Scotland. Lawes' patent was only valid up to Berwick upon Tweed. Adding to the confusion is the fact that a Scot, William Hay of Tillydesk, Ellon, according to his monument in the churchyard of St. Nicholas in Aberdeen, *"introduced and gave name to the manure called superphosphate in 1842"*. Who then was actually the first to discover superphosphate is uncertain.

The barn at Rothamsted where Lawes' "super" was first made. A pond outside was where his labourers could wash off splashes of sulphuric acid.

Inside Lawes' barn at Rothamsted where his 'super' experiments took place.
Notice the huge carboys of vitriol.
(Courtesy of Rural History Centre, Reading University, Lawes Collection No. 43)

Lawes' patent annoyed Liebig who claimed that he had been the first to produce superphosphate. Instead of going on a planned Grand Tour of Europe for his honeymoon, Lawes took his new wife on a trip down the Thames. With a keen eye for a suitable site for a factory he spotted one at Deptford Creek. He bought the plot and over the next few years had a large chemical manure works constructed that was capable of producing up to 200 tons of superphosphate a week. He sold his 'super' at up to £7 a ton and took legal action against Liebig and others to ensure that anyone who wanted to use his patent had to pay him five shillings (£0.25) for every ton they produced (Dyke, G.V. (1993), *'John Lawes of Rothamsted - Pioneer of Science, Farming and Industry'*, Hoos Press, Harpenden, p.15).

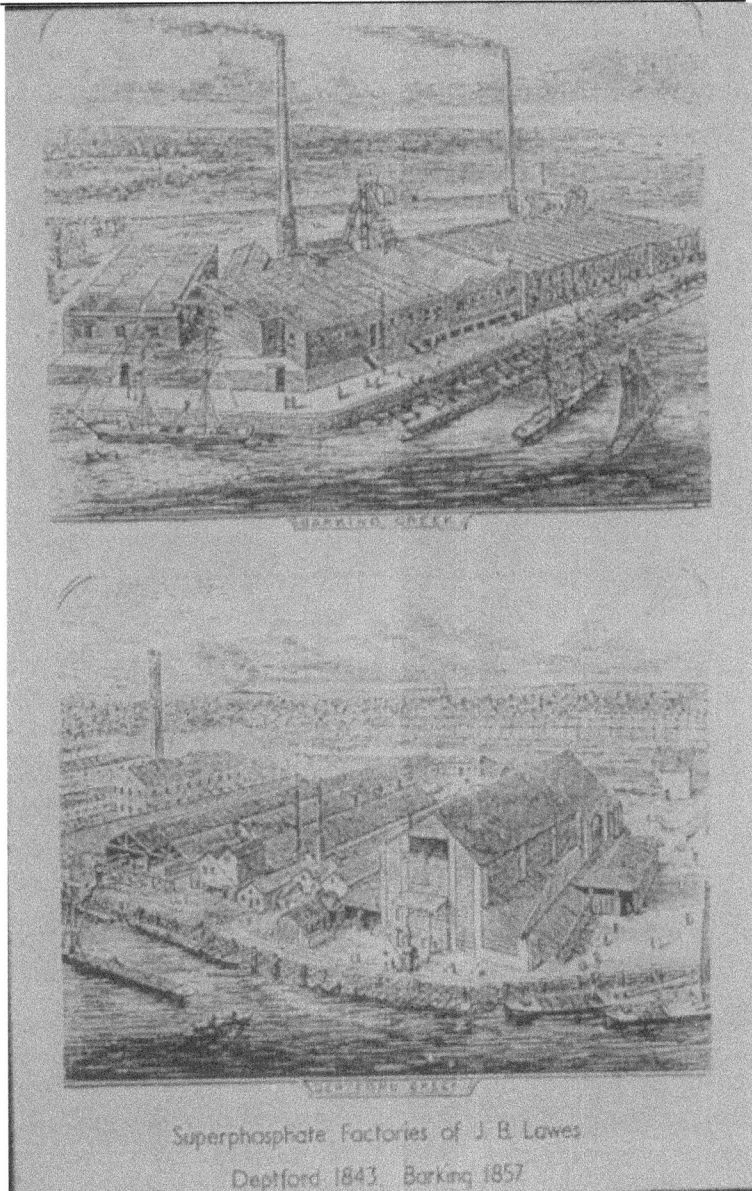

Superphosphate Factories of J. B. Lawes
Deptford 1843 Barking 1857

(Courtesy of Lawes Agricultural Trust, Rothamsted Agricultural Station)

Although Lawes' superphosphate was not as effective as the popular guano, he marketed it in the agricultural press at half the cost. As well as being used to get rid of smells from cesspits and dung heaps, it proved very popular as turnip manure, dramatically increasing yields. This in turn increased meat and milk yields that benefited farmers across the country and resulted in a growing demand for Lawes' new manure.

Rev. John Stevens Henslow 1796 – 1861, the vicar of Henslow whose discovery of 'coprolites' at Felixstowe led to the birth of a multi-million pound industry
http://www.gruts.com/darwin/articles/2000/henslow/index.php

PROFESSOR JOHN HENSLOW

A similar discovery but one with far reaching implications was made in 1843. Rev. John Henslow, the professor of Botany and Mineralogy at St. John's College, Cambridge, was given a living in the Suffolk parish of Hitcham in 1837 with £1,000 a year. He did not move in until two years later and, soon afterwards, he went on an excursion to the Victorian watering hole of Felixstowe. Accompanying him were two local men with an interest in geology, William Colchester and Charles Prestwich. Exploring the exposure created by a recent landslip in the Red Crag cliffs Henslow made a discovery that led to the development of a new multi-million pound industry that was to dramatically influence the economy of the local area. It was in 'Reminiscences of a Scientific Suffolk Clergyman' in the *Eastern Counties Magazine & Suffolk Notebook* that Henslow's contribution to "*one of the most remarkable commercial industries which arose entirely from his purely scientific knowledge of geology*" was described.

"*It was in the year 1843 that Professor J. S. Henslow and his family were staying for a few weeks at Felixstowe, a village on the east coast; and although at that time generally condemned as a watering place, yet it is seated in one of the finest bays in England, with excellent and safe bathing. It possesses a maritime flora of much interest, and cliffs consisting of some of the most remarkable of our British Strata. On the north of Felixstowe high cliffs face the sea, the lower and greater portion consisting of the Lower Eocene bed, 'London Clay', a bluish-grey clay bed, crumbling under exposure to the atmosphere, unfossiliferous, but abounding in septaria and nodular masses of stone, from one to three feet in diameter. Vast quantities of these were collected out at sea for the purpose of making 'Roman' cement. A little flotilla of boats used often be seen a mile or so out, dredging for them.*"

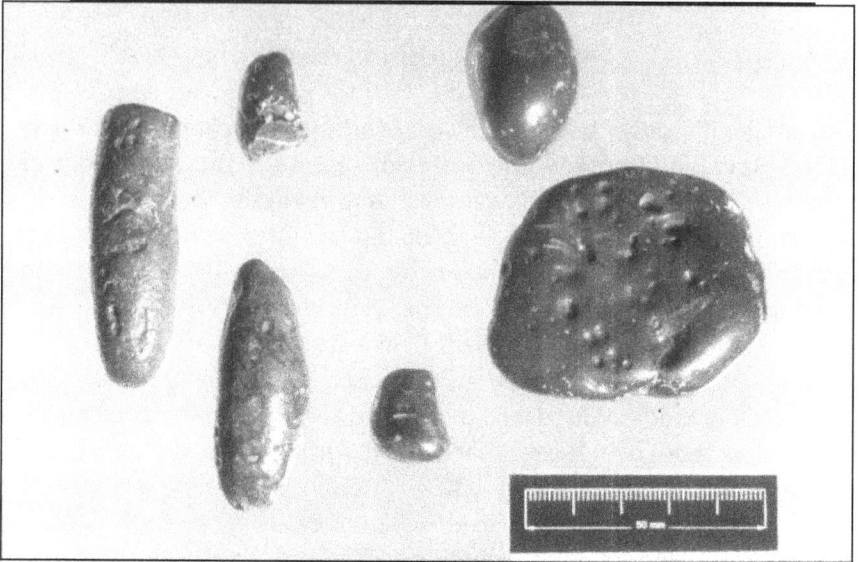

Suffolk coprolites found on the beach at Felixstowe
(Photograph courtesy of Earth Sciences Museum, Cambridge)

At the bottom of the cliffs in the north of the bay (about OS. 305343) he found some interesting fossils. There was a huge bed of them. From their smooth, brown, elongated shape he was convinced they must be fossilised dung, similar to those of the ichthyosaur discovered by Buckland. Maybe he had noticed cartloads of the Crag being removed and enquired as to their use from the local farm labourers. As they had been used on the fields for generations he suspected that there was an enormous potential of using these fossils for manurial purposes. If they could be ground into a powder and dissolved in sulphuric acid then a new industry could be created. Unaware of any chemical analysis of the deposit being done, Henslow was convinced that "they must all be considered as of coprolitic origin" (Henslow (1845), *Quarterly Journal of the Geological Society, (Q.J.G.S.),* Vol. I p.35). As a wide range of animal manure was being put onto the fields and the Felixstowe coprolites were available in vast quantities, Henslow thought that they could be used for the same purpose. As his clerical position did not allow him to engage in pecuniary speculations he made further investigations. In a letter he wrote in 1848 to the *Agricultural Gazette* he informed readers that:

"In 1844, I enquired of a person at Felixstowe, engaged in collecting the iron pyrites which are strewed along the coast, wherever the London Clay is exposed, as far as the Isle of Sheppey, and which is collected in large quantities for the manufacture of green copperas; and he agreed with me in considering that the nodules might be collected at a much cheaper rate per ton than the iron pyrites; and also that many hundreds of tons could be procured with little trouble."

COPPERAS OR GREEN VITRIOL

Tim Allen and Geoffrey Pike's research into the industry at Tankerton, near Whitstable across the Thames estuary in Kent, shows that copperas, or green vitriol, is a form of ferrous sulphate ($FeSO_4 7H_2O$), extracted from iron pyrite-rich nodules found with septaria in the Eocene clay deposits on the southeast Suffolk coast. It was used extensively in the textile and metallurgical industries but also as printers' ink, a tanning agent for leather and in the manufacture of gunpowder. In metallurgy it was a key ingredient in the production of nitric acid (*aqua fortis*) and vitriol (sulphuric acid) from which chlorine was produced. Chlorine was used as a bleaching agent in the textile industry while copperas itself was used as a dye fixative for woollens. It was a valuable raw material and its extraction stimulated a lot of local industry. The following account of the industry must have been the same in Suffolk:

"The process of producing copperas is extensively documented in 17th century sources and these accounts, together with the surviving inventories of tools and equipment, make the task of reconstructing the manufacturing process a relatively straightforward one.
"The copperas stones were collected from the seashore and placed in 'beds' which could measure up to one hundred and sixteen feet long by fifteen feet broad and twelve feet deep. The beds were lined with

clay or chalk and filled with stones to a depth of around two feet. Several such beds were attached to the Tankerton works. The stones were left to weather for up to six years, towards the end of which time they would begin to produce a large quantity of liquid, described as liquor in contemporary accounts. This liquid, a diluted solution of hydrated ferrous sulphate and sulphuric acid, flowed down plank-lined channels into a cistern housed in a boiler house. At Tankerton one large cistern measured eighty feet by nine feet and the complex included at least two other, smaller, cisterns. From the cistern the liquid was pumped into a lead boiler positioned over a coal-fuelled furnace set in a firing pit. Scrap iron was placed in the boiler and the liquid added to it. During the subsequent twenty days over which the boiling took place further scrap iron was added. At Tankerton, one of the boilers described in surviving documents measured over twelve feet square and took an initial one hundred pounds of iron, followed by a further fifteen hundred pounds during the boiling process. As the liquor was reduced by evaporation, more was added.

"When it was deemed to be sufficiently concentrated the liquor was tapped off into a cooling tank where it remained for up to fifteen days. The Tankerton coolers are described as being twenty-nine feet long by six feet and six inches wide. As the solution cooled the copperas (hydrated ferrous sulphate) crystallised on the bottom and sides of the tank, reaching a depth of around five inches. In some copperas works bundles of twigs were placed in the tank to promote crystallisation. The remaining solution was drained into a second cooler and reboiled.

"The ferrous sulphate crystals were collected, heated to melting point and poured into moulds. The resulting cakes were packed in barrels for transport.

"Some changes to the process were made during the 17th century, mainly to improve the efficiency of the boiling, but otherwise it appears to have remained relatively unchanged throughout the 18th century."

(http://www.eng-h.gov.uk/archcom/projects/summarys/html97_8/2059.htm)

In 1845 Henslow read a paper in Cambridge to the British Association for the Advancement of Science. It dealt with their potential value to the nation's farmers. Aware of its economic potential as a raw material in the manure industry he suggested that the Suffolk coprolites could be a useful source of manure. His opinion that they were *"sufficiently abundant to make it worth while to collect"* sparked the commercial interests of a number of local manure manufacturers. According to *Kelly's Post Office Directory*'s entry for Woodbridge the diggings started the same year:

"Since 1845, considerable excavations have been made in the neighbourhood for 'coprolites' so called. These phosphatised nodules are found in the crag. They are chemically prepared and are extensively used for agricultural purposes. The diggings have brought to light numerous fossils, which appear to have been washed from the London clay and other strata, as they present, like the nodules, a water-worn appearance."

The Distribution of Great Britain's Coprolite Industry 1842 - 1904

EARLY EXPLOITATION OF THE SUFFOLK COPROLITES

Lawes arranged to test two tons of the Felixstowe nodules. The services of a number of local villagers were procured to assist in their extraction (Jobson, Allan (1956), *'Felixstowe Story'*, pp.45, 46). Rothamsted Library Archives has a copy of his analysis in June 1845. It was included in his letter to Henslow (below) and confirmed that they contained a worthwhile percentage phosphate of lime:

"*Insoluble*   *6.5 %*
Phosphate of Lime *53.5 %*
Phosphate Iron   *13.0 %*
Carbonate Iron   *20.5 %*
Volatile Matter   *6.5 %*

"*I have taken some trouble to procure a sufficient quantity to be tried this year as super phosphate of lime in comparison with my own which is made from calcined bones but the owners have an exaggerated notion of their value that I have given up taken [sic] on further steps about it. I was told the other day that they were worth £14 per Ton. The Superphosphate of Lime that I make contains 50 parts of phosphate of lime and 30 parts Sulphuric acid in 100 and I sell this for £7 per ton. Therefore I do not consider the Coprolites to be worth a high price and the Carbonate of lime would consume much acid to no purpose.*"

According to Henslow, Lawes then "*abandoned the idea of their being a source to which he could have recourse, in consequence of the absurd notions which have got abroad of the extreme value of these nodules. He has been asked twice as much for them per ton as he sells the manufactured article itself!*" (Henslow op. cit. p.520) Suffolk manure manufacturers disagreed. £14 a ton would have been about six months' wages for an agricultural labourer at that time. Subsequent tests by other manure manufacturers showed that the phosphate content of the Suffolk coprolites varied considerably from as high as 70% to as low as 16%. This factor may well explain why the development of the industry in Suffolk was much more piecemeal than it was in Cambridgeshire (Morton, J.C. (1855), '*A Cyclopaedia of Agriculture*', Glasgow, p.545). Those landowners who recognised that they had coprolite deposits on their land would have sent off samples to be tested.

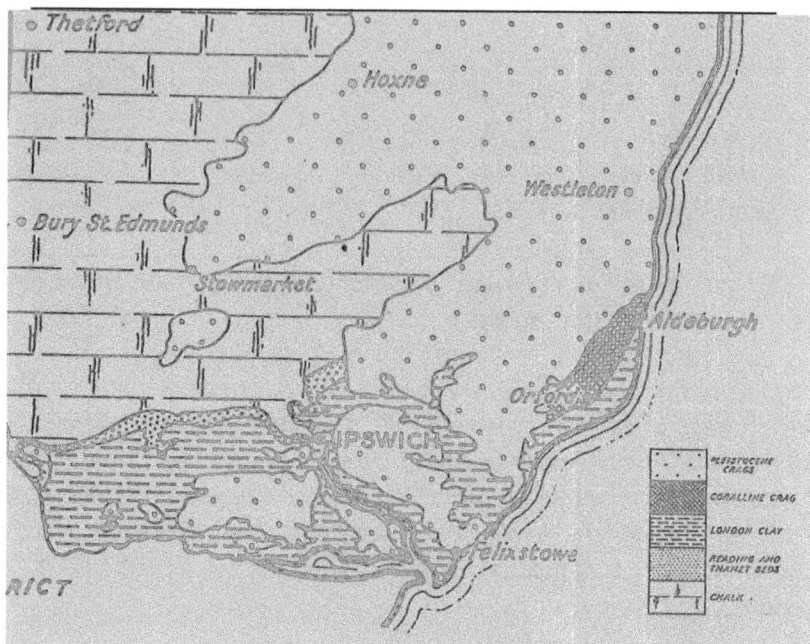

Extract from the geological map of East Anglia
(Chatwin, C.P. (1961), *East Anglia and Adjoining Areas,* HMSO)

In some cases, where the manure manufacturers suspected the deposit extended onto landowners' property, they approached them for permission to test the deposit. Naturally, the beds with the higher phosphate content would have been the most valuable and first to be exploited.

Others did not think it absurd. It was not long before a local entrepreneur recognised that their *'extreme value'* could result in extreme profits:

"At the Ipswich Museum dinner it was stated that a gentleman present was raising the nodules at Felixstowe at the rate of 60 tons weekly, and that he hoped to increase this rate, so as to be able to supply many thousands of tons within the year."

Edward Packard (1819 – 1899) founded Edward Packard and Company. In 1843 he began making superphosphate by dissolving old bones in sulphuric acid at Snape Mill. In 1851 he built Britain's first complete sulphuric acid and superphosphate works at Bramford..
(http://www.yara.com/en/about/yara_centennial/heritage/fisons_inter.html)

SUFFOLK MANURE MANUFACTURERS

Although the name of the gentleman was not stated, it was Edward Packard (1819 - 1899). After his education at Woodbridge Grammar School he gained a diploma in pharmaceutical chemistry under Mr Francis Cupiss of Diss. He began his career as a chemist in Saxmundham in 1841 when he was twenty-two and advertised as a druggist and wine and spirit merchant. He found a manager to run his business and went to London to advance his knowledge of agricultural and analytical chemistry under Dr Nesbit. On returning to Saxmundham, he read Professor Henslow's article about the Felixstowe coprolites and understood the economic potential of using them as fertiliser, In his correspondence he stated that,

"The sale of dissolved bones, my more immediate friends took a great deal of interest in the matter, and I gave an address at the Yoxford Farmer's Club, at which Mr James Cooper, of Blythburgh Lodge, presided. Mr Cooper, who had used a large quantity of raw bones (ground, of course), said he would try ten acres if I would prepare it.

He purchased a bushel, the equivalent of eight gallons, of them but, without a mill, had to have them pulverised using a pestle and mortar before dissolving them in vitriol. Cooper bought Packard's first "superphosphate" and vitriol and commenced making it himself. They recognised the labour costs were far too great using this method so, sometime in 1843, Packard approached Mr Richard Garrett about renting an engine to grind them. He was not optimistic about the venture so Packard rented Hudson's flourmill at Snape Maltings from Mr. Newson Garrett. He used the millstone, driven by a steam-pumping engine, to grind an assortment of materials: malt, linseed, rapeseed, pyrites, imported bones and Suffolk coprolites. He advertised his wares in the *Gardeners' Chronicle* under the heading of 'Pseudo-Coprolite and Fossil Bones' and *"had letters from influential people who took interest in farming, and intending manufacturers. Of course, I gave directions for using them, and this was my first introduction of the use to which coprolites should be applied for agricultural purposes"*. Three of the gentlemen were Benjamin Cooper, of Blythburgh, and Messrs. Thomas and James Girling, of Westleton Hall. (Biography of Sir Edward Packard, pp.6-9; *Fison's Journal*, No.77, December 1963; Tye, W. (1930), op. cit. p.5) There was perhaps some nepotism here as Harriot Packard of Middleton, Edward Packard's first cousin once removed, had married Richard Girling. (Communication with Giles Colchester). Given the profits to be made from selling 'super' at up to £7 a ton Packard was prepared to pay Lawes his five shillings (£0.25) a ton royalty. The financial success led to Lawes eating his words.

1861 photograph of William Colchester (1813–1898), one of the first manure manufacturers to use Suffolk coprolites.
(Courtesy of Giles Colchester)

One of the men who accompanied Rev. Henslow at Felixstowe cliffs was William Colchester (1813–1898) of Sutton, near Woodbridge. He came from a family of soap boilers, bakers and publicans. After travelling in Italy and Russia he went into the timber importing business with John Chevallier Cobbold, the MP for Ipswich and one of the brewing family. It is significant that Cobbold was instrumental in the setting up of the Eastern Union Railway in 1844. He was its chairman. The railway and river port were great benefactors to Ipswich and, over the years, they brought a great increase in heavy industry, with shipbuilding yards, iron foundries, gas and coke works, and engineering works alongside the docks.

In 1847 he made arrangements to purchase 500 tons of the fossils from Felixstowe to make into what some called his 'coprolite manure'. Thus started an industry in Felixstowe that was to last for over 40 years. William Colchester, Lawes, Fison and Prentice, other manure manufacturers successfully processed them and, with agents across the country, started marketing superphosphate on a large scale. It became much favoured by the nation's farmers, as, at prices between £6 and £7 per ton, it was less than half the price of guano, the other best selling manure at the time. It has been said that some farmers, to save money, covered a pile of coprolites with straw, set it alight and then applied the burnt mass to the soil.

Another local manure manufacturer was Joseph Fison (1819 - 1878) of Thetford in Norfolk. In 1833, when he was 13, he inherited James Fison's, his father's manure business at Stowmarket. He was part of a milling and baking family that, seeing the opportunities for profit, moved into Ipswich in 1840. Seven years later he had founded his own milling and fertiliser company and, recognising the prospects of the coprolite industry, in 1850 bought Allen Ransome's flour mill in Duke Street, Ipswich, and established a manure works on the site. It was adjacent to the new dock at Stoke Bridge. The stone flourmill was converted to process coprolites and other phosphatic material. (*Fison's*

Journal, No.77, December 1963; Norsk Hydro file, Museum of East Anglian Life, Stowmarket)

Undated photograph of Hudson's Mill, Snape Maltings. Edward Packard started grinding coprolites here in the early 1840s.
(http://www.snapevillage.org.uk/indexfr.html?framed/aboutsnape_info.html~info
)

By 1854, Joseph Fison had expanded, like Colchester and other entrepreneurs, into brick and tile manufacture, rape cake and bone-crushing, selling feeding stuffs, linseed, malting, buying and selling corn, timber, coal and wool. Two years later he was producing his own superphosphate, using Suffolk coprolites. He must have been aware of the potential profits to be made in supplying the nation's farmers with a new manure as he went on to develop his own sulphuric acid and superphosphate works at Halifax Mills. These were on the site of Mr Buttram's wind-operated corn mill at the end of Wherstead Street which ran on the west bank of Hog Highland Reach.

A steam-operated mill was installed, ran by Samuel Southgate, who lived in Mill House with his family. It is said that a number of works of art, including a Constable, show the two post mills at this site. One of the millstones from Fison's works can be seen in the Museum of East Anglian Life in Stowmarket. (*Fison's Journal*, No.77, December 1963; Norsk Hydro file, Museum of East Anglian Life, Stowmarket; Communication with Giles Colchester; *Artist's Views of Ipswich and its Waterfront over Two Centuries*, Ipswich Borough Council).

Another of the Fison dynasty was James Fison of the White House, Barningham. He too capitalised on the Suffolk coprolite deposit and the growing demand for artificial fertilisers. He expanded his milling business by moving to Thetford in Norfolk in 1853 with his two sons, James and Cornell. The company office was on Bridge Street. With the profits to be made in the lucrative manure market, he invested in the plant and machinery needed to expand into this new branch of agricultural supplies. A chemical manure works was constructed at Two Mile Bottom, two miles from Thetford. With the River Thet being navigable as far as King's Lynn, the major raw materials, mineral phosphates, coprolites and sulphur, were easily brought in by sailing barge (Norsk Hydro file, Museum of East Anglian Life, Stowmarket).

Joseph Fison (1819 - 1878) founded Joseph Fison and Company, millers and fertilizer manufacturers, in 1847. He established a fertilizer production plant adjacent to Edward Packard's factory at Bramford, Suffolk, in 1858.
http://www.yara.com/en/about/yara_centennial/heritage/fisons_inter.htm)

There was competition. Extensive artificial manure, soap and bone boiling works had been erected in Sudbury on Great Cornard Street, "... *sited on the river Stour abutting onto the Great Eastern Railway about two miles from Sudbury, in the centre of an agricultural district where artificial manure is extensively used*" (Bury and Norwich Post, February 27th 1883). Another chemical manure works was sited close to the railway line in Melford. None of these company records have come to light.

Between 1850 and 1857 the Fisons had 2,100 tons of coprolites shipped to King's Lynn from Bawdsey, Boyton, Woodbridge, Ipswich and Harwich. The proximity of the railway was an advantage, enabling easy access throughout Cambridgeshire, Norfolk and Suffolk. He had an acid plant constructed to manufacture the sulphuric acid. This was used to dissolve the imported bones, guano and coprolites to produce turnip and corn manures as well as superphosphate of lime (Norsk Hydro file, Museum of East Anglian Life, Stowmarket; *K.P.O.D.*, Norfolk, 1879,1883; Maycock, op. cit. p.29).

Coastal and foreign trade was considerable, consisting chiefly in the export of corn, malt, butter, cattle, and the various manufactures of the town, and the import of colonial produce, coprolites, phosphate, coal, iron, and timber. Ipswich's chief manufactory was the 'Orwell Works' where Messrs. Ransome's agricultural implements and machinery were made. Other dockside industries included gas ovens, a silk factory, flax mills, breweries, soapworks, tanneries, malting houses, rope yards, patent artificial stone works (using septaria), snuff and tobacco factories and stay-making using whale bones. According to the trade directory:

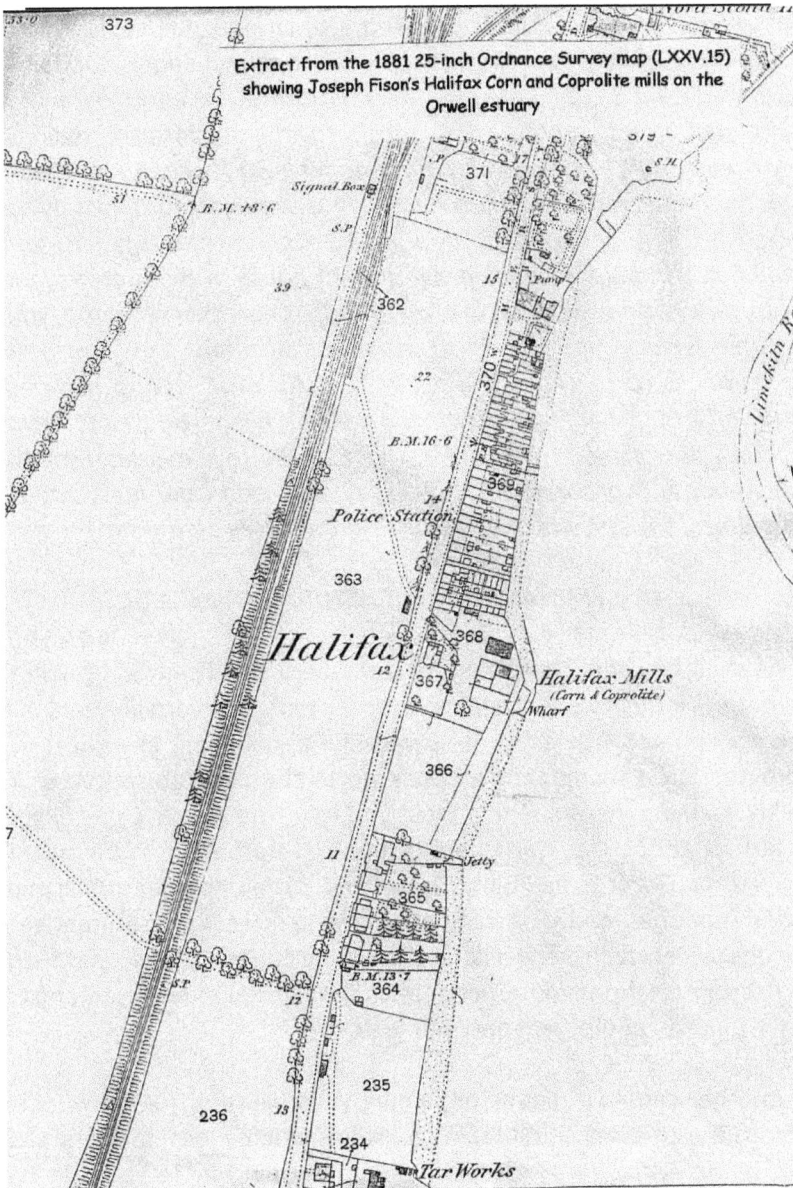

Extract from the 1881 25-inch Ordnance Survey map (LXXV.15) showing Joseph Fison's Halifax Corn and Coprolite mills on the Orwell estuary

"Among the public buildings are the town hall; the custom-house, an Italian building on the quay; the corn-exchange, capable of accommodating 1,200 persons; the post-office, recently rebuilt; the county gaol, borough gaol, court-houses for the assizes and sessions, a temperance hall, which will accommodate 500 people; a theatre; assembly rooms for balls and concerts; museum of natural history, &c., erected in 1847, and supported by a corporation rate; a public library with 8,000 volumes, occupying the ancient house in the butter-market; literary institution, held in the town hall; Church of England young men's society; young men's Christian Association; two prosperous savings-banks, a mechanics' institution, with large lecture-hall and a library of 7,000 volumes; a working men's college and club; cavalry barracks, barrack and depot for the East Suffolk militia; besides a bathing-house, arboretum, public walks and gardens, and a horticultural society, which holds three grand fêtes during the season."

DISSEMINATING AGRICULTURAL KNOWLEDGE

As shall be seen, these men became very significant figures in the coprolite industry's development. Their advertisements for superphosphate, articles on its successful application, and the use of coprolites in its manufacture appeared in the agricultural press. The weekly farming newspapers, most notably *The Mark Lane Express,* started in 1832. *The Gardeners' Chronicle* started in 1841 and *The Agricultural Gazette* in 1844. These and other popular publications carried national and non-regional news as well as summaries of agricultural research, reports and surveys, accounts of sales and shows, market information and prices, and agricultural advertisements for land, property, equipment and manures.

Another valuable means of gaining valuable information was from agricultural societies and discussion groups held by local farmers' clubs. The *Suffolk Agricultural Association* was founded in 1831. The *West Norfolk Agricultural Association* was established in 1834 and held its annual meetings at Swaffham, on the third Wednesday in June, when there used to be a great show of cattle and agricultural implements. Lord Hastings was the president, and the Earl of Leicester was vice-president. The *Royal Agricultural Society* started in 1840 and the *Norfolk Agricultural Society* in 1849. These increased landowners' and agriculturalists' awareness of the financial advantages of locating the coprolite bed on their properties, which in turn stimulated the geological mapping of the area.

However, the professors and students of the emerging science of geology disputed Henslow's theory that the fossils were coprolitic. Over the next decade they identified the Suffolk fossils as the phosphatised remains of a variety of marine life from Eocene, about 54 million years ago, through to the Pleistocene period two million years ago. The geological literature preferred to call them 'pseudo-coprolites' or 'phosphatic nodules' but in the industry, the term 'coprolites' stayed as a trade name.

THE GEOLOGY OF THE RED CRAG

The geology of East Anglia has been well studied. The emerging science of geology in the early 19th century was boosted by the discovery of a range of fossil remains found on the Southeast Suffolk coast. Here the London Clay was overlain with layers of Coralline Crag and Red Crag. Between 54 and 38 million years ago (Ma) this part of the European plate was a sea in the sub-tropical latitudes. What is now Southeast England sank steadily as the continental European plate moved steadily northward. Up to 130 feet (47.5 m) of bluish, brown or grey clay was deposited during what is called the Eocene period, sediment fed by a huge north flowing river – the forerunner of the Rhine. The habitat was warm and tropical. Deposited within the clay were the remains of a diverse range of marine and land organisms. Palm tree logs, conifers, dates, dicots, seeds, leaves and plants which now grow in the swamps and deltas of India were swept out to sea, became waterlogged and sank into the muddy sediments.

As the plate moved progressively further north the climatic conditions changed. So did the geological situation. The tectonic movement of the continental landmass caused enormous structural upheaval. An island was produced which the geologists term 'The London-Brabant Platform'. Southern England was slowly folded upwards to form a geological formation known today as the Weald. Storms, wave action and strong tides in what was a large estuary of a north flowing river draining from the European landmass washed away much of the coastal muds of the London Clay. The sun dried up and cracked the uplifted muds and clays. Wind, rain and river action exposed many of the Mesozoic fossil remains. Having a high specific gravity (2.77) they were easily concentrated on the erosional surface. Washed downstream by rivers into shallow-water bays they were broken up and many of their surface features were heavily abraded. This gave them a polished surface. In time they accumulated in hollows on the seabed, in places several feet thick, in the same way that shingle builds up on the shore during storm periods.

Submerged in warm, shallow waters there was no oxygen to decompose the bones, teeth and shells of the land and marine organisms that sank to the sea bed over millions of years. Over time they became phosphatised, acquiring a build-up of material around them. This involved two processes – under water and above. The formation of phosphatic deposits in eastern England was linked with periods when the land was covered by sea, while the periods when the land was above sea level were important in concentrating a dense mass of phosphatic material. Chemical analysis of the Crag beds shows that it contains a mineral known as carbonate flourapatite (francolite). Apatite is a phosphatic mineral that is thought to be of volcanic origin. Phosphorus washed out from the volcanic rocks of Scandinavia, Scotland and Northern England would have been one source. Ash bands have been found in the London clay that must have come from some major volcanic explosion in Europe. Maybe the carbon dioxide and sulphur dioxide given off by the explosion poisoned many of the land creatures and those marine creatures that came up for air. The ash falling over the sea slowly sank to the seabed, making the water much more acidic. The ash underwent total alteration into magnesium-rich montmorillorite, an abundant clay mineral often associated with the formation of phosphatic rocks.

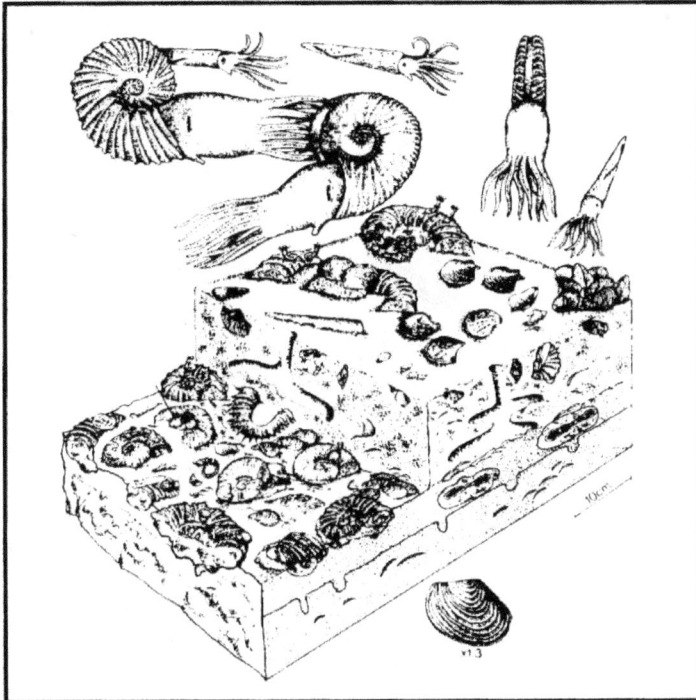

The Phosphate bed Community
(McKerrow, W.S.. (1978), *The Ecology of Fossils: An Illustrated Guide,* Duckworth, p.286)

Lower Cretaceous Terrestrial Communities
a *Iguanadon* (Vertebrata: Reptilia: Archosaur – dinosaur)
b *Megalosaurus* (Vertebrata: Reptilia: Archosaur – dinosaur)
c *Hypsilophodon* (Vertebrata: Reptilia: Archosaur – dinosaur)
d *Acanthopholis* (Vertebrata: Reptilia: Archosaur – dinosaur)
e *Equisetites* (Pteridophyta: Calamites – horsetails)

(McKerrow, W.S.. (1978), *The Ecology of Fossils: An Illustrated Guide,* Duckworth, p.297)

Along with the volcanic ash that was washed into the sea by the rivers, it produced phosphate-rich muddy waters which gradually impregnated the predominantly calcium carbonate of the Crag deposits. Ocean upwellings are thought to be another source of phosphate in seawater. Where large amounts of organic phosphate from decomposing animal tissue, their stomach, intestine and rectal contents are liberated into the surrounding water, supersaturation occurs and the apatite precipitated. The apatite replaced the original minerals of the organisms and a concretionary growth built up around them, similar to the encrusted plaque on your teeth. This replacement process also enriched the phosphate content of the derived fossils.

On the surface the organic content of the teeth and bones was greatly reduced by scavengers and bacteria. As organic phosphate is not liberated by decay like those underwater, the apatite is thought to have been precipitated in the existing structures by a replacement process.

About 5 million years ago, at the start of the Pliocene period, this area was on the same latitudes as the Mediterranean. A warm shallow sea covered what is now Southeast Suffolk and a new sedimentary deposit was laid down on top of the fossils on the clay seabed. Whitish or slightly yellow shelly sands and beds of finely broken shells or polyzoa built up to depths of 60 feet (21 m). They are known as the Coralline Crag because of the abundance of corals in it. These were subsequently identified as polyzoa, skeletons of aquatic animals with a cup-shaped body, a U-shaped alimentary canal and a sheath of tentacles about the mouth. The number of these polyzoa and oblique bedding shows that they originated as sandbanks in a shallow sea that were mostly laid down under strong currents.

Subsequent earth movements led to a sequence of foldings that from time to time shifted the area of deposition and formed a series of shallow-water bays or inlets which moved northwards as successive Crag deposits were laid down. Considerable erosion followed which removed much of the Coralline Crag.

Between 2-1.5 Ma the Pleistocene period began. This area had moved into cooler latitudes, evidenced by the shells and fossils of a number of boreal species, creatures that lived in the warmer and drier environment of hazel/pine woodland of the northerly latitudes. Throughout this period a huge northern flowing river was still depositing its load and, towards Lowestoft, shallow seabed deposits accumulated on the western banks of its enormous estuary. This Red Crag is a shore deposit up to 40 feet (14.8 m) thick in places. It is made up mostly of current-bedded sands with shells but also with some silt and layers of ironstone. The shells are water-worn which indicate drifting and analysis of the bed shows that it was deposited in banks piled near the shores of land locked bays as a result of the prevalent easterly gales.

What became known as the Suffolk coprolites were divided into three groups. They were not indigenous species. They were reworked, winnowed out of earlier deposits. The oldest were from the Mesozoic strata, 245 - 65 Mya which included the Triassic and Jurassic period. Other Cretaceous remains were washed out from the London Clay. The most common amongst these were the teeth of Striatolamia, Myliobatis and Lamna but even phosphatised wood from the Eocene Age (58 – 37 Mya) was found. The third group were washed out from Miocene strata between 25 – 4 Ma.

It was a huge fossil graveyard found today between Butley Creek and the Alde at Aldeburgh. It included the teeth of Procarcharodon megalodon, the broken rib bones, teeth and bones of mastodon (an early elephant), bones and teeth of bears, antlers of several species of deer, skulls and bones of rhinoceros, crocodile, tapir, beaver, hyena and pig. Mixed with them were the ribs and ear bones of whales, teeth and vertebrae of sharks, the remains of walrus, dolphin, spines of rays, turtle shells, fish teeth, crabs, crayfish and a host of marine organisms. The dominant species were molluscs with barnacles, brachiopods, cirripedes, corals, crinoids, echinoids, foraminifera, ostracoda, polyzoa and sponges.

Many of the fossils have boreholes on all surfaces indicating that they were periodically overturned. Boring marine bivalves (Ichno genus, Teredolites, (leymerie)) were able to penetrate their softer outer portions. The long, brown, smooth and polished nodules varied in size between half an inch and three inches (1 - 10 cm) long and averaged just over an inch (3 cm).

There were materials of very different geological ages, from far distant places coming at different times and by different means from different directions but mostly from the north. It is an agglomeration containing rolled, water-worn and phosphatised fossils as well as septaria, rounded fragments of carbon-rich London Clay. As shall be seen these too were exploited commercially. Uncommercial remains found in the bed that were sifted out by the diggers included phosphatised wood, large flints deposited by floating ice that had eroded out of the Chalk, igneous and Jurassic rocks including pieces of quartzite, granite, porphyry, mica-schist and Liassic marlstone. There were also 'box-stones'. These were rounded cobbles of brownish, quartz sandstone containing the mould of a gastropod or large bivalve. These had to be separated from the nodules as the manure manufacturers refused any supplies contaminated with them. As they did not contain as much, if any, phosphate, they tended to be sold for use as road fill or as a building material. (Charlesworth, E. (1845), 'On the Occurrence of the Genus Physter (or Sperm Whale) in the Red Crag at Felixstowe', *Proceedings of the Geological Society*, vol. IV. p.286; *Q.J.G.S.* vol. I. p.40; Lankester, (1868), 'On the Crags of Suffolk and Antwerp', *Geol. Mag.*, Vol. II pp.103 - 6, 149 - 52; Lankester (1868), 'The Suffolk Bone Bed and the Diestian or Black Crag in England', *Geol. Mag.* Vol. V, pp.254 - 8; Chatwin, C. P. (1961), *'East Anglia and Adjoining Areas'*, HMSO; Knox and Ellison (1979), 'A Lower Eocene Ash Sequence in SE England', *Journ. Geol. Soc.* London, Vol. CXXXVI, pp.251 - 3; Balson, P.S. (1980), 'The origin and evolution of Tertiary phosphorites from eastern England', *Journal of the Geological Society*, pp.725 – 729)

23rd OCTOBER 4004 BC

Whilst the discovery of fossils was one of great fascination to the country's geologists, their commercial value was not in how much they could be sold to those Victorians fascinated by fossils. Rather it was in how much the manure manufacturers were prepared to pay for them. However, the study of these fossils contributed to a huge conceptual shift in academic circles with the growing discussion of Evolution. James Ussher (1581 - 1656), Archbishop of Armagh, Primate of All Ireland, and Vice-Chancellor of Trinity College in Dublin, devoted much of his life working out from biblical references and other Middle Eastern texts that the Earth was created on Sunday 23rd October 4004 BC. Dr. John Lightfoot, a contemporary of Ussher, Vice-Chancellor of the University of Cambridge, and one of the most eminent Hebrew scholars of his time, worked it out as at nine o'clock in the morning. Adam and Eve were driven from Paradise on Monday 10th November the same year and the ark touched down on Mt Ararat on 5th May 1491 BC. The church's view when these dinosaur and other fossils were being discussed was that they all lived in peace and harmony with Adam. However, there was an increasing number of geologists and palaeontologists who were suggesting this belief and dating system were very wrong.

CHARLES DARWIN AND HENSLOW'S NEPOTISM

Charles Darwin caused a storm when his evolutionary theories were published in 1859. After qualifying as a doctor in Edinburgh he went to study theology at Christ's College, Cambridge, in 1828. He became great friends with Rev. Henslow who encouraged him to study geology. In fact, when Rev. Leonard Jenyns, Henslow's naturalist brother-in-law, declined an invitation by Captain Robert Fitzroy of HMS Beagle to go on a two-year trip round South America, Henslow was asked to go instead. His wife dissuaded him so Henslow wrote off to Captain Fitzroy recommending Darwin for the voyage.

When he returned from his five-year circumnavigation of the world in 1836, Darwin visited Henslow at his Cambridge house where he was brought up to date with the latest developments in geology and palaeontology and the current debate about dinosaurs being contemporaneous with Adam. The Christian belief that God created each distinct organism challenges Darwin's findings from his studies on the Galapagos Islands. Darwin's argument was that nature had to weed out those least fit to survive in order to save the strongest. He called it Natural Selection. By 1842 he had written a thirty-five page essay on his idea, though he kept it a great secret. In 1844 he increased it to two hundred and thirty pages but was worried about publishing it as he knew it would cause a storm in religious circles. When it was eventually published, twenty-three years later, his work, 'On the Origin of Species by Means of Natural Selection, or the Preservation of Favoured Races in the Struggle for Life', as well as challenging the established religious belief system, it further stimulated the enormous interest in geology, palaeontology, anthropology and archaeology.

A MARK OF REFINEMENT AND IMPECCABLE GOOD TASTE

Darwin never visited Hitcham, so Henslow never got the chance to show him his fossil collection from the Suffolk coprolite pits, the display in Ipswich Museum or those in other Suffolk gentlemen's private collections. It was a mark of refinement and impeccable good taste to own and display a fossil collection. Not only were they rare and precious, they hinted at a thirst for knowledge, an awareness of natural philosophy and an understanding of either God's mysterious powers on the Earth or evidence of evolution. The country houses, manor houses, vicarages and rectories of many of Suffolk's gentry had specimens from the Crag and elsewhere displayed in glass-sided cabinets in their drawing rooms. They stimulated interesting after dinner discussions over port and cigars. Geology students and their professors eagerly bought them up. Being able to have a paper published in the increasing number of geological journals or to be invited to give a lecture on the subject at some distinguished society could provide a step up the promotion ladder. Most universities had geology departments by the 1840s and they all needed specimens for their museum collections. Curators at Ipswich Museum, the Woodwardian Geology (now Sedgwick) Museum in Cambridge, Norwich Museum, the Ashmolean Museum in Oxford, York Museum and the British Museum in London were all on the look out. Excursions and field trips were organised to include the new fossil pits. Henslow had a collection of almost 400 whales' ears! A description of them can be found in Owen's *History of British Fossil Mammals and Birds*.

ACCIDENT AT BAWDSEY

On the afternoon of Thursday 19th November, 1846, there was the first recorded accident in the fossils diggings. 9-year old Rose Ann Sare was crushed to death whilst looking for coprolites at the foot of the cliffs at Bawdsey. John Wood, Jun, the Woodbridge Coroner at the time instructed the local constable to get enough men together to form a jury for an inquest to be held at the Star Public House, Bawdsey. The evidence of two friends, 21-year-old Emma Ransby and 20-yeat-old Maria Wilson, told how:

We were in the habit of collecting coprolites on the beach. We were paid a shilling a bushel for them. Rose Ann was picking up coprolites. At the spot where she was the cliff was upwards of twenty feet high. We believe she was close under the cliff. We were about four or five yards from her with our backs turned towards her. We heard part of the cliff fall and could nowhere see her. We gave immediate alarm and sent for her father. Her father and three other men came as soon as they could and dug away the sand, but she was quite dead. She was not digging a hole but merely picking up coprolites at the edge of the cliff. A verdict of Accidental Death was returned.

(SCRO. HB 10/9/60/48)

Roland Green, Rose Ann's father's great grandson, shed more light on the incident whilst researching his ancestry. He found an article published in the 1861 edition of 'The Technologist'.

Coprolites were first discovered in this part of the country about the year 1846. A celebrated artificial manure manufacturer was walking with a gentleman on Bawdsey beach and picked up some coprolites that had been washed out of the crag cliffs. Finding it contained manorial properties, he requested this gentleman to employ children to pick it up. This continued about two years, when one day the children had picked some out of the cliff so far under that the crag slipped in and killed a little girl. At the inquest the jury wanted to know what coprolite was; the consequence was, farmers discovered that their crag pits were full of it, and some began to dig for it, selling to the same gentleman at about £1 per ton. The manufacturer had obtained a patent, but it being infringed, he brought an action and lost it; and then everyone was allowed to manufacture it into manure.

('The Technologist', (1861), Edited by Peter Lund Simmonds, published by Kent & Co.)

Green felt convinced that the manufacturer was John Bennet Lawes and the gentleman was Searles V. Wood, the noted palaeontologist and elder brother of the Coroner. He suggested a speedy verdict was reached to avoid him having to explain employing young children. (Author's email communication with Giles Colchester, 17th November, 2008).

COMPETITION FROM THE CAMBRIDGESHIRE COPROLITES

The manure manufacturers' increasing demand for phosphate stimulated the search for additional supplies in other parts of the country and overseas. Fossils had been found beneath the fenland peat in Cambridgeshire from as early as 1816 (Hailstone, Rev. J. (1816), 'Outlines of the Geology of Cambridgeshire', *Philosophical Transactions of the Royal Society*, pp.243 - 250). Their discovery was related to an important fenland occupation, locally called 'claying'. This involved the digging of small pits through the 'moor' or 'bear's muck', as the bog-earth was called, to reach the clay. This lay between two and ten feet (0.74 m - 3.7 m) below the surface. Wearing waterproofed boots the diggers would use a sharp, cutting-edged shovel to dig through the peat, a light wooden scoop to get rid of drainage water and an axe or 'bill' to excavate the clay beneath. The top few feet of clay was thrown to the sides of the pit and then mixed into the peat.

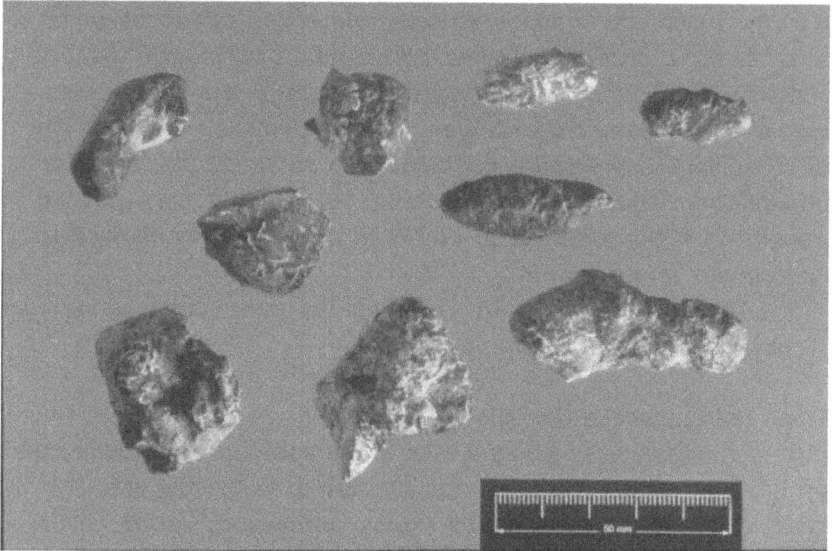

Cambridgeshire coprolites. (Photograph courtesy of Earth Sciences Museum, Cambridge)

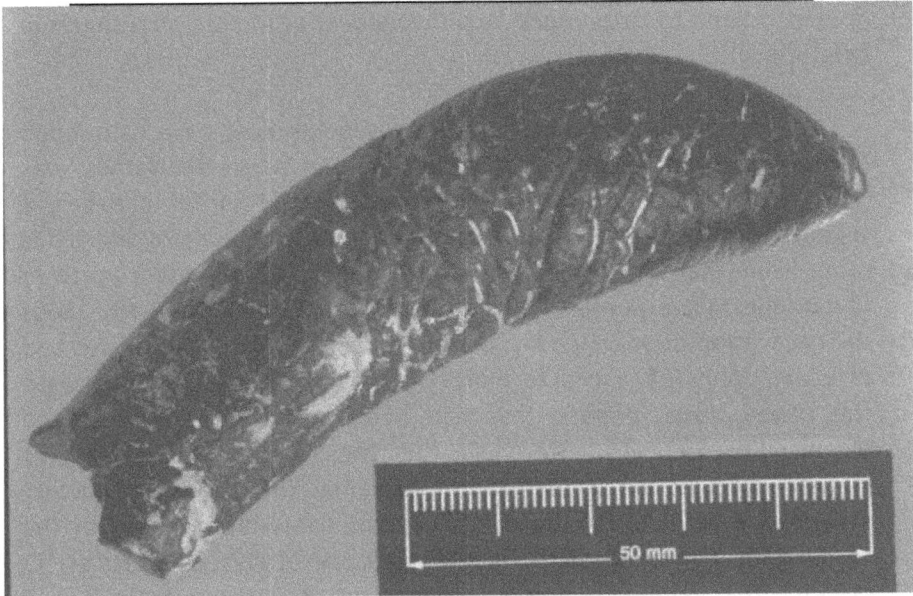

The Barrington coprolite
(Photograph courtesy of Earth Sciences Museum, Cambridge)

The material turned up by this 'claying' occasionally included fossils of what were thought to be bears and oxen. Maybe as a result of Rev. Henslow's interest in the fossils, a local farmer was prompted to show him some that he had dug up on his property. An anonymous note in Ipswich Museum's Coprolite file shows that Charles Kingsley, another of his students, must have been present as he commented that:

"My beloved friend and teacher, the late Dr. Henslow, when Professor of Botany at Cambridge, had brought to him by a farmer a few fossils. He saw, being somewhat of a geologist and chemist, that they were not, as fossils usually are, carbonate of lime, but phosphate of lime - bone earth. He said at once, as by inspiration, "You have found a treasure - not a gold-mine, indeed, but a food-mine. This bone earth, which we are at our wit's end to get for our grain and pulses; which we are importing, as expensive bones, all the way from Buenos Ayres. Only find enough of them, and you will increase immensely the food supply

of England and perhaps make her independent of foreign phosphates in case of war."

A treasure? A food-mine? Such a response must have astounded the farmer. Unfortunately, it is undocumented where the farmer was from. Whilst it could have been from one of the Suffolk parishes, it suggests that the value of the fossils had already been recognised. It is more likely that the farmer was from Burwell, a small town north of Cambridge. When Burwell Fen started to be drained in the early-1800s the excavation of drainage ditches or 'lodes' exposed an extensive bed of fossils. John Ball, a local farmer, noticed that the turnips he grew on the clayey, fossil deposit that had been mixed into his peat soil produced dramatically better yields than the crops on fields he had not clayed. Mr Lucas, the Burwell doctor, explained that the "*extraordinary liveliness*" was related to the high phosphate content of the fossils ('The Farming of Cambridgeshire', *Royal Agric.Soc.* 1847, p.71; Lucas, C. (1930*), 'The Fenman's World - Memories of a Fenland Physician'*, Norwich, p.25).

Dr. Lucas may well have heard about Henslow's Cambridge speech or read about it in the local press. Aware of the manure manufacturers' demand for fossils and maybe even knowing the farmer who had shown Henslow them, he suspected that the Burwell deposit could also be a matter of 'commercial proposition'. Their shallow depth beneath the fenland peat just above the Gault Clay would allow them to be raised without very high labour costs. The proximity of Burwell Lode allowed easy access by barge or lighter to Popes Corner - the confluence of the Ouse and the Cam - and then via Ely, Littleport and Downham Market onto King's Lynn where it could easily be transhipped to the manure works in Ipswich, London and elsewhere.

With an eye for speculation and without having first seen it, Lucas bought some eleven acres of Burwell Poor's Fen. The locals thought he had taken leave of his senses. A month later, so the story goes, he went by boat up Burwell Lode with "*an interested party*" to locate the deposit. After rowing for some time, they reached a point about a mile west of the village where the potential buyer was handed a 'sprit' and told to push it into the land below the boat (Gathercole, A. F. (1959), 'Fenland Village', *Fison's Journal*, No.64 Sept. pp.24 - 9; Suffolk County Record Office (S.C.R.O), HC 438.8728/269).

The depth of the seam was not noted but the locals were astounded when he sold the plot and the coprolites beneath it for £1,000. Realising almost £100 per acre was a phenomenal profit, given that agricultural rents ranged at that time from about ten to forty shillings (£0.50 - £2.00) an acre. The 'interested party' was William Colchester, who, according to a later geological paper, had raised 500 tons of Burwell coprolites by 1847 (Lucas, C. (1930), op. cit; Reid, C. (1890), 'Pliocene deposits of Britain', *Memoirs of the Geological Survey (M.G.S)* p.16).

Packard arranged to test them for himself. His company records show that he had started purchasing the Cambridgeshire fossils from as early as January 1847 when he bought 186 tons of Colchester's 'stones'. His three sailing barges, "*Providence*", "*Bessy*" and "*Endeavour*" brought them round the East Anglian coast to his Ipswich works (S.C.R.O. HC434 8728/310a). Tests he had done on them confirmed that they were a lot more valuable commodity than the Suffolk variety so he too expanded his operations by starting to make agreements with Cambridgeshire landowners to have them raised.

Details of the process of converting the coprolites to artificial manure in 1848 showed that seven tons of coprolites could be ground in a day and a night at a cost of twelve shillings and eight pence (£0.64). There was also the cost of 18 hundredweight of coals at a shilling a hundredweight (£0.90) which were used to drive the steam engine at 30 to 35 lb. or nearly full power. This turned three pairs of stones and rollers with the aid of one man and five boys during the day and one man and two boys at night. Paying only four shillings and four pence (£0.22) per ton as well as thirty to forty-five shillings (£1.50 - £2.25) a ton royalty for the coprolites still meant the manufacturing costs were relatively low compared to the selling price of up to £7. It was added that Joseph Fison and Son had experimented mixing 56 pounds of what they termed 'Coprolithes' with 26 pounds of sulphuric acid with no water and there were subsequent notes as to their best combination. 28 lb. of Coprolites, 10 lb. of Sulphuric Acid and 7 lb. of water seemed a favoured method (S.C.R.O. HC. 434/8728/310a).

In 1848 the fossil seam was noticed in the Chesterton brickfields, near Cambridge. The owners sold some of what they had previously considered *"troublesome annoyances"* to Mr Deck, a chemist of Fitzroy Street, for £2 per ton. He probably was not told the royalties the Suffolk manure manufacturers were paying but would have known that similar 'phosphatic nodules' were being raised in the Felixstowe and Burwell areas. The tests he did on them showed that the Cambridgeshire 'coprolites' had between 50% - 60% calcium phosphate, up to 10% higher than the Suffolk variety. It stimulated their extraction as *"a matter of commercial proposition"* (Cambridge Independent Press (CIP), 18th January, 1851, p.3).

42-foot sailing barge *Ethel*, typical of the Suffolk lighters that carried coprolites to manure factories in Ipswich and London. (http://www.schooneryacht.com/resume.html)

When it was found that the seam extended to the south under Coldham's Common in Barnwell, the industry took off on a large scale. The Suffolk manure manufacturers and entrepreneurial coprolite contractors, keen to capitalise on the demand, moved into the area to win agreements with brickyard and other landowners to raise the fossils. Gangs of experienced diggers were brought over from Suffolk but demand for labour was so great that men walked to the Cambridgeshire diggings from all the adjoining counties (O'Connor, B.

(1998), 'The Dinosaurs on Coldham's Common', Bernard O'Connor, Everton).

FOSSIL PHOSPHATES IN THE WEY VALLEY

Another seam of Upper Greensand was found to outcrop above the Gault clay at the foot of the North Downs. At its base was a similar bed of phosphatic nodules that was exposed along the side of the Wey Valley, near Farnham. Evidence suggests that these nodules were not converted into superphosphate, simply carted from the pits by the farmer to be spread on their fields. Messrs Paine and Way, two local agriculturalists, published their findings about these phosphates in 1848. They acknowledged that the coprolites were extremely hard, requiring very powerful machinery to grind them, and that the resulting powder was insoluble.

"It may occur to some persons to ask, to what purpose if there already exists an abundant and cheap supply of phosphate of lime in the coprolites of the crag - to what purpose should the agriculturalists be troubled to look for another? or in what respect are the beds of the chalk formation about to be described, of interest in a practical point of view? The answer to these questions may be readily given - the mechanical and chemical processes necessary to prepare the Suffolk coprolite for agricultural use must doubtless, to a certain extent, prevent them being brought into the market, at so low a price as they might be, were such preparation unnecessary."

TAKE OFF IN SUFFOLK

Gradually the technology improved with bigger and more powerful grinding stones being introduced. The millstone grit was not hard enough and was replaced with a much harder buhrstone, specially imported from a granite quarry in La Ferte-sous-Fauarre in France. This produced a much finer phosphate and in time led to reduced costs. This further increased demand for the Suffolk coprolites. Recognising the huge potential of this new industry, Packard was concerned at his inability to obtain a site to build a larger mill at Snape Maltings. Both he and his wife were acquainted with Mr Allen Ransome, who helped him locate suitable premises on Ipswich Dock in St Clement's ward. In 1850 he bought the flourmill on Ipswich Dock north of Ransome's 'Orwell Works' and installed a powerful condensing pumping engine. He commenced business there the following year. He began by sending his artificial manures to Scotland, then Ireland and later to Russia,

According to his company records, the county gentry gave him a cold reception. It was not done for gentlemen to engage in the manure trade. The profits to be made compensated for such problems. So much did his power and influence grow that twenty years later he was elected Ipswich's mayor! He went on to specialise in the manufacture of his superphosphate and the grinding of coprolites and rock phosphates for resale to a growing number of manure works that had been set around the country. In an article in *Fison's News* entitled 'Ipswich Firm's Remarkable Development' it stated that:

"The building of superphosphate and fertiliser factories had been going on all over the country in the same manner as in the Eastern Counties, and at almost every important port in the U.K. works sprang up between 1845 and 1860."

In 1849 Buckland wrote a paper on the manurial potential of the 'nodules' and pointed out that their equal value with guano and bone-dust had led to the exploitation of "*this newly discovered storehouse of fertility*". A sample of the Felixstowe fossils had been analysed by Professor Edward Solly (1819 - 1886), a distinguished chemist and Fellow of the Royal Society, who found that their chemical composition was almost identical to Rev. Buckland's coprolites. As a result the Dean similarly encouraged agriculturalists to take full advantage of them. He published a paper, 'Causes of Presence of Phosphates in the Strata of the Earth', in the 1849 Journal of the Royal Agricultural Society.

"Many thousand tons of these pebbles and bones have been collected from the shore near Felixstowe; whilst many occupiers of inland farms near Felixstowe and Woodbridge have been and are still collecting similar pebbles and superficial beds of gravel of the crag formation, varying in thickness from one foot to many feet, and extending over areas of variable extent and irregular forms..."

By the 1850s the fertiliser industry had taken off, exploiting fossil beds in Suffolk, Cambridgeshire and Hampshire. In Buckland's 'Study of Abstract Science Essential to the Progress of Industry' published in the Memoirs of the Geological Society in 1850 he questioned the possibility that these

"...excretions of extinct animals contained the mineral ingredients of so much value in animal manure. The question was in fact not yet solved by the chemist, and we took specimens, in order to confirm by chemical analysis the views of the geologist. After Liebig had completed their analysis, he saw that they might be made applicable to practical purposes.

What a curious and interesting subject for contemplation! In the remains of an extinct animal world England is to find the means of increasing her wealth in agricultural produce, as she has already found the great support of her manufacturing industry in fossil fuel - the preserved matter of primeval forests - the remains of a vegetable world! May this expectation be realised! and may her excellent population be thus redeemed from poverty and misery!

I well recollect the storm of ridicule raised by these expressions of the German philosopher, and yet truth has triumphed over scepticism, and thousands of tons of similar animal remains are now used in promoting the fertility of our fields. The geological observer, in his search after evidences of ancient life, aided by the chemist, excavated extinct remains which produced new life to future generations."

In 1851 the Agricultural Society published Mr Way's comprehensive analysis on the various sources of phosphates available for making superphosphate. In it he pointed out that there were only two sources in England, those of the coprolites from the Suffolk Crag beds and those in the Greensand formation in Hampshire. It was clear that he had not heard of the Cambridgeshire coprolites.

"The former has up to a late period stood alone in practical importance, and yet it remains to be seen whether the phosphoric strata of the chalk and greensand will at any future time offer a more available supply of phosphate of lime. .. The coprolites of Suffolk occur in rounded lumps and masses in a shelly gravelly soil, and in many places very near the surface. They are separated from the gravel by an easy process of sifting. These coprolites are sold in London, with a profit to the collectors, at about 30s. a ton. To grind them to a tolerably fine powder (and as they are intensely hard, this operation requires very powerful machinery) a further expense of from 15s. to 20s. a ton is incurred. It is probable that the ground coprolites could not be sold at a much lower rate than 3l. a ton. But it is to be remembered that the coprolites are not entirely composed of phosphate of lime; on the contrary, not much above one-half of them consists of this substance. The average proportion of phosphate of lime in the coprolites is 56 per cent. A ton of them contains therefore 1332 lbs., and by an easy calculation it will be found that a ton of phosphate of lime as supplied by ground coprolites will cost 5l. 9s.1d. which is the rate of 100 lbs. for 4s. 10d., or rather more than 0.5d. for each pound of phosphate of lime."

As the Farnham phosphates worked out to be five pence (£0.025) and guano three farthings (£0.0075) for a pound of phosphate of lime, Way's article must have left manure manufacturers thinking about which supplies to go for. Certainly demand for the Suffolk coprolites continued. Documentation of the financial arrangements made between the manure manufacturers and local landowners is scarce. However, insight into the dealings was provided in a lecture given by Dr Thornton Herapath, a chemical analyst, two years later. He pointed out that:

"The contract which is usually entered into in this county for the labour of raising these remains, namely for digging, screening, washing, and storing, amounts from 4s.6d. to 5s. per ton; whereas, delivered on board the vessel, the charge to the purchaser is 30s. to 45s. per ton. This difference in price, it must be understood, has no respect whatever to the chemical value of the fossils, but is to be attributed solely to the cleverness, or rather cupidity of the seller. Taking the lowest price, however, a clear profit of 20s. or 25s. per ton is gained by the owner of the land. So large, indeed, is the profit thus obtained, I have been told that the produce of a few acres in fossil bones, &c., when sold, has been often known to realise the full value of a small estate; whilst at the same time it must be recollected, that the land itself is actually improved by the course of treatment to which it is subjected when excavating for the fossils. 60l. to 70l. and even 80l., have been repeatedly given for the liberty to dig over a two-acre field."

The financial success of the industry has been attributed to Henslow. In a letter written by Rev Gunn, the vicar of Beccles, to the Norwich Geological Society he commented that:

"The idea of the nature of these nodules being coprolitic originated with Professor Henslow - a mistake, but one, perhaps, one of the happiest mistakes ever made by a man of science; for had not Professor Henslow believed these stones to be coprolites, (fossil dung), he would never, in all probability, have had them analysed, and the phosphatic nature and consequent agricultural value of these stones might possibly for centuries have remained unknown."

Henslow had been made President of the Ipswich Museum by 1850 by which time it had built up quite an extensive fossil collection. He wrote to the Suffolk Chronicle regarding a lawsuit Lawes had brought and wanted to correct an error he had made in his speech at the Museum dinner.

"I was supposed to have said I had received a subpoena to attend a trial in which the sum of £7,000 was involved, in respect of the nodules, commonly called "coprolites", found in the neighbourhood of Felixstowe. It will be seen by the sequel, that I must have said "£7,000 per annum". The trial to which I referred was brought to an issue last Monday, and the verdict was adverse to the claims of the plaintiff, who had taken out a patent, in 1842, for the manufacture of superphosphate of lime... A host of witnesses were subpoenaed, and among them I recognised at least seven Professors in Chemistry, geology, anatomy, etc. Considering the pains that had been taken with this case, and the great expense to which the opposing parties had been put themselves, it seems to me strange that the newspapers the following day should merely have stated that, "the Exchequer Court had been occupied all day with a patent case which contained nothing of sufficient interest to be reported". I venture to believe the case will prove to have been one of interest to some of the landed proprietors of East Suffolk, and possibly some in Essex also, who happen to possess property on the Red Crag formation. I also think it is a case which might be adduced with success against some of the absurdities of our patent laws...

In company with seven gentlemen, who had been attending the anniversary last week, I visited the "diggings" at Felixstowe; and from what I then observed, in addition to what I knew before of the positions of the phosphatic nodules in the crag, I feel strongly inclined to believe they will be found (here and there) dispersed over a very extended area. It is more than two years since I visited the locality, in company with Dr. Daubeny, the chemical professor at Oxford, and until then I had not been to the spot since I have communicated, through the Bury Post, in 1845, what I had previously observed of the abundance of these materials in that locality. We saw 1,000 tons of the nodules lying in a heap in a field, from which another 1,000 had been previously extracted, only a short time before. I had no opportunity at that time of remarking the exact position of the bed in which the nodules lay. I now find that they lie on patches immediately above a continuously abraded surface of the London Clay, and consequently beneath the general mass *of the Red Crag. The fact of their being slightly rolled, as well as mineralogically altered from the condition in which they were originally formed in the London Clay, has been noticed in a report of the proceedings of the British Association at their meeting in Oxford in 1846; but I had not then observed that they were so specifically located at the bottom of the Crag.*

The extent to which the nodules have already been raised is enormous, considering how short a time has elapsed since the spirit and energy of Mr Lawes were first brought to bear upon the question of their being made serviceable to the manufacture of superphosphate of lime. Hitherto, I understand, the demand has exceeded the supply; but the extent to which I am inclined to believe they may yet be procured is an hundredfold greater than I had ever before supposed to have been likely. It may afford some idea of the importance of these "diggings" when I state that I have been assured by those who appear to have possessed excellent opportunities of knowing the fact, that £10,000 per annum is within the income which has recently been derived from the sale of phosphate of lime obtained from these "diggings".

£10,000 a year was an enormous fortune. Whilst this could have been an attempt to limit Lawes from capitalising further in the area it provided an opportunity for local entrepreneurs. It was said by his contemporaries that, being a man of the cloth, Henslow did not wish to benefit financially from his discovery, but by including such details, it appeared he had an ulterior motive. He went on in the article to state that:

"...If any of the landed proprietors of the neighbourhood should profit by these hints, I may probably some day venture to remind them, cap in hand, that a small fragment of their gains might advantageously be appropriated to the funds of Ipswich Museum."

A few weeks later, a letter appeared in the Suffolk Chronicle criticising Henslow. It was from Dr W. B. Clarke, of 14 Berners Street, Ipswich. He felt that Henslow ought to have acknowledged his assistance as he claimed that it was him who had helped in locating and describing the deposit. He also had an article published in the Magazine of Natural History (Clarke, W.B. (1851), 'A few remarks upon the Crag of Suffolk', *Annals of the Magazine of Natural History*, ser. 2, Vol. VIII, pp.205 - 11). Maybe this was an attempt to let landowners know that he could be contacted for similar advice. From his letter it was apparent that some of the earlier workings had been exhausted and that the diggings now extended beyond Felixstowe.

"I conducted them to the spot where I had previously examined the "formation", but found the men had ceased operations, and the pits were covered in; but the results of the workings were lying upon the field in one or two large heaps... I also informed Professor Henslow I had found the deposit to vary in thickness from about a foot and a half to three to four inches... I also recommended the Professors to speak to some of the neighbouring villagers and labourers, which was done, and from these they obtained a good supply of various remains, principally auditory bones of whales, and the teeth of sharks..."

It is said that the diggings into the cliffs at Felixstowe resulted in a considerable increase in their erosion. High tides were capable of removing thousands of tons of rock. Faced with the potential loss of real estate the owners of cliff top properties probably put pressure on the town's fathers to curtail the operations and initiate sea defences. It is thought that this explains the construction of a sea wall of limestone blocks in 1850 (Correspondence, Allied School, Felixstowe, 11th Nov. 1855). As a result the workings were forced further up the coast as well as in inland parishes. New pits opened across the estuary on the marshes. Henslow observed this expansion and in a letter to the Raynbird Bros, Suffolk agriculturalists and prospective purchasers, he described the scale and profitability of the operations at Felixstowe:

"We saw 1,000 tons lying in one field, and 1,000 more had been raised during the past winter. This is independent of the many

thousands of tons raised by Mr. Lawes. Raised for 8 - 10s. a ton, sold at 24s. a ton. Manufactured phosphate sold at £7.0s.0d. a ton."

Getting up to £1,600 from just one field must have provided all the incentive they needed but no records of any arrangements Raynbird made have come to light. To be able to cut out the middleman and control the transport explains why so many of the manure companies wanted to be involved in every stage from raising to marketing. Landowners and farmers would have been approached directly by the manure companies, their agents or independent coprolite contractors. A coprolite manager and foremen were taken on to supervise the workings and they made arrangements with coprolite merchants to purchase their supplies and have them transported by barge or cart to Ipswich and elsewhere.

EXPANSION BEYOND FELIXSTOWE

In 1850 the diggings expanded across the Deben estuary into Bawdsey as well as further up the coast towards Boyton. In Colin Maycock's *'Charity, Clay and Coprolites – The Story of a Suffolk Almshouse Foundation,'* he states they were raised on the 690-acre Valley Farm (TM 367469), one of the properties in Boyton owned by the trustees of Mary Warner Charity. They were the major landowner in the parish. 43-year old William Miller was the tenant farmer and evidence shows that in 1850 he sold 71 tons from one pit to Edward Packard.

On 29th July John Crabtree, the clerk to the Trustees, was visited by two Bawdsey men, Edward Ransby, the landlord of 'The Star Inn', and Francis Robinson. They enquired about the possibility of raising the coprolites themselves from the Charity farm just northeast of Valley Farm (TM 374477). It was tenanted by John May. This was the present day Laurel Farm on the northern side of the Tang valley below Capel Wood. Here the crag was exposed on the hillside and the coprolites found beneath it where it overlay the London Clay. They did not get the contract. Packard did (S.C.R.O. HC 434 8728.310a; Boyton Charity Papers; Maycock, op. cit. pp. 28 - 29). His arrangements were that he pay the trustees two thirds of the sale price. This was thirty shillings (£1.50) for every ton at the dock. The trustees formalised a legal agreement with him on 5th November. This is the world's first documented coprolite agreement whereby the trustees agreed

"...to sell the Coprolite that may be found on Mr Miller's Farm at Boyton to Mr Packard who is to be considered the owner thereof. Mr Miller to dig, sift, and cart the same in a proper marketable state to be delivered free of all expense at Boyton Dock and put on board a vessel or at some other place of shipment equally convenient for shipment but not exceeding that distance. The same to be dug in such a manner as in the least possible way to affect the property. Mr Packard to pay to the Trustees the net sum ten shillings per ton free of all deductions and to pay Mr Miller one pound per ton on delivery - the Trustees or Mr Packard to have the liberty of putting an end to this arrangement upon giving one month's notice."

(S.C.R.O. CB412:4125 Box 2)

May's labourers got to work on the fields on the northern slopes of the Tang, just below Capel Wood. Whilst there is limited evidence of agreements in the Suffolk area, considerably more is known of the work in Cambridgeshire where surveyors' and solicitors' records have been deposited in the Record Office. Suffolk landowners in this area owned much smaller estates than the Cambridge Colleges, the Church and the Charity Commissioners. Many landowners made their own arrangements to have the fossils raised and, as a result, fewer of their records found their way into the local Record Offices or Museums. Farmers with the freehold got their labourers to dig them out during the winter months, once the harvest was in.

Fossil bones from the Cromer bone bed at West Runton, just west of Sheringham on the north Norfolk coast, were shipped down to Ipswich along with whale bones. Whether the latter were from the fossil bed or from the whaling fleet is unknown. Despite the expansion of the diggings into Cambridgeshire, Norfolk and Essex there was still a good demand for the Suffolk coprolites. A lot of the local traffic was by lighters and sailing barges that provided a boost in trade for those involved in the transport industry. Where the pits were too far from the coast or estuaries, horse-drawn tumbrils would have been seen carting them into Ipswich along the country lanes. Although Slater's 1850 trade directory for Suffolk did not mention the coprolites, perhaps as a direct result of the trade, it was mentioned that:

"The roads in every part of Suffolk are excellent, the improvements of them these last few years being almost inconceivable. The sea ports depend much on the exploitation of malt and corn, some are noted for making fine salt, burning lime from fossil shells."

The better fossil specimens were sold at anything from a few pennies to a few guineas, depending on their size and quality. There were a growing number of fascinated Victorian geologists who visited the many pits that opened in the area in the hope of getting some good specimens. Colchester and his sons built up a valuable collection of fossils from pits that were opened in Sutton. They were acknowledged as being generous in giving samples to visiting geologists. This naturally attracted the attention of a group from the British Museum who visited several pits on the Sutton estate in 1866. Exactly where they were located is uncertain. They did not use grid references in those days and it was common in the early years of geology for students and professors not to give accurate details of the location in case someone else found their site, got some other interesting specimens and then wrote a paper on them. Henry Woodward, an assistant in the geology department at the British Museum and co-founder of the Geological Magazine, reported how:

"Near Bawdsey Ferry we noticed in front of the cottage-doors small heaps of the dark-brown, shining, water-worn pebbles called "coprolites," which ten years ago created an extensive trade here, and

the preparation of which for artificial manure gave employment to numbers of peasantry....

"Leaving the river, we ascended the hill towards Mr. Colchester's farm at Sutton. We saw the first large accumulation at the entrance to a field, probably 220 tons; we picked up a water-worn tooth of the great shark Carcharadon, and another of Lamna, but no good examples of coprolites, although some pieces showed the twisted form slightly. On enquiring for Mr. Wood (Mr Colchester's steward), he soon appeared, and was most obliging and attentive to us throughout. He amused us by pulling from his pocket a handful of shark's teeth, two fossil crabs, and a very fine corkscrew coprolite, the best specimen I ever remember to have seen. These he presented to us."

DEATH OF A FOSSIL EXPERT

Woodward and his colleagues' enthusiasm for good specimens led them to the pits in Sudbourn. Indirectly this enthusiasm led to the death of the local fossil expert. He went on to tell the readers that:

"After leaving the village of Chillesford (where the Norwich Crag occurs) we came to Sudbourn Park gate, but not being quite sure of the way through the park, we kept to the turn-pike, and soon hailed the Orford lights. Every village in Suffolk, of any importance, has its "King's Head" and "Crown" inns; we went to the former, and after a night at the "Ramsholt Dock Inn", were both prepared most thoroughly to appreciate this comfortable little place. Having ordered supper, we sallied forth to enquire for a celebrated character at the "White Hart", known as "Jumbo" (alias William Brown). This oddity is a thin, wiry old man, between sixty and seventy years of age, and the most handy fellow in the parish. He is* the living oracle here on Crag-pits and shells, and must be invoked and propitiated with beer and shillings if you want to find the best of both. He is, however, troubled with fits of "brooding melancholy" (the effects of over potations), when he will not respond to any call, and must be dispensed with.

1887 photograph of a horse-drawn coprolite tumbril (cart) and washing pit on the banks of the River Deben beside what is now Waldringfield Sailing Club, Suffolk. (Suffolk Photographic Survey, Abbot's Hall Museum).

Horses, men and boy working at the coprolite washing pit beside the River Deben at Waldringfield. (Suffolk Photographic Survey, Abbot's Hall Museum).

Undated postacrd of Bawdsey Ferry close to the 19th century coprolite workings.
(Postacrd Picture by Judges Ltd. Hastings)

Such was his mood at this time. His knowledge of crag shells places him in a very exalted position, and among the rustics he is considered quite a distinguished palaeontologist. Having obtained this information, we returned to our inn, and after supper cleaned and packed our day's collection of Crag. We were up the next morning, and... As we could not get "Jumbo", we persuaded the landlord to accompany us to the pit in the park where the same great beds of Cyprina Islandica and Terebratula grandis, which we had observed at Sutton the day before, were again visible. All the best shells were however too brittle (owing to the wet state of the soil) to be obtained entire, so we got very few rarities. After dinner "Jumbo" presented himself, and said he had some Crag-shells for sale. We condescended to receive his overtures, and bought 10s. worth off him, which made up a pretty complete series, and the whole afternoon was occupied with packing them for London.

"He is", we ought rather to say "he was", for "Jumbo", like the crag itself, is now a thing of the past. Stimulated by a sovereign given him by

my friend Professor Suess of Vienna, "Jumbo" took an overdose of brandy, and, alas! went to the spirit land."

Coprolite wheelbarrow on the plank which probably led up to a barge. The large front wheel allowed the workers to see the plank in front of them. (Suffolk Photographic Survey, Abbot's Hall Museum).

Woodward pointed out for the benefit of prospective entrepreneurs who might be interested in venturing into the business that each operation was not always successful. He commented that Colchester had arranged to have a pit opened up on the south side of the hill but, when it proved unremunerative, it was filled up one or two years later and the ground levelled between 1861 - 1862. A lot of the rubble from these pits was used to reinforce the sea walls along the banks of the river. It is thought that the pits were around the 50-foot (15 m) contour line just north of Sutton Hall (TM 305454) (Whitaker, W., *Proceedings of the Geological Society,* vol. v.).

A long, water-filled trench was dug from the river and the coprolites were washed in wooden trays before being shovelled out into a pile. The brushwood fence protected the workers from the cold wind. (Suffolk Photographic Survey, Abbot's Hall Museum).

VISIT BY THE BRITISH ASSOCIATION FOR THE ADVANCEMENT OF SCIENCE

Two months after the opening of the Great Exhibition in Hyde Park in May 1851, a number of the great and the good of British Science met in Ipswich for the 21st meeting of the British Association for the Advancement of Science. It was attended amongst others by Prince Albert, Queen Victoria's German husband, George Airy, the Astronomer Royal, Charles Darwin and Thomas Huxley, the biologists, James Nasmyth, the engineer, Sir James Ross, the Antarctic surveyor, Rev. Henslow. On 8th July *The Times* reported on its outing down the

Orwell, visiting, amongst other sites, the coprolite pits and chemical manure works.

The labours of the association in the sections were suspended today and were diversified by some of those outdoor excursions which the members know so well how to turn to the best account, both physically and morally. No wonder, indeed that they should, with all their devotion to science, be glad to see her now and then al fresco, and that they should joyfully turn for a time gram gazing on her in her dress of black and white diagrams to the natural decoration of green trees and waving foliage, and exchange the heated atmosphere of the lecture room for the fresh breezes of the sea coast or open downs. The programme of excursions was rather extensive. In the first place there was a party for Woodbridge and Orford by land, a journey of 20 miles, presenting many agreeable features, not the least of which was a splendid breakfast offered to the members by Mr G. Thomas, of Woodbridge. The price of the tickets was 5s. and the numbers who went on the excursions proved that the route had very considerable attractions. After breakfast they inspected the creditable collection of British, Roman, Saxon and medieval antiquities of Mr Whincopp, in the Lecture hall of Woodbridge, and intimation was given to those members who "specially desired to examine the superposition of red on coralline clays, and the excavations for coprolites at Sutton," that they might gratify their desires by hiring a carriage. ...many little migrations were made by philosophical explorers well provided with sandwich-cases and hammers.

As it was impossible to be in all those places at once, I had, in compliance with the exigency of the case, to make a selection, and determined on "steam on the Orwell and along the coast". The River Queen left Ipswich soon after 9 o'clock; but, as the boat was not large and as the crowd of excursionists was very large, some little supplementary and independent trips were made in the same direction. The scenery on the Orwell is familiar to most of those who have a knowledge of the works of our landscape painters. It presents pleasing subjects for the pencil, as the shores are clothed with fine trees and undulate with many graceful windings from the water edge to the horizon, so as to form apparently chains of little lakes which are generally thickly studded with vessels beating up and down the tortuous channel. At the ancient port of Harwich a detachment of the Saxons landed at Ship-yard stairs, and were received with all proper courtesy; several of the craft in dock being dressed with flags and streamers of the occasion; they inspected a very old (barrel) crane erected in the time of Elizabeth, and visited Morton's patent slip, were in the course of building, and then went over to the coprolite factory of Mr Colchester, where the fossils are made into manure.

They proceeded to the handsome seat of Mr Bagshawe, M.P. where...a they were conducted to a temporary building in the grounds, in which was exhibited an interesting collection of fossils and curiosities, the property of Mr Bagshawe, and most of which were found in the vicinity of his residence. Coprolites, sharks' teeth, whales' bones, puddingstone, an ancient hoop cannon found off the coast, the femur of a mammoth &c. were all duly admired, noticed and criticised. Some beautiful specimens of fossil turtles, belonging to the Rev. Mr Bull, and of the crag on the seashore, the property of Mr Cricker, also attracted attention.

(The Times, 8th July 1851, page 8)

After a visit to Dovercourt, on the return trip they called in at Felixstowe and Bawdsey Ferry *"where there are numerous geological curiosities."* They also alighted at Ramsholt, to see the fossils being raised and to have the possibility of purchasing any interesting specimens.

"The coprolite was found in adjacent coasts, and there was a large stock of it at the mill. Many specimens of sharks' teeth, crabs, and other fossils were found in the coprolite and they were presented to the

visitors." (*Proceedings of the British Association for the Advancement of Science,* (1851), Ipswich)

Offices, Ardleigh Hall, and Colchester,

Ramsholt.

To be SOLD by AUCTION,
By B. MOULTON,

In the middle of October, unless previously disposed of by private contract,

NINE valuable detached pieces of Land, containing in the whole 18a. 2r. 82p., by the Tithe Survey, lying by the several roads in the parish; some adjoining the Estate of Lord Rendlesham; one abutting on the river Deben, adapted for a landing place, and the remainder intermixed with the estate of Joseph White, Esq.; the whole supposed to contain Coprolites; together with three Cottage Tenements.

Printed Particulars and Conditions of Sale, will be published in due time, and may be had of Messrs. Clayton, Cookson, and Wainwright, Solicitors, New Square, Lincoln's Inn; and of the Auctioneer, Woodbridge.

Undated **cutting from the Ipswich Journal, courtesy of Giles Colchester**

THE KYSON MONKEY

In the 1830s William Colchester was living at Little Oakley, near Harwich, where he had business interests. He still managed the Kingston (commonly called Kyson) brickworks just outside Woodbridge from 1837. His interest in fossils was sharpened that year when he found a mammal tooth in the London Clay. Members of the British Association for the Advancement of Science, on their excursion to Woodbridge in July 1851, were

informed that Kingston Kyson, where the remains of Macacus and Hyraeotherium were discovered by Mr Colchester, was within a easy walk of Woodbridge. Macacus, who is suggested to be so interesting an object that it will be worth while to visit the very spot of his discovery by coach, is, it appears, a fossil monkey, a fragment of the right side of whose lower jaw Mr Colchester was lucky enough to discover, in 1850, beneath a stratum of blue clay in a bed of whitish sand, thus proving that animals of this organisation lived in the Eocene period. Of Hyraeotherium I could glean no creditable information.

(The Times, 8th July 1851, page 8)

It sparked considerable interest when two geologists, Searles Wood and Charles Lyell, saw it. Lyell was from Scotland whose interest in geology was sparked by one of Rev. Buckland's lectures at Oxford University. He went on to write books on geology and was assisted in identifying fossils from the Tertiary formation by Searles Wood. Wood had settled in Hasketon, Suffolk, when he retired from the East India Company's mercantile fleet and devoted his life to palaeontology. He amassed a large Crag fossil collection, particularly from Ramsholt and Sutton. They showed Colchester's tooth to Sir Richard Owen of the Royal College of Surgeons in London who identified it as from an old world monkey. It was thought to date from 55 - 52 Ma. A newspaper critic suggested "*it might be nothing more than the remains of some monkey belonging to a travelling menagerie, which had died in Suffolk*". Subsequent investigations determined that it was from a hyracothere, a rabbit-like creature, or an early horse! It was kindly donated to Ipswich Museum. Over the next few years Colchester found jaws and teeth of other marsupials and his contacts with professors in London and Oxford got him really interested in palaeontology (Markham, R., Notes on the Kyson Monkey, Woodbridge and Fossils in Ipswich Museum).

TAKE OFF IN THE 1850s

By 1851 the diggings had taken off. Mr. Herapath, writing on the agricultural value of the deposit, pointed out that:

"Several thousands of tons of fossil bones, &c. are annually sold in this country under one form or another, and the consumption of them is daily and rapidly increasing."

John Wiggins, a fellow of the Geological Society, was probably one of those who had visited the pits and in his article in their quarterly journal commented that:

"Near Ramsholt Creek, Sutton, as in other parts of the Suffolk Crag, large quantities of fossil teeth, bone and coprolitic substances are found. These are rich in phosphate of lime and are now collected for agricultural purposes. They are found mixed with sand and gravel from 2 - 4 feet below the surface and about 300 tons had been procured from about a rood of ground which had been turned up."

THOMAS WALLER IN SUTTON

Such a shallow depth and yields of up to 1,200 tons an acre would have meant an enormous fortune for the landowner. When labour costs ranged between eight and ten shillings (£0.40 to £0.50) a ton and the fossils with the highest phosphate content could be sold to manure manufacturers at prices up to £3 per ton, big profits could be made. According to several sources, this pit was most likely on the estate of Thomas Waller, who lived in Sutton Hall (TM 305451) (Wood, S.V., (1858) 'Fossils of the Red Crag', *Q.J.G.S*, pp.40 - 41). In W.G Arnott's description of the estuary it was mentioned that Stonner Point, on Waller's estate (TM 292447), had been used as a landing place throughout the period of human settlement in the area.

"Quite a large settlement formerly existed round the Green at the back of the Point and it was a busy part of the parish when the coprolite industry was in full swing during the 19th century. Stonner Quay was built by Thomas Waller of Sutton Hall about 1850 for the purpose of shipping coprolite when the old barge channel was deepened. Coprolite, which is fossilised animal dung, was used as a fertiliser for the land and

was dug in large quantities all over the neighbourhood and particularly at Ham Woods. It fetched about £3 a ton and thousands of tons were shipped annually from the Debenside quays to all parts of the kingdom. The industry gave employment to hundreds of men, women and children between Bawdsey and Woodbridge, and there were men living in Waldringfield now who were earning 6d. a day "coproliting" and sleeping on benches in the bar of the Maybush Inn on a Saturday night because they were too tired to go home."

In Herapath's article he indicated that the diggings had expanded into neighbouring counties but made no mention of those in Cambridgeshire. He pointed out that the remains

"... are met with in such enormous quantities on the coasts of Suffolk, Norfolk and Essex, where several hundreds of persons are now actively employed in exhuming and collecting them, with the view to their future conversion into artificial manures. It is from these counties, indeed, that Mr. Lawes of Rothamsted, obtains nearly the whole of the material he employs in the preparation of his well-known "coprolite manure"; and so extensive is the demand for this description of fertilisers for wheat and turnip growing lands, I am credibly informed that several thousand tons of fossil bones, &c. are annually sold in this country under one form or another, and the consumption of them is daily and rapidly increasing... The Suffolk crag being exceedingly rich in fossils, both as regards number and quality, and the expense of water-carriage to any part of the Eastern coastline being at the same time very trifling, this county offers peculiar advantages to those who are engaged in this branch of traffic."

EVIDENCE FROM THE 1851 CENSUS

William Colchester was living only a few miles from his manure works in Harwich in Little Oakley, with his wife, nine children and six servants. He described himself as a merchant and ship-owner. There's no supporting evidence of coprolite diggings in Essex. The several hundreds employed were not referred to in Suffolk's 1851 census. Apart from eight people in Capel St Andrew, there was no reference to fossil or coprolite diggers, coprolite contractors or merchants in any of the parishes where it was then being worked. It is thought that the work was just considered as general labour, or, if they were employed by a farmer, as agricultural labour.

Another explanation is that the work generally took place over the winter months, once the harvest was in, and by late spring when the census was taken, the diggers were engaged on farm work. Hence they would not have described their occupation to the census enumerator as "diggers" or "coproliters". Analysis of the population changes over the decade to 1851 shows only some evidence that the diggings had any affect on numbers.

Boyton had its largest population that century – 320, thought to be directly related to the diggings. There had been a 34% increase over the decade of 81. Agriculture still dominated the economy but, despite its small size, the village had the full range of trades people and craftsmen to stay self-sufficient. They included a butcher, blacksmith. carpenter, dressmaker, grocer, miller, shoemakers and wheelwright - a lot of trades for a small community. The wealth generated from the sale of coprolites and the employment engaged in raising and transporting it would have been a significant stimulus to the economy. Despite this new occupation, no one in the census was described as involved in the diggings. This suggests that Miller and May used their farm labourers to do the work and they simply considered themselves as 'labourers' or 'agricultural labourers' rather than 'fossil' or 'coprolite' labourers.

Sutton experienced a 12.6% increase over the decade to 241. Although Mr. Waller was involved in 1850, he was described in the census as a "Farmer of 560 acres employing 26 labourers". Given that Henry Edwards of Sutton only employed thirty labourers on his 1,000 acres there is the likelihood that Waller's labourers were raising the coprolites for him (S.C.R.O. FC47.A1/1).

Capel St. Andrew was the only parish where there was any evidence of the diggings in the census. It had experienced a 9% decline over the decade to 202. There were diggings further along the slope from May's Farm towards Stonebridge Marshes, possibly on the site of the small ponds marked on today's map as Bushey Hole (TM 379484). 57-year old John Lucock was described as "*a farmer of 31 acres employing 1 labour, employing 4 labours after coprolite*". 48-year old James Stebbing farmed 64 acres with "*2 labours & son & 2 labours after coprolite*" (S.C.R.O. 1851 census; Strong, B. 'The Accounts of a Suffolk Blacksmith 1859 - 1881', *Journal of the Tools and Trades History Society*, Vol.9, p.55). How much they raised and what arrangements they made with the coprolite merchants remains unknown.

FURTHER DIGGINGS IN BOYTON

Late in 1851 John Crabtree visited both farms but only wrote in his notebook about May's Farm. Perhaps this was because Packard's workings were going on according to his instructions.

"Examined the coprolite diggings at Boyton. Up to this day Mr May has sold 50 tons of Coprolite to Packard which went to the North. There is now lying at Boyton Dock from Mays about 60 tons, 40 tons of which is sold to Packard. There is now lying at the back of May's barn about 100 tons in heaps. Memorandum: May pays Bennington (the tenant of Dock Farm) 7d. per ton for Dock charges. Bennington to this time has worked and screened about 42 tons and there is another heap in progress." (S.C.R.O. FC47.A1/1)

The work that was going on was described in 1885 by William Whitaker, one of the numerous geologists, who came looking for interesting specimens for their fossil collections or to sell to the new museums springing up around the country. He was employed by the

Geological Survey of Great Britain who specialised in the Cretaceous, Tertiary and post-Tertiary deposits. In particular he was interested in the water supply of the London area and south-eastern England. He was the author of numerous Geological Survey publications, and papers in the professional (*Quarterly Journal of the Geological Society of London*) and amateur (*Proceedings of the Geologists' Association*) geological journals, as well as in the publications of several local societies. He served as President of the Geological Society of London, the Geologists' Association, and the Croydon Natural History and Scientific Society. He was elected a Fellow of the Royal Society and, as we shall see, was instrumental in mapping the geology of the Ipswich area.

"*The [Boyton] pit, through overlying Crag and Drift, is made in successive steps, each three feet deep, except those at top and at bottom, which of course vary according to the surface of the ground and to the lie of the nodule bed. The sand, etc. is separated from the stones and nodules by screening, the unprofitable stones are picked out from the phosphatic nodules, bones, etc., which are carted off and taken to the distant manufactory. In this way a large area is sometimes worked over, the part first dug out being filled up with the material from the next attacked, and so on, the whole field in the end being levelled and returned to cultivation.*"

Without access to the railway network except at Ipswich, the industry did not develop in Southeast Suffolk as quickly as it might. The line to Cambridge was completed by October 1851 that allowed Colchester, Packard and Fison to bring in increased quantities of Cambridgeshire coprolites. However, the lack of a railway infrastructure provided a valuable boost to local carters and bargees. With super being sold across Britain and overseas, more and more businesses joined in the rush for manures. Demand for coprolite rose. Royalties paid to landowners ranged from seven to fifteen shillings (£0.35 - £0.75) a ton in the early 1850s. They depended on a range of factors: the depth, extent, continuity of the seam, the angle of dip, its cleanliness, the nearness to a water source, road, wharf or station, the volume coming onto the market, knowledge or ignorance of current prices and, inevitably, nepotism - how well the contractor knew the landowner.

WHAT DID THE DIGGERS LOOK LIKE?

The diggings were an alternative and much more profitable line of work than digging clunch, clay or turf. Enid Porter, a Cambridgeshire local historian, was told that the diggers wore thick union flannel shirts, fustian trousers tied with 'lalley gags', a fustian jacket with the commonly-used red handkerchief. To keep the rain off their heads and the sun out of their eyes they wore a black cap with a patent leather peak. On their feet they wore fen-type boots with two or three tongues that reached four inches above the ankle. To give them a better grip in the bottom of the pit some diggers fastened iron creepers to their boots. Iron insteps helped to prevent the boot from wearing away with the regular spade-work (Porter, E., Notes in Cambridge Folk Museum on her conversation with C. A. Swann; Examples of the iron work can be seen in Ashwell Museum, Cambridgeshire).

Tye's investigation into the life of the diggers led him to comment: "What a dirty job the old coproliters must have had! What with the red Crag around them and slush underfoot, they must have looked like bedraggled Red Indians when emerging from the pit at night."

EXPLOITING THE COPROLITE DEPOSIT

It was hardly a coincidence that the geological mapping of the country started around this time. Whilst the exploration was mainly for scientific reasons, knowledge of the extent and distribution of the Red Crag and Cambridgeshire Greensand was of commercial importance to those who had money to invest in what was to become known as the coprolite diggings. The seam averaged about thirty inches (about 39 cm) thick but in Potton in Bedfordshire it was up to six feet (2.1 m). In

1866 Iguanodon bones, teeth and claws were unearthed which sparked intense geological interest. In some areas the seam was non-existent, locally called 'dead land', due to a slight rise in the seabed whilst the fossils had tended to accumulate in the hollows. Yields therefore varied.

In Cambridge itself it was about 300 tons per acre (0.404ha.). In one pit in Wicken it was as high as 2,000 tons but the average was 250 tons per acre (Kingston, A. (1889) *'Old and New Industries on the Cam'*, Warren Press, Royston p.16). When annual agricultural rents were rarely over fifty shillings (£2.50) an acre and the coprolites could be sold at over £2 per ton, potentially several hundred pounds could be realised from an acre! Wages of agricultural labourers at that time would not have been over £25 in a year and £200 could have bought a small estate. No wonder there was a lot of interest in them. So began what has been termed by the historian, Richard Grove, as *'The Cambridgeshire Coprolite Mining Rush'* (Oleander Press, Cambridge, 1976).

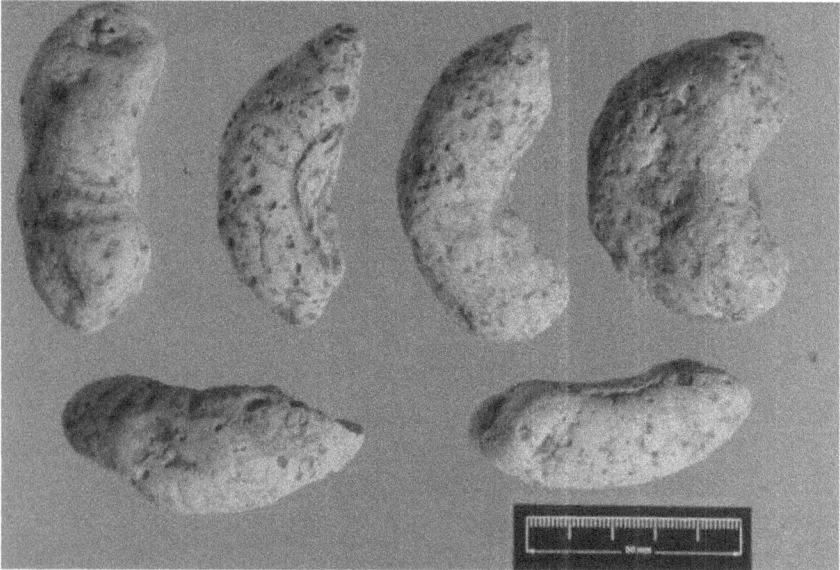

Bedfordshire coprolites from Potton. Whilst they resemble droppings they are actually broken sections of ammonites.
(Photograph courtesy of the Earth Sciences Museum, Cambridge)

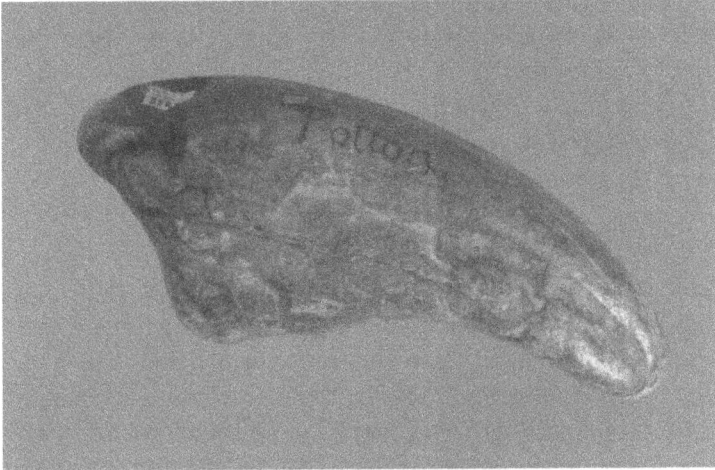

The Potton iguanodon claw
(Photographs courtesy of Earth Sciences Museum, Cambridge)

The depth and extent of the bed had to be determined. This was done initially by digging a coffin-like pit. A cheaper method was by using a two-man corkscrew borer. Walter Tye, in his account of the Suffolk industry, included an interview with one of the diggers who said that:

"To test the depth of the coprolite he made use of a tool like a giant corkscrew, called a 'dipper', which shuddered in his hands when striking the mineral. Local cottagers always knew what the foreman was after when he came into their gardens carrying his 'dipper'. Naturally, they strongly objected to their gardens being turned topsy-turvy, however much coprolite he might find there, and they were always delighted to see him go. Old residents today say that a sixpenny tip usually had the desired effect."

In many places in Suffolk the deposit was found outcropping on the surface but in Cambridgeshire it generally had to be dug from between ten and twenty feet (3.7 - 7.4 m) of chalk marl. Where it was found on a small property it was a simple matter for the landowner to take on a gang of labourers and have the fossils dug up, washed and sorted and then carted off and sold to a manure manufacturer. In Suffolk it was commonly the farmer's own agricultural labourers. They used to dig the fossils during the low season, once the harvest was in. The work continued over the winter months and then the pits would be left to allow farm work to start in spring.

If the land was copyhold then the tenant might get permission to raise any minerals underneath the property using their labourers, paying a royalty to the landowner. Occasionally, where a large-scale operation was envisaged, sub-tenants were evicted and a coprolite manager was allowed to move in to the farmhouse. There was no security of tenure in those days. On larger properties an advertisement might be placed in the local press and tenders invited for a contractor to do the work. Farmers and others set themselves up as coprolite contractors and took on a gang of men and boys. Pick axes, crowbars, shovels, spades, planks, dog irons (supports for the planks), wheelbarrows, trucks and tramway had to be bought and, away from the coast, a horse or steam-operated washmill had to be erected to clean the soil and clay from the fossils. In some places a well was sunk or a pump installed to raise water. One of the farm buildings was used for storing tools and machinery, otherwise a new shed was erected. These were sometimes needed for sorting the fossils from any unwanted pebbles or stones. They were also used for having lunch or sheltering from the rain. All this cost money and local bank managers were keen to make loans to enterprising individuals in an industry that had such high returns.

No details of female employment in Suffolk have come to light but women and girls were employed in large numbers where the deposit was found in sandier areas. Here the fossils needed sorting to remove any unwanted stones that would reduce the quality and therefore the price paid by the manure manufacturers. The main areas of female employment were in Wicken in Cambridgeshire and Potton, near Sandy in Bedfordshire.

Contractors agreed to do the work over a set number of years with them paying the landowner a royalty of so much per ton. The tenant farmer was often compensated for the loss of revenue from those fields out of cultivation by up to £10 an acre. Once work got started, the topsoil and subsoil was barrowed to one side of the field to be replaced later. In many cases it was used as the base of the washmill. As the coprolite seam was exposed, the diggers shovelled it into wheelbarrows or drop-sided trucks. These were then pushed by hand or pulled by horses along a tramway specially laid that ran out of the pit, along the edge of the field or trackway to the washmill. Here their contents were unloaded to create large piles before they were washed and sorted.

Coprolite Diggings at Orwell, Cambridgeshire. 1860s – 1870s

(Courtesy of Cambridgeshire Collection W27.1J80 25358)

Coprolite Diggings in Cow Pasture, Abington Pigotts, Cambridgeshire, 1883
(Courtesy of Mr and Mrs Sclater, Abington Pigotts)

Coprolite pit at Great Brickhill, Bedfordshire in 1875.
(Courtesy of Mr A. T. Bates)

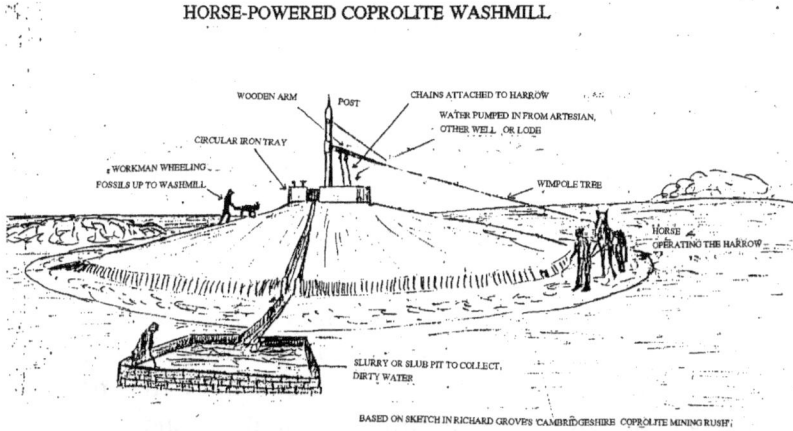

HORSE-POWERED COPROLITE WASHMILL

Postcard c.1884 showing coprolites being taken by tumbril to Millbrook Station, Bedfordshire. Similar scenes would have been common in Suffolk taking coprolites to the estuary for washing or to the manure works for grinding.

The soil above the seam on the new face was removed after undercutting, a process that caused considerable danger. Crowbars, pick-axes and shovels were used to make it collapse and, for convenience, it was just thrown into the trench already worked. This 'backfilling' meant that the labourers gradually progressed across the field and onto adjoining property where a new lease was sought. Sometimes pits were opened at opposite ends of the field and two gangs of diggers gradually dug their way towards each other.

In Cambridgeshire and Bedfordshire there were numerous cases of accidents in the pits caused by these collapses. Broken limbs, smothering and even death by suffocation were reported. Addenbrookes Hospital in Cambridge was so concerned that they encouraged those in charge of the pits to employ 'watchers' to warn the diggers of an impending collapse. Not many did and the accidents continued. Apart from Rose Ann Sare being killed in a cliff collapse, little other evidence of accidents in the Suffolk pits has come to light.

The job of washing the fossils got progressively easier over the years. Initially, the technique in Suffolk was to dig a trench into the side of the estuary or the riverbank. The actual washing and screening process was described in Walter Tye's fascinating insight into the diggings:

"That was an old man's job when he became too old for the pit. A long tank some thirty feet in length, was specially provided for the job. The coprolites, along with a certain amount of dirt and bones, were shovelled into sieves which, when full, were placed on a ledge in the tank, just under the surface of the water; to each sieve was fastened a long pole, which the washer pulled backwards and forwards until the stones were clean. When there was a shortage of water, in or near the pit, the washing was done at the quayside before loading."

This was often done sheltered by high straw fences to protect them from the cold winter breezes coming in off the North Sea. (Special Rpt. on Mineral Resources of Gt. Britain No.5, *Mem. Geol. Surv.* 1916; Tye, W. op. cit). In Cambridgeshire, without access to a tidal estuary, innovative engineers used their skills to develop sophisticated washmills powered by horse or steam engine. A mound was constructed using the top and subsoil. On top of this mound a circular brick base was laid onto which a circular iron tray was placed. Barrowloads of fossils were wheeled up the mound and emptied into the tray. A pump was often installed to bring the huge quantities of water needed from a nearby water source. Wells sometimes had to be dug and lined with bricks. At one time there were eleven such mills in operation in the Bassingbourn area that were claimed to have been responsible for lowering the water table of the area (Whitaker, W. (1921), 'Water Supply of Cambs', *Mem. Geol. Surv.* London, p.84). There is a photograph of a circular coprolite harrow in Cambridgeshire Collection: W27.1. KO. 19554).

Mr Lucas, the son of the Burwell doctor described the working of these mills. Once the coprolite had been brought to the surface:

"The first thing to do was to throw up a hill in the middle of the ground, and this was done by first erecting a post about ten or twelve feet long, and throwing the soil around it to a height of eleven or twelve feet and of thirty feet in diameter. Three feet from the centre a ring would be formed six to eight feet wide and four feet deep. This would be paved with bricks and the sides would be sheets of iron. On one side of the hill a platform was made from a wooden tank, to which was connected a pump eighteen feet long; a pipe from the tank would go with the ring and opposite the tank was a trapped outlet, and on the outer side of the hill a square of about two chains would be earthed up a little to form a sort of pan. From the central post a wooden arm would be attached about twelve to fourteen feet long; to this would be attached a wimpole tree, to which a horse would be yoked. Connected to the centre of the post would be a light rail which was fixed to the

horse bridle to keep the horse always in its track; from the arm would be suspended two iron harrows which ran well in on the bottom of the ring. When the soil containing the fossils was wheeled up to the ring a sufficient quantity of water would be let in. As the horse went round a creamy fluid would be produced and the fossils would drop on the floor. Then the trapped outlet would be opened and the creamlike fluid, called "slurry" would flow into pans. This operation having been repeated a number of times, the fossils on the floor would be washed clear of earth and weighed up".

The cost of constructing these mills in the late-1840s when they were first developed was £100 but by 1875 the "coprolite contractors had become so expeditious that a hill could be put up for £5!" (ibid.). A description of such mills was recorded in David Eades' 'Rambles in Cambridgeshire', a 19th century tourist's account of his trip to the fens:

"As we return from Burwell our eyes rest on several raised circular enclosures, round which a number of often grey horses are almost ceaselessly walking. These are the mills erected for washing the fossils. These fossils or coprolites are valuable on account of the calcic phosphate contained in them."

These mills were probably used in those Suffolk parishes away from the estuaries. Whether the following method was used has not been documented but in Hinxworth, Bedfordshire, a water-powered wheel was set up in a barn. In Audrey Kiln's research into the industry she interviewed a Mr Street who described the process:

"The eaves in the barn he estimated at 20 feet high. Housed in the barn was a portable steam engine, fired by wood and coal, which was connected by a belt to a huge wooden wheel which Mr Street said missed the roof by inches. Underneath the wheel was a large washing trough. The wheel had large metal cups attached to each strut. The fossils were placed into the trough and water was let in through a pipe. The wheel was driven by the engine and as the cups passed through the *trough they picked up the fossils, carried them round, and replaced them in clean water at the bottom of the trough. The slurry was then released from the trough by removing a large plug. Until recent years, part of the wheel could be seen standing outside The Barn, but unfortunately there is no record of its existence now."*

In some areas a less expensive but more efficient process was developed. This was a cylindrical wash mill, rather like an early version of today's vegetable washer. They were in use over at Potton in Bedfordshire where they were described in an article in the Bedfordshire Times:

"... the coprolites are wheeled in barrows to another portion of the ground where a cylindrical sieve is fixed for the purpose of freeing them from the sand. This machine, which is worked by horse power, is a round cylinder of sheet iron, perforated with holes of a quarter inch diameter and placed horizontally in a tank of water, the cylinder being half submerged. The drum of the cylinder is two ft. in diameter at the larger end and 1 ft. at the smaller and 10 ft. in length.

"The fossils are put in at the larger end, and as the drum revolves the smallest stones and the sand fall through the holes into the water tank, and the larger are carried along by a screw arrangement, and emptied at the smaller end into barrows. When these are filled they are wheeled by men into the sorting sheds where women are engaged in sorting. These sheds, 28 ft. long by 8 ft. wide, have on each side a bench, separated by partitions with room for one woman to work.

"The fossils being largely mixed with sandstones, it is necessary that they should be removed before they are ready for market. The fossils in their mixed state, are emptied on the benches and sorted, the stones being thrown onto the floor and the fossils passed through a hole at the back of the benches into a box outside. They are then wheeled into heaps ready for sale."

As the technology improved, contractors who could afford it, introduced steam-powered washmills. After several such washings the dirty water, locally termed 'slub' or 'slurry', was run back into banked-up 'pans' to dry out before the topsoil was replaced. The idea was that, once dried, the cracks in it would allow better drainage.

As the work progressed across the field the mill was transferred to a more accessible site. Drainage pipes were laid, the topsoil was barrowed back into the trench or slurry pit and the land was levelled ready for cultivation. Whilst the theory was that this process would improve the soil, in practise the operation was not always done thoroughly. It was cheaper for a contractor to cover it up quickly and move on. A farmer, however, would take care as he would benefit from improved cropping. In parts of Cambridgeshire white chalk markings can still be seen on the fields which indicate where slurry was not properly covered or the topsoil replaced. Aerial photographs may well show the same problem in Suffolk. Astute land agents ensured that agreements included very precise instructions for the drainage, levelling and seeding.

During the 1850s there were four manure factories in Ipswich and four in Cambridge. With them paying an average forty-three shillings and sixpence (£2.18) a ton in 1856 for Cambridge coprolites and less than £2.00 a ton for the Suffolk deposit there were still reasonable profits to be made by coprolite contractors and merchants. With 'super' being sold successfully across the country it was not long before sales were being promoted across Europe, in America and throughout the Empire. There were reports of sales as far afield as Russia and Queensland (Grove, op.cit.).

There was now a commercial incentive for the geologists to map the Red Crag deposit in Suffolk and Essex. Work started in other counties. Although the Upper and Lower Greensand beds were not continuous, the fossils at their base were worked in parts of Norfolk, Cambridgeshire, Hertfordshire, Bedfordshire, Buckinghamshire, Oxfordshire, Hampshire, Yorkshire and Kent. Its enormous extent allowed many new manure companies to capitalise on this raw material and take a share of the increasing market for artificial fertilisers. Accordingly, many new chemical manure works were opened on the coprolite belt in Burwell, Duxford, Shepreth, Royston, Bassingbourn and Odsey.

FINANCIAL ARRANGEMENTS

In the early 1850s coprolite contractors were paying landowners royalties per ton for all the coprolites they raised. This entailed having a weighbridge set up by the works and for accurate measurements to be recorded. To avoid errors and dependence on the contractors' weighings, the land agents for the larger landowners in Cambridgeshire suggested an alternative scheme whereby royalties should be paid according to how many acres were dug over the year. This entailed having the pits surveyed around Lady Day (May 1st) and Michaelmas (September 29th). The surveyor's measurements could then be used to determine how much the contractor owed. This provided companies like Bidwell, Francis, Smith, Carter Jonas, and Mann and Raven a valuable additional source of income for the next forty years. Unfortunately, very few records of Suffolk surveyors who did coprolite work have come to light.

Royalties ranged from as high as £400 to as low as £30 an acre but the average was about £100. This was about forty to fifty times the revenue the landowners could get from agricultural rents. After labour and other costs were deducted the contractors could make a big profit.

In October 1852 Packard got his first delivery of 158 tons of Boyton Charity coprolites from Felixstowe Ferry (TM 329377). They were unloaded at the Ipswich docks from the "Celerity" and the "Active". This was to become a regular source of supply over the next thirty years (S.C.R.O. HC 434 8728.310a; Boyton Charity Papers; Waldringfield HD 328/1; Tye, W. op.cit. p.5).

The Ipswich Dock in 1890. This picture was taken from Flint Wharf, near where the Last Anchor restaurant is now, looking across to Neptune Quay close to Fore Street
http://www.eveningstar.co.uk/Content/columns/kindred/htm/030304docks.asp

By the end of 1852, 200 tons of Boyton coprolites had been sold at prices which fluctuated between twenty-four and twenty-five shillings (£1.20 and £1.24) per ton. May estimated *"the expense of digging, screening, carting, wharfage, porterage, barrows, sieves, pump, etc. equal to 12/- (£0.60) a ton"*. This gives one a good idea of the profits being made. As the Trustees took two thirds of these revenues and allowed May the other third one can understand that this new activity was more profitable than farming. A total of 344 tons were raised that year and such was Packard's demand he had bought 712 tons by the following November paying twenty-eight shillings (£1.40) a ton. Demand by the end of 1855 was so great that he was paying a staggering £3 a ton. Documents also show that Ransby was paying fifty-nine shillings (£2.95), suggesting he was acting as an agent, arranging sales to other manufacturers. Prices dropped to forty-five shillings (£2.25) by the end of 1856 but with 'super' selling at between £6 and £7 there were enormous fortunes being made.

The hard work involved resulted in the labourers being given higher wages and as a result, expenses rose to between twenty-eight to thirty shillings (£1.40 and £1.50) per ton. By 1854 about 12,000 tons of Suffolk coprolites were being raised each year. The industry was booming with reports of coprolites being traded at Woodbridge, Felixstowe, Bawdsey Ferry, Ipswich and Harwich.

THE STOWMARKET NAVIGATION

The Stowmarket Navigation, often referred to as the Ipswich & Stowmarket Navigation, was constructed by 1793 making the 17-mile (27.2 km) River Gipping navigable. Fifteen locks, each 55 ft by 14 ft (20.3 x 6.8 m) with a draught of 3.3 ft (1.17 m) allowed barges carrying up to 35 tons to rise the 90 feet (31.5 m) between the two market towns. The return trip took about 16 hours. By the beginning of the 19th century over thirty barges a week were carrying coal, slates, manufactured and imported goods upstream, whilst gun-cotton, beer and agricultural produce were carried on the return run. Manure, by order of the original Act of Parliament, could be carried free of tolls! When coprolites began to be exploited in the 1840s they provided a significant boost to the company's profits. Stowmarket prospered after the navigation opened. Within a few years the population had doubled and industries were springing alongside the river (Bob Kearney, Ipswich IWA).

BARGES, LIGHTERS AND SHIPS

Packard realised there was tremendous potential for profit in the coprolite and fertiliser industry and decided to invest on an even larger scale. He owned a number of canal barges named after rivers and, with other members of his family, had a large proportion of the shares in three sea-going sailing barges, appropriately called the *Fossil* built at Blackfriars in London in 1843 and purchased in 1847, the *Ammonite* in 1859 and the *Nautilus* in 1870. The *Dewdrop* was built in 1867. William

99

Bell of Harwich was the skipper of the *Fossil* and owned eight of the sixty-four shares. He later moved to Ipswich to become ship's husband of Packard's barges. As well as sailing barges, Packard also operated a small fleet of steam coasters. His shipyard built other ships, notably the *Express* in 1854, the *Albatross* in 1869, *Mabel* in 1875, *Fearless* in 1876, the *Davenport* in 1877 and *Kingfisher* sometime later (Moffat, op.cit.).

With the fossils being exploited from the London Clay, William Colchester got involved. He recognised that there were profits to make in the transporting of the fossils and invested in shipping, particularly the barges and lighters. He ran a small slate importing and shipbuilding business in No. 6 yard in Old Carpenter's Row in St Clements where his first sailing barge, the *Raven* was built in 1841 under the management of James Hubert. The second was the *Primus*. The construction of the wet dock in Ipswich in 1842 was hailed as the largest construction of its kind in the country and allowed vessels drawing 15 feet (5.55 m) up the Orwell and float in the dock. Seeing the economic potential of getting larger ships and more trade stimulated entrepreneurs to develop the site. Colonel George Tomline inherited Orwell Park six years later with plans to develop the Orwell Works. This encouraged Colchester to move further downstream to a site he purchased between the Bayley's yard, the major Suffolk shipbuilding family, and the tree-lined roadway running along the lower dam of the New Cut dock, just north of the Cliff Bight. It was later called Dock End Yard. Subsequent barges he had built before 1863 were named *Secondus, Tertius,* (*Quartus* was built elsewhere), *Quintus, Sextus, Septimus* and *Octavius.* By the beginning of 1860 he had 14 barges, two schooners, two billyboy sloops and three other sloops.

By about 1870 Colchester had more than thirty vessels, which included fourteen barges, two schooners, the *Ann* and the *Rose,* a couple of 'billyboy sloops' and three other sloops. Sometimes as many as fourteen of his vessels were waiting in turn to load at his Ipswich works. He also had a fleet of shrimpers, smacks sailing from Harwich that had previously been used for raising septaria for use in the cement industry (*Geological Magazine*, March 1899; Author's correspondence with Giles Colchester, London; Moffat, op.cit, p.36).

RAILWAY TRAFFIC

As the extension of the Eastern Counties Railway brought freight and passenger traffic as far as Colchester in 1843 a group of Suffolk entrepreneurs saw financial opportunities to develop it further to Ipswich. John Chevallier Cobbold, the Ipswich MP, managed to get an Act through parliament to establish the Eastern Union Railway. With him as chairman the company purchased land between Ipswich and Colchester and began constructing the connection. When the trustees of the Ipswich and Stowmarket Navigation realised the line was going to run adjacent to the canal they were worried about losing trade. Careful negotiation resulted in the railway company leasing the navigation. In 1846 an Act was passed allowing them to rent it for 42 years but to be kept in the same condition as it was on the date the Act was passed.

The line between Ipswich and Colchester, the terminus of the Eastern Counties Railway from London, duly opened in June 1846. The line to Bury St Edmunds was completed a few months later and to Hadleigh the following year. This facilitated the rail transport of coprolites and a whole range of other goods to Stowmarket, Cambridge, London, Norwich and other parts of the country. It was not uncommon for frequent special trains to be running laden with thousands of tons of the newly discovered mineral. Railway trucks had COPROLITES painted in red on their sides.

The railway from Manningtree to Harwich was completed in 1854 which would have boosted Colchester's business. It is worth noting that washed coprolites were transported by train as 'loose traffic' in the 'mineral class' of goods but when they were in ground form, they were treated as 'special class'. Being more valuable in ground form, the freight charge was considerably higher. This caused the manure manufacturers to complain as it made the difference of between four shillings and sixpence and ten shillings (£0.22 and £0.50) a ton. As it was quite likely that some of the shareholders, directors of the manure companies, and coprolite landowners also had investments in the railway boards, pressure could well have been brought to bear. The Eastern Union Railway Company decided to compromise and agreed to truck it all at the rate of six shillings and eight pence (£0.34) per ton, the same class as stones and slate (Cambridge Railway Station, notes 15-D-2).

Packard's first recorded coprolite agreement in Cambridgeshire was in 1854. He gained permission to raise them from Coldham's Lane in Cambridge. The archives of Cambridge City Council, St. John's and Corpus Christi Colleges show his men were working pits on Coldham's Common, in Grantchester and Barton and it is almost certain he made other agreements with smaller landowners whose records have not been kept. He stayed on in Cambridge until the early 1870s when the shallower coprolite seams were becoming exhausted ('The Early Fertiliser Years 1843 - 1929', *Fison's Journal*, 1963; O'Connor, B. '*The Dinosaurs on Coldham's Common*', Bernard O'Connor; Bedfordshire County Record Office, Peel's Estate Papers).

CROSSKILLS OF BEVERLEY

Although the use of portable steam engines on tramways laid across the fields has not been documented in Suffolk, it is possible they were used on large operations. Crosskills of Beverley, North Yorkshire supplied farm railway equipment and low-sided, wooden tipping trucks to coprolite contactors in Cambridgeshire. William Crosskill set up his first foundry business in about 1825, producing the first clod breaker. By 1830 he was supplying rails and trucks for farm railways. When the fossil diggings took off in the 1840s he may well have supplied Suffolk landowners and coprolite contractors with much of the equipment needed to transport the coprolites to the nearest road, wharf or railway siding. (Paar, Harry, (2003), *'The Industrial Locomotive,'* pp.329-

335;   Correspondence   in   *'Steaming'*   2003,
http://www.ruralhistory.org/nof/victorianfarming)

MOVING OUT OF IPSWICH

The processes involved in making superphosphate proved objectionable to some of the Ipswich residents. In 1851:

"The fumes of silicic acid so affect the nostrils of the worthy citizens of the borough and the dimensions of their business had so increased in the meantime, that the firm [Packard] were compelled to carry their mixing departments some miles into the country, keeping the old premises exclusively for grinding and storing purposes."

(*Norwich Argus*, 'How Chemical Manures are manufactured', undated article in Bury St Edmunds Record Office)

He purchased land in Bramford from the Eastern Union Railway Company and Sir George Broke-Middleton, between Papermill Lane and the railway and south of the River Gipping and the Ipswich and Stowmarket Navigation. In 1854 construction of his Bramford Chemical Works began (TM 126477). When it started operating in 1857, it was the first sulphuric acid and superphosphate works of its kind in the country. The bargees, in addition to their wages, were paid four pints of beer a bottom (emptying a barge of coprolite at the factory).They probably drank in the White Elm just up Paper Mill Lane. The plant had its own sulphuric acid works, gasometer, a wharf and railway sidings where cranes hauled the coprolite from the barges coming in from Ipswich and the covered trucks coming from Cambridgeshire (25" Suffolk, 1881 75.2).

Joseph Fison followed suit. He expanded his business by moving from Levington to a site in Bramford in 1858. His Eastern Union Mills were erected with only a wall separating his works from his competitor (TM 126479). Being closer to the river meant easier loading and offloading for the sailing barges. That year he advertised as a manufacturer of Chemical Manures, Sulphuric Acid and Artificial Manures. His company was to become a specialist in the manufacture of compound fertilisers, mainly for home use, but also for abroad. They were sold as far afield as New Zealand, Australia and South Africa. The manure companies' business provided a valuable stimulus for the dock trade at Ipswich (*K.P.O.D.*, 1858; Norsk Hydro file, Museum of East Anglian Life, Stowmarket).

In summer 1857 they arranged to purchase regular quantities from Frederick Laws, a Suffolk coprolite contractor who lived at Foxhall Hall (TM 229436). Laws was also raising them from Coldham's Common in Cambridge from where they were sent by train to be processed at Prentice's chemical manure works.

Laws was one of the first coprolite contractors to lease land in Cambridge. He worked part of Coldham's Common for two years from 1854. When the City Corporation realised how profitable the deposit was they wanted more than the guinea (£1.05) a ton Laws was paying them. Unwilling to renew his lease with them he returned to Suffolk. Evidence shows that he had coprolite pits in operation in Foxhall between 1855 and 1858. One of his workmen uncovered a human jawbone in a 16-foot (3.3 m) deep pit. This is referred to later (Spencer, H.E.P., '*A contribution to the History of Suffolk*', Suffolk Naturalists' Society, early 1970s, pp.118 - 20; *Mem. Geol. Surv.* Mineral Statistics, HMSO.1860, p.375).

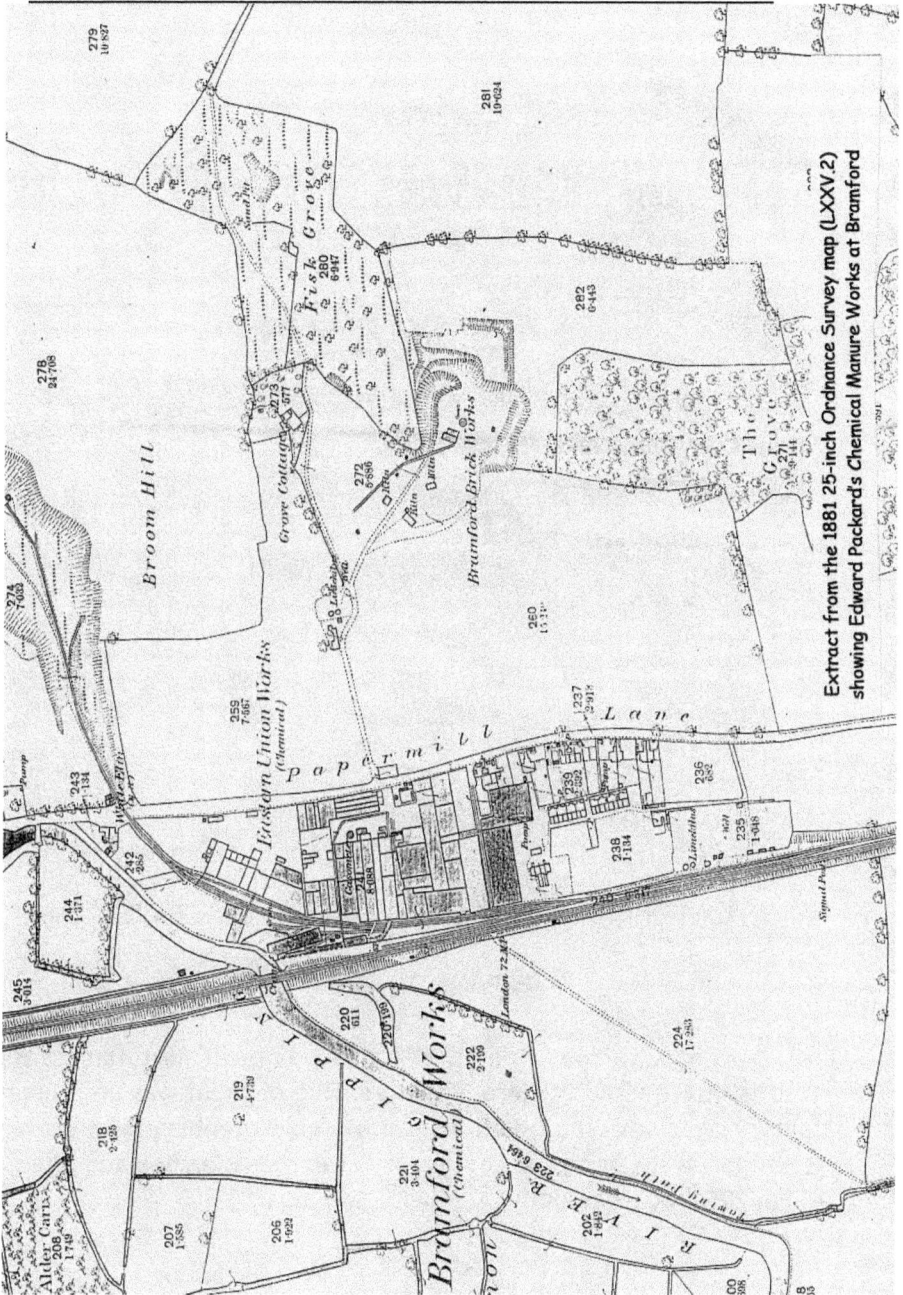

Extract from the 1881 25-inch Ordnance Survey map (LXXV.2) showing Edward Packard's Chemical Manure Works at Bramford

EASTERN COUNTIES MANURE WORKS,
IPSWICH;
BONE MILLS AND ACID WORKS,
BRAMFORD.

EDWD. PACKARD & CO.

Have the pleasure to inform their Friends and the Public, that they are prepared to supply the following manufactured and other Manures, which they guarantee of the best quality.

Packard's Top Dressing for Grass and Wheat	Mineral Bi-Phosphate of Lime, 20 to 25 per Cent. Soluble	Sulphate of Ammonia
Ditto Manures for Barley and Oats	Super-Phosphate of Lime, containing 35 to 40 per Cent.	Sulphuric Acid
		Ditto Concentrated
	Packard's Wheat Manure, a most efficient autumnal application	Ground Coprolites
Ditto for Mangold Wurtzel and Clover Leys		Ditto ditto Dissolved
		Ditto Bones—Ditto Calcined
Ditto Turnip Manure, yielding 25 per Cent. Soluble Phosphate of Lime	Peruvian Guano, guaranteed Gibbs' Importation	Ditto Dissolved
		Ground Gypsum
	Nitrate of Soda	Agricultural Salt
		Linseed and Rape Cake

From the complete state of our Bramford Works, we have been enabled to bring our Manures generally to a high state of perfection, and in particular we would refer you to the high per-centage of Soluble Phosphate the Turnip Manure and Super-Phosphates contain, believing that the quality has not been equalled by any other Manufacturer. The prices of these manures are also, in proportion to their increased value, much lower in price than they have hitherto been sold.

E. P. and Co. having been engaged for the past twelve years in the Manufacture and Sale of Manures, with an ever-growing trade, feel convinced that to continue to receive the favours of the Agriculturists of the Eastern Counties they must produce good results, affording a profitable return for the outlay incurred, and thus they will secure the confidence, support, and recommendation of their customers, which it will be their earnest endeavour to merit.

WORKS: IPSWICH AND BRAMFORD.

Kelly's 1858 Post Office Directory for Cambridgeshire, Norfolk and Suffolk

EXPANSION IN THE 1850s

As Felixstowe was one of the many popular Victorian seaside 'resorts' it attracted numerous visitors. One of them was an eccentric Cambridge fellow who called himself 'Humble Gumble'. He must have gone for a walk along the coast past Felixstowe Marshes and after his trip in 1854 recorded that:

"*When you approach the Deben the cliffs disappear; and by the side of the river you will see a large extent of salt-marsh, which is not very ornamental. By the side of the river stands a bunch of houses, which appears to take its name from the Ferry, it is called Bawdsey Ferry; the people inhabiting them are very poor, subsisting chiefly on lobsters and coprolites. In the summer they also pick up a little money by letting their boats and taking Felixstowe people for a quiet toss after dinner 'with the blue above and the blue below'... In the winter their abode must be rather trying; one of the ferrymen told me that they were frequently disturbed in the winter nights by the summons of ships in distress.*"

The discovery of the fossils would have provided the cottagers with a welcome extra source of income but it appeared it did not particularly improve their standard of living. Those who owned their own property under which the fossils were found would have profited from selling them but generally it was the large landowners who made considerable fortunes from having them raised from their estates. White's trade directory for 1855 revealed just how far the industry extended:

"*Immense quantities of COPROLITE are got in all parishes on or near the coast from Bawdsey Haven to Boyton. It is a valuable mineral, and is extensively used as manure and in the finer sorts of earthenware, and thousands of tons of it are now shipped yearly from the Deben to various parts of the kingdom, and great quantities of it are burnt and used as manure by the Suffolk farmers.*

Eustace Prentice (1833 – 1884), one of the founders of Prentice Brothers,
fertiliser manufacturers of Stowmarket
(http://www.yara.com/en/about/yara_centennial/heritage/fisons_inter.html)

Its name coprolite, or dung-stone, is expressive of its fertilising qualities which were first discovered in 1718 by Mr. Edmund Edwards, a farmer of Levington. Veins and ridges of it are found and got at various depths from two to twenty feet, and as much as £20 worth has been got out of a cottager's garden. It is mostly found near springs of crystal water, surrounded by crag and abounding in fossils of the antediluvian world; including relics of enormous species of fish, animals and shells, most of which are now extinct. When thrown up, it is carefully sorted, washed through sieves, and laid in heaps, ready for carting. It gives employment to many hundred hands; gangs of 20 to 25 men, women, and children, being daily at work in many parts of the district between Bawdsey, Boyton and Woodbridge. Gold stones, used in the manufacture of copperas and sulphuric acid, and immense quantities of septaria or cement stones, are collected by numerous boatmen employed in dredging for them along the coast from Harwich to Orford Ness."

There was a similar description in other directories that was repeated in the three subsequent publications *"There are large strata of coprolites, and the cliffs are celebrated for geological and fossil remains"* (*K.P.O.D.* and Harrod's *County Directory*, 1858, 1873, 1877, 1883).

Those crossing the estuary by ferry would almost certainly have been aware of the business, especially when they went to The Ferry Boat Inn. The thirsty 'diggers' must have increased its trade. The earliest documentary evidence for the coprolites being sold there was in 1855. Packard made his first recorded purchase in August of 95 tons which were loaded onto the lighter, *Duckle*. They were then shipped up the Orwell and Gipping to his new chemical manure works at Bramford. From which farm they were raised was not specified but demand by that time was very high. Ransby was very much involved at this time, purchasing Boyton coprolites at up to £3 a ton! Whether this was Edward was not specified but a George Ransby was landlord of The Star Inn in 1877 (Prestwich, *Q.J.G.S.* vol. XXVII, p.337; *K.P.O.D.*, 1877; S.C.R.O. HC.434.8728.310a Boyton Charities).

A fossil bed at Newbourn had attracted the attention of geologists as early as 1840. When the 'coprolites' were first worked in this parish is unknown. The first reference was in 1856 when Sir Richard Owen's geological paper mentioned that William Colchester was purchasing fossils from Newbourn. None of his arrangements have come to light.

Sir Charles Lyell, the Scottish geologist, was also collecting Newbourn fossils from as early as 1840. He built up his collection with contributions from Mr Edwards of Bushill Row, Woodbridge and George Ransome, from Felixstowe (Lyell, C. (1847?) *Annual Magazine of Natural History,* vol. IV, p.186; Owen, (1856), *Q.J.G.S.* vol. XII, p.217).

Colchester was elected a Fellow of the Geological Society of London in 1857 and was also a member of the Geological Club. He was a friend of Charles Darwin and Aldous Huxley.

EIGHTEEN MANURE WORKS BY 1857

By 1857 there were at least eighteen manure works in Britain and with Laws opening a second works on a 100-acre (40.8 ha.) site on the Thames at Creekmouth, Barking. Ships carrying up to 150 tons were able to offload nitrate of soda from Chile, guano from Peru, animal bones from around the world and coprolites from Suffolk and Cambridgeshire. Demand was increasing and anyone with coprolites on their land was about to make a fortune.

LORD RENDLESHAM GETS INVOLVED

One major landowner in this area was Frederick Brook Thelluson, the 5th Lord Rendlesham. Records show that he made arrangements to have the coprolites raised from numerous parts of his Suffolk estate. When he made the first arrangements is uncertain. The earliest evidence is in 1857 when he allowed Thomas Easterson, one of his tenant farmers in Bawdsey, to raise them from his fields. Over the winter of 1857-8 200 tons were raised and sold to William Colchester at fifty shillings (£2.50) a ton. His labour costs were twenty shillings (£1.00) a ton leaving a profit of almost £300! Out of this Easterson had to pay income tax of sixty-five shillings (£3.25).

Over the following winter, perhaps because of bad weather, the records show that only twelve tons were raised and despite similar labour costs, prices had dropped to £2 a ton. This price did not improve. Easterton's men raised 143 tons in 1860 and he must have been disappointed as, after investing in a "*New Buin* (sic) *for depositing coprolite*", prices fell to thirty shillings (£1.50) a ton. Only £70 profit was quite a drop and, although he may have exhausted the pit, it may explain why no further records have come to light (S.C.R.O. HB416/F.2 pp.13, 31, 63, 91, 127, 153).

Undated photograph of coprolites being unloaded at Lawes' Chemical Manure
Works at Barking, London
(Courtesy of Rural History Centre, Reading University Neg. No. 35/23594)

Rendlesham's records show that he allowed another tenant, William Johnson of Cauldwell Hall, about a mile (1.6 km) south of Boyton (TM 377457), to raise them from his estate. Over the 1857 - 1858 winter Johnson sold 106 tons to Colchester at fifty shillings (£2.50) a ton. With costs of forty shillings (£2.00) a ton it would have given a profit of £137.80. The trade directory for 1858 did not mention the coprolite pits. It only reported there being "*several crag pits*"

(*K.P.O.D.*, 1858). Maybe it was from these that the coprolite was raised. Prices dropped to thirty shillings (£1.50) a ton by 1860 by which time Johnson's labourers had raised a further 336 tons. This reduced the profit to £120 in 1859 and only £56 in 1860. These fluctuations remained a regular phenomenon over the years of the industry but, when a labourer's annual wage was only twenty pounds or so, the profits were worth having (S.C.R.O. HB416/F.2 pp.13, 31, 63, 91, 127, 153).

The earliest documentation of diggings further inland in Bucklesham was in 1858. Where they were worked at that time is not certain but subsequent evidence showed pits on Church Farm. Which of the modern day farms was previously known as Church Farm is uncertain. It could have been Steel's Farm (TM 244424) on the western bank of a small tributary stream that fed into Mill River. Like many streams in this area it had cut through and exposed the fossil bed on its slopes. The trade directory the same year pointed out that *"There are several crag pits in the parish, containing many fossil shells, some of them very curious"*. Work in Waldringfield on the west bank of the River Deben had started by 1858 as the same directory stated that *"Coprolites are excavated here"*. The entry for Shottisham, a few miles south east of Sutton on the east banks of the Deben, reported that *"The parish is rich in antediluvian shells and fossils; the coprolites are also dug here"*. Who was involved is unknown and the 1861 census gave no indication (*K.P.O.D.*, 1858, 1873).

In 1858 they were being raised in Alderton, a few miles north of Bawdsey. Lord Rendlesham, as Lord of the Manor, arranged to have them raised from one of his farms tenanted by Mr. Hiller. Exactly which one was not documented. His records reveal that sixty-two and a half tons were dug over the winter of that year with labour costs of eighteen shillings (£0.90) a ton. They were worked from pits on his farms in other parishes where, possibly in regards to the depth of the pits, costs ranged from fifteen to forty shillings (£0.75 to £2.00) a ton. As well as bills from the carpenters, Messrs. Fairhead and Read, presumably for sheds, planks, tools and other work, there were bills for sieves, chains and 'coprolite skeps'. These would have been used to carry the fossils. Total costs were £67 but the accounts did not detail how much they were sold for nor for how long the work continued. There was a note that in 1859 that the parish trustees rated the coprolite land at a half yearly payment of thirty-two shillings and sixpence (£1.63) (S.C.R.O. HB416/F.2 pp.31, 81, 91). This would have contributed to the parish's Poor Relief for the less well of members of the parish.

Over the winter of 1857 – 1858 Lord Rendlesham made similar arrangements with Thomas Crisp, one of his tenants in Foxhall. Between 1857 and 1860 there were two coprolite contractors involved. Maybe Crisp got them to do the digging for him and they took on his labourers. By 1858 one pit had realised 75 tons. Another in 'Bush Covers' produced 101 tons. The coprolites were sold to Colchester for forty-five shillings (£2.25) a ton. The labour costs at the two pits were very different, seventeen shillings (£0.85) a ton at the first pit and forty-four shillings (£2.20) a ton in 'Bush Covers'. Perhaps it was due to the depth of the seam? Rendlesham's annual profit of almost £200 was quite a handsome return for an almost minimal investment.

The following year a Mr Button was paid £7 for sinking another coprolite pit. He may well have been one of the contractors referred to earlier. The other was a Mr Lucock, who, by 1860, had raised a further 49 tons. Prices then had dropped to thirty shillings (£1.50) a ton. After the costs of "skeps, new sieves, wheelbarrows and carting" were deducted, profits of only sixpence (£0.025) per ton were well down (S.C.R.O. HB416.F.2 pp.13, 31,91,127,153).

Lord Rendlesham also owned 1,760 acres of land in Capel St Andrew, a mile north of the Boyton diggings. In 1857 he allowed John Lucock to raise them from his fields. These were probably those on the north bank of The Tang (TM 378478). He could have been the John Lucock who, in the 1851 census for Capel St. Andrew, was described as a farmer employing *"4 labourers after coprolite"*. Over that winter 75 tons were raised and sold to Colchester at forty shillings (£2) a ton. As his labour costs were only twenty shillings (£1) a ton, Lucock realised a profit of £75.

The following year Lucock's costs went up to twenty-five shillings (£1.25) a ton but production fell to only 60 tons which led to a reduced profit of only £45. Although this was the equivalent of about two farm labourers' annual income it would have been a welcome addition to his income. Records show that over the 1859 - 1860 winter, Lucock was working further north in Butley, again on Lord Rendlesham's estate. The tenant there, Thomas Crisp, was engaged in his own workings so Rendlesham had brought in Lucock and another contractor to work the deposit (S.C.R.O.HB416/F.2 pp.13, 31,63,127,153).

Yet more of Lord Rendlesham's property was worked in 1857. He arranged to have the coprolites raised from part of his 578-acre holding in Ramsholt, on the east bank of the Deben, a few miles southwest of Shottisham. They were worked from fields farmed by Charles French. Documents show that a Mr. Ling was the contractor. Whether he was the George Ling who took on coprolite work at nearby Boyton in 1870 is uncertain. He would probably have taken on French's labourers after the harvest was in, supervising the loading onto Mr French's carts which took them down to the river. Here they would have been washed and weighed.

Records show that between 1859 - 1860, a Mr Guard, another local man, was involved. Whether he had a licence or made arrangements with French is unknown. With his 189 tons and the 219 tons raised on Mr French's farm, Lord Rendlesham made a profit of £89. As the records did not continue after 1860 it is uncertain whether they continued being raised but they probably did. Up to that time 749 tons had been worked, which, due to fluctuations in demand, resulted in less than expected profits. Mr Ling's charges were only fifteen shillings (£0.75) a ton which would have given Lord Rendlesham a profit from these diggings of just over £550. However, this was enough to have improved his properties or bought considerably more land.

By 1860, the work at Ramsholt had not been completed very well. French was allowed £31 10s.0d. (£31.50) compensation for the damage done to his fields over the previous three years, £20 7s.0d (£20.35) for carting costs and £5 16s.7d. (£5.83) for implements (S.C.R.O. HB416.F.2 pp.31, 91,127,153). When the government published its mineral statistics in 1858 it listed nine villages in Suffolk as exporting coprolites. They were Alderton, Boyton, Bucklesham, Butley, Felixstowe, Nacton, Ramsholt, Shotley and Shottisham (*Mem. Geol. Surv.* Mineral Statistics, H.M.S.O. 1860, p.375).

THE DUKE OF HAMILTON vs. CLARKE

Like Lord Rendlesham, other landowners were not slow in making arrangements to have the coprolites raised on their property. In July 1858, William, the 11th Duke of Hamilton, the Lord of the Manor of Walton, Trimley and Felixstow, took legal 'action to trover', recover damages for the wrongful taking of his personal property. The case was reported in *The Times*.

Duke of Hamilton and Brandon v Clarke
Mr O'Malley and Mr Couch appeared for the plaintiff, and Mr Keane and Mr Marriott for the defendant.
This was an action to trover bought by the Duke of Hamilton to assert his right to the coprolites found upon the beach between high and low water, in the manor of Walton, Trimley and Felixstowe Priory of which he is lord. In 1854 the Duke advanced his right to gather coprolites, which have during the last few years become of considerable value being crushed and then used for manure. In 1854 tenders were sent in for the right of collecting them, and an agreement was entered into by which the sole right was granted to defendant for one year at a rent of 50l. On the termination of that agreement another persons named Packard purchased the right and now holds it. Clarke continued

to collect without a lease, and now disputes the Duke's title. He keeps a boat, and collect the coprolites which boys and girls gather together. The manor rolls were put in evidence, and they with a great deal of other evidence showed that form 1739 moneys had been paid to the Duke's account, some the proceeds of the sale of wreck other payments for the groundage of vessels and for salvage others for the licence to take shingle. Among other acts of ownership, it was shown that leases of the right to take the stone for cement found on the beach had been granted and acted upon, and it did not appear that any adverse claim had ever been set up.

Mr Keane submitted that there was no case, as the exclusive right had been granted to Packard. Leave was reserved to the defendant's counsel, if, on consideration he should consider that there was anything in the point.

Mr Keane then addressed the jury for the defendant, and His Lordship having summed up, The jury immediately found a verdict of the plaintiff – damages, 40s.

(*The Times.* 29th July 1858 page 10)

It would be interesting to know whether the defendant was Dr W. B. Clarke, of 14 Berners Street, Ipswich, who helped Henslow locate and describe the coprolites in 1842.

OUT-MIGRATION TO CAMBRIDGESHIRE

With Colchester, Packard, Prentice, Fison, Laws and others winning licences to raise the coprolites in Cambridgeshire, managers were appointed who engaged many of the experienced Suffolk diggers. Wages were up to £1 a week – nearly double agricultural wages. Gangs of up to 500 were recorded in some fenland villages. This out-migration was referred to in the 1861 census. The population decline in Bawdsey, Boyton, Newbourn and Sutton was attributed to the workings in Cambridgeshire *"where more available deposits have been discovered"* (S.C.R.O. 1861 census Vol. I, p.353). Analysis of the census returns for the Cambridgeshire 'coprolite' villages confirms this migration (Cambridgeshire Census 1861,1871,1881,1891 returns). 34-year old Nathaniel Warren Johnson, living in Chesterton, was Mr. Packard's agent. His entry revealed the domination of the industry by Eastern Counties Manure Company as he was described as a

"Coprolite Merchant and tenant farmer holding about 13 acres employing 8 men and 5 boys. Raising of Coprolite the undersigned employs about 375 men and boys in various parts of Cambridgeshire."

EVIDENCE FROM THE 1861 CENSUS

Over the decade to 1861 numbers in Bawdsey decreased by 52 to 426, an 11% fall. This was the first decrease in numbers that century. Boyton experienced a 21% reduction of 66 to 254. After a 34% increase the previous decade the out-migration must have caused concern. Newbourn's numbers fell 55 to 317, a drop of 15% after a 31% increase the previous decade. Sutton's numbers fell by 13 to 228, a 5% drop.

But these were not the only parishes that experienced population decline. Ramsholt's numbers fell 8% to 186. Felixstowe's numbers fell 3% to 673. Nacton had a 15% increase of 77 to 582. Shottisham experienced a 1% drop of only two people to 239. Yet the other coprolite parishes saw population increases. Alderton increased by four to 634. Bucklesham increased by 44 to 362. Butley increased ten to 385 and Shotley increased by 77 to 582, a 15% change.

Despite all the work going on only two parishes had records of coprolite diggers. Nine were reported in Bucklesham whose population had increased 14% to 362. One lived at Church Farm, where the deposit was being worked. The others lived on Bucklesham Street. It was generally a young man's job as their average age was 22.3. The eldest was 33-year old John Moor and the youngest, 11-year old James Fulcher. As five were born outside the parish it seems they had been attracted to the parish by the better pay in the diggings. Three of them were lodgers.

Three people in Newbourn were described as involved. Two 20-year olds, John Geggins and Henry Goodall, were described as *"coprolite miners"*. Both were lodgers. With 15-year old John Farrow, also born outside the parish, it suggests that they had been attracted to Newbourn by the possibility of work. None of the farmers gave any indication that they were involved but that is not to say that they weren't. As in 1851 it suggests that most farmers employed their own labourers to raise them and the work was described by many as agricultural or general labour.

Although no one described themselves as coprolite labourers in the 1861 census for Butley, 50-year old Thomas Crisp was described as a *"Farmer of 3,700 acres employing 58 labourers, 2 millers, 10 shepherds, 28 women and children and 31 boys"*. Some of them must have been involved in the coprolite work.

It is unknown whether the coprolites were exploited in Levington. Its population experienced a 24% decline to 168. The manufacture of horticultural products had been going on since 1858, a practice that continues to this day. There is the possibility that they were worked on land farmed by John Dawson of Nacton. The census described him as a *"Farmer and Merchant of 1,600 acres in Nacton and Levington employing 40 men and 9 boys"*.

In Sutton, 61-year old Waller had done very well for himself out of the business. He was described as living at *"Sutton Hall, Owner and farmer of 800 acres employing 38 men and 15 boys"*. William Ely was recorded as a *"coprolite miner"* and evidence shows he bought *"irons, rivets and sives"* from the Boyton blacksmith (S.C.R.O. 1861 census; Strong, B. op.cit. p.55).

The population of Walton, a small village to the north of Felixstowe, had increased by eleven to 385 but there was no mention of anyone involved. Two farmers employed what seemed to be a particularly large number of farm labourers. 47-year old Thomas Woodgate farmed the 333-acre Gulpher Farm (TM 305369) with 14 men and 28 boys and 38-year old William Williams farmed the 300-acre Hill House Farm (TM 298367) with 21 men and 8 boys. If they were the freeholders they may well have employed them to raise the coprolites from the fields above Rosier Marshes.

William Colchester was recorded as Justice of the Peace for Harwich, ship-owner and stone merchant. He was renting Grundisburgh Hall, *"a beautiful mansion, pleasantly situated in the midst of a well wooded park & shrubs."*, where he lived with his wife, five daughters, two sons, a governess, coachman, page, three housemaids, a cook and kitchen maid.

"PATTRICK'S SHAFT"

Although Packard was the major purchaser of the Boyton coprolites there were also 80 tons sold in November 1851 to Mr. Pattrick of Dovercourt, in Harwich. Maybe he was Colchester's agent as he had 'coprolite works' in Harwich. However, he may have been making his own 'super'. What was locally called "Pattrick's Shaft", the chimney at the works, was demolished at the beginning of the Second World War to prevent enemy aircraft using it as a landmark. Although the coprolites were used for artificial manure, Allan Jobson, a local historian, in his book *'In Suffolk's Border'* thought that they had another use *"...vast quantities were collected by a perfect flotilla of little boats, taken to Harwich to be shipped to London to be made into Palmer's Roman Cement"*. No other evidence confirms this.

SEPTARIA AND ROMAN CEMENT

It appears there was confusion with septaria. Some sources say that septaria is fossilised excreta, coprolites, others that they were limestone nodules. They were also called pudding-stone as they looked like flat dough criss-crossed by cracks that resembles string. These nodules, up to several feet wide, were found exposed at low tide in the London clay along the banks of the Stour estuary. As the calcium also contained clay material, mainly silica and alumina, they were baked in a coal or coke-fired kiln, to produce a pink/red/brown coloured powder which, when water was added, produced a plaster which hardened like cement. It was very similar to the mortar used by Romans in the construction of domes and cupolas. James Parker, using septaria from the Solent and Stour estuaries, patented the method of manufacture in 1794. He called it Roman cement. He sold his patent to the architect, James Wyatt and his cousin Charles Wyatt, and went over to the United States but the manufacture continued, mostly at Christchurch on the Isle of Wight, but on a smaller scale at Harwich. One of its uses was to restore damaged statues in Lichfield Cathedral. A cement industry developed in Dovercourt, exploiting septaria and limestone from Beacon Hill cliff. To prevent the harbour silting up a limestone pier was built in 1849.

By the middle of the 19th century there were about a dozen 'stone dredgers' that worked in the Stour estuary dredging septaria. What was called 'Colchester's Fleet' of shrimpers were originally involved in this line of business. His Harwich cement manufacturing business was in partnership with John Watts. Colchester's attention was drawn to the range of interesting fossils dredged up while searching for these large septaria. White's trade directory, in its description of Shotley in 1874, mentioned *"Sea Boats are employed here in collecting stone for the manufacture of Roman Cement"* (White, (1874), op.cit.). In 1871 Lucas C. King was described in the census as a *"Farmer of 76 acres employing 4 labourers and 2 boys, Cement Stone Merchant employing 6 men"*. This had been going on at least since the 1850s when many men described themselves as cement stone dredgers and loaders. The *Geological Magazine* of March 1899 commented that:

"These dredging operations were also of great importance in deepening the channel at the mouth of the River Orwell, which owing to the set of the tides, was liable to be obstructed by the formation of a bar across its estuary."

Similar operations were going on in Waldringfield around 1870 on the banks of the river. Whether it was the result of the coprolite workings exposing suitable deposits of chalk marl is undocumented but having experienced diggers in the locality must have been an advantage for what was to become the Portland Cement Works (TM 286445). The manager was George Mason, who may well have been the same man who had been a timber merchant and farmer in Foxhall in 1861 (S.C.R.O. 1861, 1871 census). The social and economic impact that these industries had on Waldringfield was detailed in the village's website:

"Having its own farms, gardens, shop, inn and craftsmen Waldringfield in those far-off days was almost self-supporting. Only occasionally did anyone, even the parson, venture as far afield as Ipswich or Woodbridge, which were said to be a 'long way orf'. The roads were full of holes and ruts, slushy in winter and dusty in summer. Should they be ice-bound or flooded, then the only way out was by the Deben, where a local boatman was always glad to earn a shilling. Vital necessities, such as groceries and clothing, were brought in by the carrier, and even he did not venture out when the roads were icy, unless his pony's shoes were 'roughed'.

"Most men worked on the farms, whilst a few were employed as gardeners and coachmen at the bigger houses. Not many women went out to work, being far too busy at home. Mrs Walter Brown, for instance, who lived in a four-roomed cottage near the Maybush, wouldn't have much time to spare after she had cooked, washed, and sewed for her husband and sixteen children. Young women, however,

occasionally went out to work in the fields, stone-picking, hay-making and gleaning. As for the children, boys did the bird-scaring, singling beet and tending hogs and sheep, whilst the girls, barely in their teens, were usually employed as maids by the local gentry, with whom they often stayed till they were married. There was no village school in Waldringfield a hundred years ago.

"Very little time was given up to leisure and entertainment in Waldringfield during those mid-Victorian days. Like country folks in general, they were quite happy at work. Their most exciting events of the year were the summer outings to the sea-side or Ipswich, and the unforgettable Christmas parties. What a picturesque scene it must have been when newly painted wagons, drawn by magnificent Suffolk Punches and crowded with men, women and children, all dressed in their Sunday best, could be seen ambling along the pretty country lanes. And what a happy crowd they were, singing and cheering to every wayside cottage and passerby. Then the Christmas parties, too, where they played every game from blind-man's buff to charades, what joys those simple pastimes seem to have brought into otherwise uneventful lives. Last, but by no means least, there was the Sabbath, to which everybody in Victorian days looked forward, being the one day of the week in which they had a real change. To them the meeting of old friends, the singing of hymns and psalms, the saying of simple prayers and above all, the hearing of a good sermon were as satisfying as meat and drink. Thus, despite the lack of modern transport, entertainment and wireless the people of Waldringfield in those bygone days seem to have been quite happy and contented.

"Waldringfield continued to pursue the 'even tenor of its way' until the sixties when, within the space of a few years, two industries, viz. Coprolite and cement, suddenly sprung up in their midst. This mushroom development was entirely due to the existence of vast quantities of coprolite in the nearby fields and acres of mud lying under the tidal waters of the Deben. Coprolite was the raw material, largely phosphate in composition, which firms like Fisons and Packards were searching for to grind into manure. Mud was one of the two main essentials later used by Masons in the manufacture of cement. Thus it

was that Waldringfield, almost overnight, suddenly embarked on its own industrial revolution and in the course of a few years was dispatching thousands of tons of coprolite and cement to all parts of the East Anglian coast.

"What a busy place Waldringfield was in the early eighties, when its two industries were at their height of prosperity. By that time some two to three hundred men and boys were employed in the pits and in the kilns, many walking in from miles around, some even rowing down the river from Woodbridge. Every day barges were either loading or unloading at the quayside, others waiting their turn to come in. Never a day passed without tumbril loads of coprolite trundling down the hill, depositing it on the beach, where it was washed before loading. Thus, with the busy quayside, the noise of engines and machinery, the hurrying and scurrying of workmen, and the piercing blast of the 'wonnerful wissel', the whole scene much resembled a miniature Tyneside. Then occasionally the old manure barge from London arrived, exchanging manure for hay and straw. All windows and doors were closed when this barge was unloading."

(http://www.waldringfield.info/1850-1950.htm)

COADE STONE

In White's 1855 history of the county it revealed that the coprolites had another very little acknowledged use.

"Coprolite is a valuable mineral extensively used as manure and in the finer sets of earthenware. It was mostly found near springs of crystal water, surrounded by crag, which abounded in fossils of the antediluvian world, including relics of enormous fish and animals mostly now extinct."

These finer sets of earthenware were known as 'Coade stone', high quality garden statuary. A Mr Coade set up a manufactory on Narrow Wall in Lambeth in London in 1769 to make stone casts. They had the benefit of being easily carved and resistant to frost and acid pollution. His wife, and then relatives, continued the operations into the 19th century. Examples can still be found in some of the antique shops in the area but the best are reported as being the stone lion on the south side of Westminster Bridge in London, statues outside the John Soane Museum, two tombs in the Museum of Garden History, Lambeth Palace, vases on the balustrades of Somerset House and Egyptian caryatids in the breakfast room of Pithanger Manor in Ealing. More locally they can be seen in statues in the graveyard at Saffron Walden. Whether the coprolites were mixed with the clay or used in the glaze is uncertain. The manufacturing technique is claimed to have been lost (White, W. op.cit. 1850 and 1855).

Giles Colchester relates how a stone lion, thought to be made from coade stone, stood in the garden of his great-grandfather, Herbert Mason of The Grove in Bramford. It broke the springs of his Rolls Royce when it was transported to Lady Packard's house near Woodbridge..

THE BOYTON FOSSIL DIGGINGS

There was no mention of anyone being involved in fossil or coprolite digging in the census returns for Boyton. 59-year old Edward Bennington farmed the 416-acre Dock Farm (TM 383478) by the river employing sixteen labourers. This suggests he was not involved in raising them himself and a contractor was engaged with his own gang of men. 56-year old William Miller was farming 600 acres with 17 men and 6 boys. William Johnson of Cauldwell Hall farmed 500 acres but as he employed 16 men, 13 women and 4 boys, it seems likely that some of them would have been working on his 'diggings'. Further evidence was 15-year old James Richardson who was described as a carter. He probably took them down to the Dock (TM 392474) where cargoes of coal, wheat and manure were unloaded and barrowloads of coprolites emptied into the holds of the lighters.

The 'diggings' had a tremendous impact on the economies of Boyton and the other coprolite villages. In many cases workers were attracted to the diggings from the surrounding countryside and there must have been extra money coming in from lodgers. More accommodation would have been constructed and, as happened in other areas, there is every likelihood the farmers supplied the men with beer at the diggings and by the docks. It was not just the Trustees who were benefiting from their land being dug. The documents showed that they were also dug from adjoining smallholders' land and even May's sister managed to get five tons from her cottage garden. Mr. Crabtree, the surveyor, was called in to examine the Boyton workings. He wrote that "*May thinks there is no more on the farm*". In fact, a further sixteen tons were raised taking the total to over 1,203. Over seven years their sale made an invaluable contribution to the Charity funds. After May had received his third, the rest was invested in 3% Consuls. Evidence shows that most of this money was used to purchase two cottages and pay for a roadway.

DIGGINGS ON IPSWICH RACECOURSE

There is evidence that the bed was worked in Ipswich itself. It was listed as one of nine Suffolk coprolite mining areas in 1858 (*Mem. Geol. Surv.* Mineral Statistics, H.M.S.O.1860, p.375). Who was responsible for the operation is unknown but there were said to have been extensive workings on the Racecourse (approximately OS. 183429).

COLCHESTER JOINS THE GENTRY

Such were the fortunes made by the manure manufacturers that Colchester rose into the realms of the gentry. His social aspirations were high. In 1857 he was elected a Fellow of the Geological Society of London and became a member of the Geological Club. He was a friend of Charles Darwin and Aldous Huxley with whom he probably had engaging discussions about the Suffolk fossils. After some years in Dovercourt he moved with his wife Mary, first into Grundisburgh Hall,

Woodbridge, in 1860 and then into Springfield House in Ipswich a few years later. To compete with Packard and Fison, he too had his own manure works on Griffin Wharf in Ipswich between Harland and Bath Street that also had its own railway sidings for unloading the Cambridgeshire coprolites. The local trade directory listed him as not just a chemical manure manufacturer but also as a ship owner and boat builder (*K. P.O.D.* Ipswich).

In the 1861 census he was described as a Shipowner and Stone merchant. Seven of his ten children lived with him, five daughters and two sons. He also employed a governess, a coachman, three housemaids, a cook and a kitchen maid (S.C.R.O. 1861 census). In line with many Victorian entrepreneurs who wanted to establish themselves in society, William Colchester invented tradition. He is reported to have filched the coat-of-arms of the Gloucester Colchesters to display on his silver tableware and had a carpet made with them on. A completely false family tree was written up purporting a descent from Oliver Cromwell's sister and some Welsh princes, hence his second son being called Edward Cromwell Colchester. It was Edward who managed the coprolite workings in the Cambridgeshire area around Bassingbourn (Author's correspondence with Roy Colchester, Mendlesham, Giles Colchester, London; O'Connor, B. (1998), '*The Dinosaurs on Bassingbourn Fen*', Bernard O'Connor).

On the eastern side of the River Orwell there was another manure works belonging to Edward Packard. His family owned the site in the early 1800s. Because so many tumbrils loaded with raw material passed along it, the name Coprolite Street was adopted (TM 170440). (*K.P.O.D.* 1892). Bob Markham, the Suffolk geologist, commented that people have travelled miles to have their photograph taken beside it.

RAILWAY MERGER IN 1862

The Eastern Union Railway was in bitter competition with the Eastern Counties Railway throughout most of its history. John

Chevallier Cobbold, as company chairman, agreed the purchase of three steamers to ply the coastal route between Harwich and London, in direct competition with the Eastern Counties Railway. They retaliated by speeding up the traffic via Cambridge and not providing very good connections for the Eastern Union trains arriving at Colchester. The movement of raw materials and finished products between Ipswich and Bramford had been mainly by rail, but by the early 1860s the Eastern Union Railway was in financial difficulties and its services were in a deplorable state. Its shareholders eventually agreed to amalgamate with the Eastern Counties Railway and the Great Eastern Railway was born in 1862.

A photograph dated 1910 of the wharves alongside Edward Packard's Manure Manufactory on Coprolite Street. The Orwell Iron Works are on the right.
(http://www.eveningstar.co.uk/Content/columns/kindred/htm/040906water.asp)

Geologists are said to travel miles to have their photographs taken beside
Coprolite Street on the north side of what was Edward Packard's Manure Manufactory.
(http://www.bbc.co.uk/suffolk/nature/walk_thru_time/05.shtml)

STOWMARKET NAVIGATION

Rail traffic between Ipswich and Bramford during the 1860s was described as 'chaotic'. Delivery of coprolite to Packard's chemical manure works was so unreliable that he decided to transfer all his phosphate traffic to sailing barges. He then took over the Ipswich and Stowmarket Navigation Company (Hugh Moffat, 'East Anglia's Railways', p.153).

With such poor connections Packard decided to transfer all his traffic from the railway to the river navigation and invested in an iron-built, twin-screwed, steam barge called the *Orwell*. It was considered unusual at the time as steam barges were considered uneconomic for inland waters because the machinery took up valuable space. Also, speed on the navigation was necessarily slow to protect the banks from erosion by the wash (Moffat, op.cit. p.69).

MAKING SUPERPHOSPHATE IN THE 1860s

Other companies similarly ventured into the coprolite business, including Chapman and Co. They advertised as Chemical Manure Manufacturers, oil-cake and guano merchants as early as 1858 with an office in Cornhill, Ipswich (Kelly's P.O. Directory 1858). Unfortunately, no records from this company have come to light that might have shown that they similarly had made agreements with landowners to raise the fossils. It is possible they were responsible for the Eastern Counties Manure works, acting as Packard's agents but no evidence has emerged of this.

Laws' agent in Ipswich was Charles Everedge. He was involved in arranging purchases of the Suffolk coprolites and their transport to London. There were two other manure companies in the area, Yarmouth and Bagshaw and Co. of Haddiscoe, about six miles west of Lowestoft, and Bailey and Sutton of Runham, about four miles west of Great Yarmouth. None of their records have yet come to light. It can be seen then that this new artificial fertiliser industry must have provided Ipswich with a considerable business, both in terms of the numbers employed in its transport, manufacture and marketing and the income generated from its imports and exports (Kelly's Directories 1873; V.C.H. 'Suffolk' vol. ii pp.285 - 6; 25" Maps Suffolk 75.12, 75.15).

Extract from the 1882 Ordnance Survey map of Ipswich showing the manure manufactory to the south of Coprolite Street.

There have been several published accounts of the conversion process and it is interesting to see the development through time of the technology involved. Some of Packard's early company books detailed the process he had learned from the Newcastle Agricultural Meeting. To mix bones with vitriol he noted one had to:

"Make a conical heap of Earth or Ashes with a mouth at the top; for two acres put 8 bushels of half inch Bones to 160 lbs. of Sulphuric Acid. Mix the Acid with 40 Gallons of hot water. Place alternate layers in the cone of Earth of bones and acid. Stir and cover over for a day or two and turn over twice or thrice."

(S.C.R.O. HC. 434/8728/310a)

This method could easily be done in the farmyard and in the early days of the industry some farmers processed the coprolites locally. In A. N. Gray's *'Phosphate and Superphosphate'* it was stated that:

"...on many parts of the Suffolk coast, the manure was prepared directly on the spot; that is to say, the coprolites and bones are reduced to a coarse powder in mills of a peculiar construction and great power, furnished with vertical granite and buhr stones; they are afterwards mixed with about an equal weight of strong sulphuric acid or oil of vitriol, in tubs, &c., and are thus converted into superphosphate of lime; whilst in other cases they are transported by water to other places, where large manufactories have been erected for the preparation of artificial manures."

There is every likelihood that local iron founders, like the Ransomes of Ipswich, would have found a considerable market for the assortment of associated coprolite plant and machinery as well as in the manufactories themselves. In Packard's Bramford Chemical Works the original process was somewhat more sophisticated. It attracted the attention of a party of members of the Geological Association on 20th July 1863. They went on a river trip to see some of the coprolite pits, hopeful of finding a few good specimens of fossils. The only one mentioned specifically was Mr Everett's pit in Foxhall. Whether he was a landowner, farmer or coprolite manager is uncertain. The visit to Bramford was given much more detail. As in most industrial processes at this time, there was a significant lack of safety precautions for the labourers. Gray described the method the visitors saw:

"...for calcined bones to be reduced to a very fine powder and placed in an iron pan, with an equal amount of water (a cast iron trough, such as is sold for holding water for cattle, will do), a man with a spade must mix the bones with water until every portion is wet; whilst the man is stirring, an assistant empties at once into the pan sulphuric acid, 60 parts by weight for every 100 parts of bone; the acid is poured in at once, and not in a thin stream as is commonly recommended; the stirring is continued for about three minutes, and the material is then thrown out. The larger the heap that is made, the more perfect the decomposition, as the heap remains intensely hot for a long time. It is necessary to spread the superphosphate out in the air for a few days that it may become dry."

To leave it on a brick floor or in a brick-lined pit to be stirred with rakes was understandably described as *"a very unpleasant job"* and this practise was discontinued when the 'Den' was introduced. In a lecture to the Institute of Chemical Engineers, W. Packard later described it as:

"... a square or rectangular chamber lined with bricks with a top inlet through which the semi-liquid mass was dropped from a small mixer. The dens usually held from 30 to 50 tons of superphosphate, although there were evidently some that held 100 tons... They were lit by flaring gas jets. Half-naked men worked in a cloud of steam and gases, their mouths covered by handkerchiefs, shovelled superphosphate into barrows and wheeled it away. The mouth of the den would be sealed with huge timber blocks held in position with iron bars. During the early days escaping gases were drawn through wooden passages affixed to a chimney. The dens remained closed for about four hours and when opened gave off vast quantities of foul smelling gases."

The fumes would have been noticeable by the people of Bramford who lived in the wake of the prevailing south-westerly wind. Ipswich's city fathers had objected to this work going on in the city. It would have been bad enough with the smells from the dockside factories and the smoke from the industrial premises as well as from domestic coal fires. The result of the manufacturing process, when it cooled, was a dry, friable, honeycombed mass that was dug out of the pits and once more reduced to powder in a disintegrator. At this stage, to produce more specialised fertilisers, nitrogenous material such as Ammonium Sulphate was added, or, where a manure specially adapted to corn, grass, mangel, potato or other crops was required, potash salts were added (Thorpe, *Dictionary of Applied Chemistry*, pp.507 - 10; O'Dell, I. (1951), *'A Vanished Industry'* (original MS in Luton Museum) pp.7 - 8).

SUFFOLK COPROLITES

From Messrs. Way and Evans.		From Dr. Augustus Voelcker.	
Moisture	1.72	Moisture and a little	
Organic Matter, &c.	4.98	Organic Matter	6.34
Sand &c.	10.31	Phosphates	60.30
Triassic Phosphate of Lime	55.08	Carbonate of Lime, Magnesia,	
Carbonate of Lime	16.48	Flouride of Calcium &c.	21.46
Sulphate of Lime, Oxide			
Insoluble Siliceous Matter	11.90	Of Iron, Alumina &c.	11.43
	100.00		100.00

From Hy. K. Bamber, F.C.S.

Water and Organic Matter	5.400
Chloride of Sodium	Trace
Sulphate of Lime	1.632
Phosphate of Lime	53.400
Carbonate of Lime	17.500
Magnesia	Trace
Alumina	4.400
Oxide of Iron	6.000
Flouride of Calcium	1.450
Silica	9.750
	99.532

(St. John's College, Cambridge, Muniments 162.7/4)

This artificial manure was then sacked and marketed locally to many of the East Anglian farmers but such was its fame that Packard was able to sell it in Scotland, Ireland and as far afield as Russia. Packard advertised it at the 1862 International Exhibition and included three analyses.

Bringing his fertilisers to the world's attention brought Packard international medals throughout the 1860s and 70s. He got a medal at the London International Exhibition in 1862, medals at Riga in 1865 and 1867, a gold medal at Lyon in 1871, medals in London in 1872 and 1873, a progress medal at Vienna in 1873, and medals at Norkopping and Brussels in 1876. The import and export taxes he paid, rates paid to Ipswich Town Council and the employment he provided at his factories and in the coprolite pits provided a significant contribution to the Suffolk economy. He was duly rewarded when he was appointed mayor in 1869 (*East Anglian Handbook*, 1870s).

In 1862 72,000 tons of superphosphate were produced in the country with a value of £360,000, of which Ipswich would have had a significant share (Midland Counties Herald, Feb.20th 1862). With increasing quantities of Cambridgeshire coprolites coming onto the market and greater demand for fertilisers, Fison's profits allowed him to expand his operations into King's Lynn and East Dereham in 1868. The *Victoria County History* of Suffolk mentioned that Fison's' fertilisers were:

"used to raise the flower crops of the Scilly Isles and Guernsey, and the fruit and potato crops of Kent, and who claim to have adapted the reactive qualities of artificial manures so as to meet the peculiar needs of hothouse grapes, cucumbers, hops, flax and tomatoes."

As well as guano, bones, local and other counties' coprolites, the manure manufacturers were keen to investigate other sources of phosphate supplies. In 1861 Carter Jonas, one of the Cambridgeshire surveyors, reported that:

"Sombrero phosphates... have recently become important in commerce from it being extensively used in the manufacture of Superphosphate of Lime for Agricultural purposes. It is obtained from the island of Sombrero, a small hat shaped island, one of the West Indian group noted for its white cliff like appearance hitherto uninhabited and of no importance but now of great value for the entire surface being farmed for the phosphate which rises in high cliffs from which it is quarried and easily shipped to England."

(Cambridge University Library, Add.7652 II Q)

The ships would have been seen sailing up the Orwell to Ipswich where their cargoes were unloaded for grinding at the dockside factories and transhipped by sailing barges up the Gipping to Bramford and by the Ipswich and Stowmarket Navigation to inland manure works. By 1870 there were at least eighty manure works established around the U.K. and many others in continental ports (Packard, W.G.T. 'The History of the Fertiliser Industry in Britain', The Fertiliser Society, p.8; Suffolk Chronicle, 23rd Dec. 1949).

MAJOR LANDOWNERS

There seems every likelihood that other Felixstowe landowners like Captain Ernest Pretyman and Sir Cuthbert Quilter, stockbroker and MP for Ipswich, would have capitalised on the deposits found on their estates. As yet the only documentation to emerge is from Colonel George Tomline's estate in Felixstowe (S.C.R.O. HA 119 50/3/209). Tomline was described as 'a man of enormous wealth', the second largest Suffolk landowner, who inherited Orwell Park in 1848 when he was 35. He later inherited estates in Shropshire and Lincolnshire. He was an MP, High Sheriff for Suffolk and a magistrate, and had acquired 18,479 acres (7,542 ha.) in the county by the time of his death in 1888.

It included land in Nacton, Levington Manor, Brightwell Manor, Falkenham Manor, Kirton Manor, Kesgrave Manor, Martlesham Manor, Seckford Hall, Grimstone Hall and Felixstowe Manor. Packard had an agreement with him to take all the coprolites on his Suffolk Estates, which included the farms in Walton.

Kenneth Goward's research into Tomline's history revealed that he had one of the finest art collections in England, including works by Holbein and Murillo. He also built up one of the finest libraries of the day, with many first and rare editions. Orwell Park mansion became something of a treasure store. Over the years his coprolite revenue and estate rents paid for much other work around the building, including the observatory tower and eastern extension, upon which work was not started until the turn of the 1860/70s. The village of Nacton was extensively remodelled. It was his wish that houses close to the mansion were to be knocked down and local stories have it that the front doors of those along the main village road were altered to make side entrances so that he wouldn't be stared at when passing by.

One of his hobbies was shooting and he had a decoy set up at Levington Heath. Many of his guests contributed to the toll. The most fowl ever captured in one year was 3,000, in 1853, 2,380 were taken, in 1854, 2,279 and in 1855, 1,803. Over eighteen years he bagged 27,991, of which 5,711 were wigeon.

THE FOLLOWING ARE EXHIBITED

IN CLASS I,

INTERNATIONAL EXHIBITION, 1862,

By E. PACKARD and Co., IPSWICH.

COPROLITES (so called) AND FOSSIL BONES,

The remains of Animals from the Upper Green Sand, washed and reduced to a fine powder, ready for mixing with Acid, contain 58 to 61 per cent. of Phosphates.

Price 50s. to 55s. per Ton.

COPROLITES (so called) AND FOSSIL BONES FROM THE SUFFOLK CRAG.

This variety of these Mineral Phosphates (which form the cheapest source of Phosphate of Lime yet discovered) similarly prepared, yield 55 to 60 per cent. of Phosphates.

Price 45s. to 50s. per Ton.

SUPER OR BIPHOSPHATE OF LIME,

Manufactured exclusively from the above, well adapted to Root cultivation.

Price 80s. per Ton, and quality guaranteed.

These Fossil remains are very valuable for Agricultural purposes, forming the basis of the Manure sold under the name of Superphosphate, Turnip, and other Manures, of which it is estimated 200,000 Tons are now used annually in the British Isles. For this enormous quantity 100,000 Tons of Phosphates at least are required, the supply being obtained in about equal proportions of Bones and Coprolites; it is thus apparent how important an addition the latter form to our sources of Manure.

(St John's College Muniments, Cambridge Box 162 7/4)

EXPANSION INTO CAMBRIDGESHIRE

Edward Packard's son, also called Edward (1843 – 1932), was trained in chemistry at King's College, London and in agriculture at the Royal Agricultural College in Cirencester and was appointed manager of the Bramford's works in 1863 when he was 20. He took on an active part in Ipswich's social, business and political life and kept up his interest in the scientific world. When his brother Henry became a partner in 1866 they opened an office in London. Both the Packards and Colchester invested in the coprolite industry, expanding their operations to capitalise on the newly discovered coprolite deposits in southwest Cambridgeshire in 1863. Chemical analysis had determined a significantly higher phosphate content than the Suffolk coprolites. They won contracts at only £50 an acre to work some fields (Cambridge Chronicle, 17th October 1863; Cambridgeshire County Record Office (C.C.R.O.) Francis Bill Books A-N 1863 pp.347, 362).

By 1865 Colchester had gone into partnership with Thomas Thwaites Ball of Burwell and erected a Chemical Manure factory on Burwell Lode, just outside the town. This reduced transport costs and capitalised on the extensive fenland coprolite deposits. It also indicated a move away from Suffolk to capitalise on the more profitable supplies (Author's conversation with owners of the Burwell works).

FURTHER EXPANSION OF THE SUFFOLK DIGGINGS

The first documentary evidence of coprolite diggings on the Shotley peninsula was not until 1864. They had started in Erwarton on the north banks of the River Stour and continued for at least the next ten years (White (1874), op.cit.). The 1861 census returns gave no indication of anyone involved. Two local farmers may have been working them, Walter Wrinch of Ness Farm (TM 216339) and Jack Hempson who farmed Erwarton Hall (TM 224353). Hempson also advertised as a maltster of Ipswich. The first 25" map of the area shows a "Coprolite Pit" about half a mile south of Lower Houses on the northern side of the small hill. Interestingly, the footpath to Harkstead ran alongside the pit which suggests the diggers may have created it (TM 198348, 25" Suffolk, 89.1). It was not far from Burnthouse Queach and Lower Houses Road would have allowed the carts to get down to Johnny All Alone Creek where the coprolites would have been washed.

William Whitaker, the geologist employed by the Geological Survey to cover the Ipswich area, identified other pits just west of South Hall (now Ness Farm OS. 214339) and a third of a mile southeast of Erwarton Hall (TM 226347) (Whitaker, (1885), op. cit. p.48.). There were others further north on the south bank of the Orwell estuary next to Hill House and not far north of Church Farm, near Long Wood and Pages Common half a mile northwest of Chelmondiston (TM 272403). They were probably washed and sorted before loading onto sailing barges at Pin Mill. No evidence of the landowners' financial arrangements with farmers or coprolite contractors for these workings has come to light (Wood, S.V. and Harmer, F. W., (1877), 'Later Tertiary Geology of East Anglia', *Q.J.G.S.* vol. XXXIII, p.75).

The following year, 1865, there was a reference to them still being worked in Waldringfield. The records show that Mr. Kersey, a local farmer who was probably involved earlier, started work on Church Farm (TM 283442). The arrangements he made with the landowner as to the coprolite royalties were not specified. At that time it was a proportion of what he received from the manufacturers for each ton. When the subsequent operator took over in 1876 it was revealed that Kersey had paid a total of £7,881 6s.10d. to the landowner, an average of about £770 per annum. This was a veritable fortune in those days, the equivalent today of about a quarter of a million pounds. Parish records estimated *"the expense of digging, screening, carting, wharfage, porterage, barrows, sieves, pump, etc. equal to 12/- a ton"*. Eighteen shillings (£0.90) a ton profit would have been very welcome when yields of several hundred tons per acre were being realised (S.C.R.O. GB412: 4125, Box 2, Minute Book 21/9/1867 - 6/8/1941; Thursk and Imray, (1958*), 'Suffolk Farming in the Nineteenth Century',

Ipswich, p.81; Account book in possession of Mr. C.A.P. Waller, Bury St. Edmunds).

Undated photograph of William Colchester and John Ball's Chemical Manure Works beside Burwell Lode, Cambridgeshire. It was bought in the early 1880s by Prentice Brothers of Stowmarket. (Courtesy of the Cambridgeshire Collection)

MANNING PRENTICE'S EXPANSION IN STOWMARKET

'The Early Fertiliser Industry' an article in *Fison's Journal* tells readers that by 1866 Eustace and Edward Prentice, who had taken over Thomas' fertiliser side of the business, were joined by another brother, Manning Prentice. They had works at Flint Wharf in 1870. Manning was considered:

"...*an outstanding chemical scholar who was to prove the mainspring of the future success of the company. He became well known as the inventor of a process for concentrating sulphuric acid in a platinum pan and he also developed a continuous nitric acid still.*"

Undated photograph of William Colchester's barge building yard at Burwell
Chemical Manure Works. (Courtesy of the Cambridgeshire Collection)

The Prentice Brothers described themselves as 'merchants'. They recognised that the future prospects in the chemical fertiliser industry necessitated expansion of their works. They went on to purchase a 99-year lease on a plot of land in Stowupland between the railway and the river known as Claypit Bottoms. The extensive Great Eastern Chemical Works were erected, supplied by rail with coprolites from Suffolk and Cambridgeshire as well as rock phosphates from overseas (S.C.R.O. HC 434.8728. pp.227 - 9; *K.P.O.D.* 1873). The extra seventeen miles (27 km) of the Ipswich and Stowmarket Navigation would have only added half a day's travelling time for the sailing barges. Below is one of their advertisements:

ROOT CULTIVATION is The Basis Of Profitable Farming. PRENTICE's Manures.

Mangold Manure..........8 Pounds 10 Shillings per Ton.

Turnip Manure..............6 Pounds 10 Shillings per Ton

Superphosphate............6 Pounds per Ton

Soluble Guano...........12 Pounds per Ton

Are especially prepared to produce large crops, and may be used with equal advantage for Cole Wort, Kohl Rabi, etc, with or without farm yard manures. Address early orders to Thomas PRENTICE & Co., Agricultural Chemical Works, Stowmarket. Or to any of their Agents:--- Mr John CRISP, Beccles; Mr H. LING, Bulcamp; Messrs BULLOCK Brothers, Aylsham; Messrs T. and J. W. BUNN, Great Yarmouth; Mr Z. LONG, Attleborough; Mr G. SMITH, Dereham; Mr F. SMITH, Ryburgh; Mr R. D. SAVORY, Burnham Sutton; Mr D. SAYER, Barnham Broom Mill.

(Beccles & Bungay Weekly News 25 September 1866 Page 1, column 2)

THE FATAL EXPLOSION AT STOWMARKET

Not only did the company make chemical manures, in 1863 they expanded into the manufacture of gun cotton as a way of using the excess acid produced in their other work. The government needed it for the army's munitions across the empire, so demand was high. It was a simple process but potentially dangerous. The Patent Safety Gun Cotton Company was set up on the site where the ICI had its industrial plant in the 20th century. Clean cotton wool was immersed in a mixture of equal parts of the strongest nitric and sulphuric acids. It was lifted out, allowed to cool for a minute and then washed in plenty of cold water. It could be dried in the sun or by using a very gentle artificial heat. However, it was highly inflammable. On 11th August 1871 an explosion occurred at 2.00pm that shook Stowmarket, blowing out windows in the town and as far away as Haughley station, some three miles away. It was heard as far away as Diss. Naturally it got into the pages of *The London Illustrated News:*

Particulars were given last week of the terrible explosion, on the 11th inst., of a gun-cotton factory at Stowmarket, by which twenty-four persons were killed and seventy-two others injured. A local journal says: —"The scene of the accident is one of perfect ruin. The only thing that appears intact is the tall, handsome white brick chimney shaft. At the base of this lies a confused mass, extending over a wide area, of broken walls, rafters, tiles, slates, masses of half-burned cotton, iron rods and beams, twisted into the most fantastic shapes, corrugated iron fencing and all the remnants of what had been an hour before an extensive pile of buildings. The site of the magazines is, however, the most telling of all the strange and horrible spectacles on the spot. There the only thing to be seen is a huge chasm, nearly circular in. form, and more than 100 feet in diameter. The soil is boggy, and has been turned out in huge, boulder-like lumps, leaving the bottom nearly twenty feet below the natural surface of the surrounding soil. Scarcely a brick or tile, or vestige of any building is to be seen near this centre, and the trees which stood around, some of them of large growth, were torn out by the roots or broken short off, and the fragments scattered around, affording testimony of the awful force which dug one in an instant the huge pond-like hole where the magazine had stood. It may be mentioned that the telegraph wires on the railway have been torn off, the rails themselves being started in many places from the sleepers and scattered about with portions of the trees and fragments of the buildings. A farmhouse in the occupation of Mr. Woods, on the Ipswich road, about 400 yards from the factory, is all but ruined. The windows are blown in; the tiles cleared entirely from portions of the roof, and in the centre the framework of the roof looks as if crushed in by some mighty blow. The cottages in that neighbourhood are similarly damaged. Window-frames may be seen forced out and hanging only by a nail or shred; tiles are scattered in all directions. In the town a like scene presents itself. In the district called California the houses, principally cottages, are wrecked as to the glass and the roofs. The streets in other parts of the town are strewn with glass, and at five o'clock all the shops have closed shutters, simply as a matter of precaution to save the goods, for the glass is gone from nearly every frame. The church windows are all broken, the leads and glass having been forced inwards upon the iron framing, and in some cases blown entirely away. The cast window of the north aisle has suffered even more severely, for the mullions have given way to the pressure, and hang tottering to their fall.

An inquest has been held. Yesterday week, evidence of an important and painfully interesting character was given by Mr. Trotman, manager of the works. He was in his office when the explosion occurred. He heard a heavy thud, and at that moment found himself standing amid the ruins of the building. He at once ran to the shattered sheds by the river side, and calling out to know if anyone was there, he was answered by moans. He dragged away the bricks, and discovered two men, whose lives he was instrumental in saving. He then met the two Messrs. Prentice, and had scarcely left their side when the second explosion occurred, which blew one of them to atoms. On the Friday preceding the explosion there were twenty-one tons of gun-cotton, on the premises, but ten tons were sent away. The place was so full that a packing-shed was made temporarily into a magazine. The cotton made for Government was of the greatest dynamic strength. An explosion occurred some years ago through too much hot air being admitted into the drying-house. No heat-meter is kept in the magazine. He believed that heat had something to do with the present explosion, such accidents having always occurred in this unlucky month. With his present experience, he considered the factory too near the railway station and the town. The earth mounds between the buildings had been removed and brick walls substituted. The rules of the license had, he contended, been generally adhered to. The inquiry was resumed last Saturday, when the examination of Mr. Trotman was proceeded with. Witness was questioned at some length respecting a suspicion that some of the cotton had been tampered with in the process of manufacture, but upon this point the evidence was not clear. Mr. Trotman stated that he could not account for the occurrence at all. Colonel Younghusband, superintendent of the Royal Gunpowder Works at Waltham Abbey, described the results of some experiments showing *the explosive qualities of gun-cotton by ignition, which were carried out several months ago by direction of the Government. These established the following points: — 1, The non-liability of compressed gun-cotton to explosion by accidental ignition when stored in magazines in the proper boxes; 2, the ignition of a package of compressed gun-cotton, forming part of a store, was not necessarily attended by the immediate ignition of the neighbouring boxes, as would be the case with gunpowder; 3, gun-cotton was perfectly non-inflammable when stored in the damp condition. Colonel Younghusband added that further experiments ought to be made with gun-cotton in a dry state, and that its storage should be conducted with great care. The further hearing was adjourned.*

(*The Illustrated London News*, 26th August 1871)

No trace of the remains of Edward was found other than a battered gold watch found later. Its hands had stopped at five minutes past three, the time of the second explosion. Miss Susan Prentice, Edward's sister, wrote in her diary:

"This is the most terrible day of our lives ... Papa saw William blown to pieces & Edward too. William had only just arrived from
Heidelburg University & had called to see Papa before coming home. All laughter has left our house. Will Papa ever smile again I wonder. His sadness enfolds us all."
(http://www.stowman.fsnet.co.uk/prentice_family.htm)

William Colchester's second cousin once removed, Henry Thompson Colchester, or one of his siblings, was also injured in the blast (Author's communication with Giles Colchester) Following Edward's death, Manning Prentice assumed the bulk of the responsibility running the business, employing about 40 people, but he died in 1875. Although little documentation of his business has come to light, it is likely he made similar arrangements for coprolite supplies from the contractors working the deposit from the Cambridgeshire Greensand and the Suffolk Crag.

FURTHER DEVELOPMENT UPRIVER

Although there is little reference to the Suffolk workings during the 1860s demand must have been so high as to elicit concern from a number of geologists. Their interest had been sparked by Edwin Lankester's concern about them becoming exhausted. From 1839 he had been the Secretary for the biological section of the British Association for the Advancement of Science. In 1845 he became a fellow of the Royal Society and in 1865 founded and edited the Journal of Social Science. He regularly examined the fossils bought up by Mr Whincopp and Mr Baker of Woodbridge which included *"teeth of Sus, Rhinoceros, Tapir, Mastodon, Castor, Ursus, Felis, Hyaena etc., tusk of Trichedon, and earbones and rostra of whales"*. He duly reported his findings in the *Quarterly Journal of the Geological Society* but there was no indication as to which coprolite pit they came from (Lankester, E. (1865), 'Mammalian Fossils of the Red Crag', *Q.J.G.S.*, pp.221 - 32). From 1875 – 1891 he was professor of Comparative Anatomy at Oxford and Director of the British Museum until 1898 during which time he received a knighthood.

In 1848 Edward Charlesworth, a keen geologist and fossil collector, gave a lecture to the Norwich Geology Society entitled 'The Prospective Annihilation of the Suffolk Red Crag, Phosphatic Stone, Coprolite' (Charlesworth, (1868), *Geological Magazine*, vol. v. p.577). This prompted further visits to the Suffolk pits but, as shall be seen, only the superficial deposits had been exploited. Deeper deposits were still available but at greater cost.

Joseph Prestwich, the son of a noted London wine merchant, gained much experience of continental geology whilst on his father's business. In particular he had plans for a Channel Tunnel and an improvement to London's supplies of drinking water. His interest in the Suffolk fossils must have led him to visit the Butley pits in 1868 as he noted *"a shallow pit now worked between Butley Abbey and Butley"*

(TM 371509) (Prestwich, J. (1868), 'Structure of Crag Beds', *Q.J.G.S.*, p.460). He was appointed professor of Mineralogy at Oxford University in 1874, a post he held until 1887. William Johnson-Sollas was a student at St John's College, Cambridge, who was later appointed professor of Geology at Oxford. When he visited the Suffolk diggings in 1872 he referred to a large crag pit on Neutral Farm, near the Butley Oyster Inn (TM 371509). It was 300 feet (105 m) in length and 35 feet (12.35 m) at its deepest point (Prestwich, J. (1871), 'Structure of the Red Crag', *Q.J.G.S.* p.326; Johnson-Sollas, W. (1872), 'Upper Greensand Formation of Cambs.' *Q.J.G.S.* p.402; Taylor, J.E., *Geol. Mag.* July, 18--). Johnson-Sollas was one of the Oxford geologists accused of faking the Piltdown man fossils of 1912 but theorists now target other suspects. In Whitaker's account of the geology of the area, a section of the Sutton workings was taken in 1868. The section clearly shows five pits around what was appropriately termed Coralline Crag Hill (TM 303453) (Whitaker, (1885), op. cit. pp.67 - 9).

The financial success of these workings, in terms of labour for the diggers and carters, royalties for the landowners and compensation to the tenant farmers, stimulated the local economy. It encouraged nearby landowners to allow the bed to be worked on their land. The owner of Pettistree Hall had the deposit on their land raised. In 1871 Prestwich referred to a working on the slight rise to the south of Pettistree Hall (TM 303439), close to the Deben. Here the bed was excavated to a depth of 22 feet (8.1 m) (Prestwich, (1871), *Q.J.G.S.* vol. XXVII, pp.116 - 8).

In March 1870 Miller of Boyton sold a further 104 tons from Valley Farm to a George Ling of Bedfield. Who he was and his role in the diggings has not come to light. Bedfield is a few miles northwest of Framlingham, about 25 miles (40 km) north of Boyton. Could he have been acting as a coprolite merchant, selling them on to another manure manufacturer? In subsequent years he advertised as a *"Coprolite Raiser"* from Great Bealings (TM 233486). This village was about a ten-mile (14 kms.) horse ride from Boyton so he may well have lodged in rented accommodation (White, (1874) op.cit.). These new pits must have been from deeper seams which were possibly too expensive to extract earlier. Where exactly they were worked remains unknown. In 1871 914 tons were sold but at a lower rate of only thirty-five shillings (£1.75) a ton. A Captain Saxby took it in two vessels, the *Industry* and the *Lady of the Wave*, from Boyton Dock to the manure works in Ipswich. Maybe this was Stephen Saxby, a naval engineering instructor, writer of several naval books and weather forecaster.

INTEREST IN THE OVERSEAS MARKET

A significant influence on the coprolite trade was the devastation of the French wine industry in the late 1860s. Phylloxera, a deadly virus, had attacked the roots of most of the vines. To recover from their demise, French viticulturists had to import vine stock from California that had been taken over there by French emigrants. In order to ensure it took root, the best fertiliser on the market was required (Yates, R. *'History of Potton'*, unpublished paper, Potton History Society, p.44). This led to a significant trade with Bordeaux and Boulogne from which Ipswich profited. Between 1869 and 1871 coprolite was the port's second largest export after ballast which had 60,000 tons. When the third largest was iron with less than 4,000 tons, it confirms the importance of coprolites to the port of Ipswich.

However, expensive British coprolites prompted the exploitation of a French coprolite deposit. This was found in the same geological strata on the other side of the English Channel. They had first been worked in the Ardennes in 1846 and later in the Pas de Calais. Edward Packard had investments in these supplies from the end of the 1860s. When they came onto the market at the end of the decade the export market for British coprolite dipped (S.C.R.O.HA 65/2/46-48). It also saw the manure manufacturers start a concerted effort to secure cheaper supplies from other areas of Europe and the empire, a move that was the start of the decline of the British coprolite industry. The 1871 Ipswich Dock Commission Report included the following figures:

COPROLITE EXPORTS FROM IPSWICH 1869 — 1871

	1869	1870	1871
Tonnage	21,942	17,883	14,589
Number of ships	324	265	224

Following the end of the Franco-Prussian War in 1870 there began a period of relative peace and stability which brought a brief upturn in Britain's and France's economy. Increased farmers' demand for fertiliser stimulated renewed interest in the coprolite industry. Although the phosphate content of the Suffolk coprolites was not as high as those in Cambridgeshire, it still fared well in comparison to those in Bedfordshire, Buckinghamshire and France.

EVIDENCE FROM THE 1871 CENSUS

Analysis of the 1871 census returns revealed only sixty-nine people described as involved in the Suffolk coprolite industry. Although this was a 458% increase over the decade there must have been many more. As in previous decades it is thought that many did not describe their work as a fossil or coprolite labourer because a farmer employed them. However, after almost a quarter of a century of the diggings, six parishes had it as a recognised occupation by the enumerators. To give one an idea of the scale of the Suffolk industry, there were 2,013 recorded in Cambridgeshire, 347 in Bedfordshire, 14 in Buckinghamshire and 10 in Hertfordshire.

Colchester had installed two of his sons in Bassingbourn, Cambridgeshire, where 28-year old William was described as a *"Coprolite Raiser employing 176 men, Farmer employing 16 men and boys and Engineer and Iron Founder, employing 11 men and 5 boys"*. The iron foundry produced much of the plant and machinery needed in the diggings. Living with him was his 27-year-old brother, Edward, who was described as a *"colinist in New South Wales"* (C.C.R.O. RG 10/1361

1871 census). He had returned from Australia after losing his farming investment in a disastrous fire and ran some of his father's coprolite workings in Trumpington and Great Shelford (author's correspondence with Giles Colchester, London).

Edward Packard was living at The Grove House on Paper Mill Lane, Bramford. He was described as a 27-year old *"Merchant and Manufacturer of Chemical Manure"*. Living with him was his 24-year old wife Ellen, his three children under three and four female servants. At Grove Cottage next door lived 52-year old Frederick Buttram, the *"Manager of Chemical Manure Works"*. He had only a general servant but his two nieces lived with him as governesses. .

Felixstowe's population had increased by ninety-seven over the decade to 760 but only one person was described as involved. That was 54-year old Micah Frost, a *"Trinity Pilot, Coprolite Merchant"* of Felixstowe Ferry. Whenever the master of a ship entered unknown waters he would ask a Trinity House pilot to join his ship to guide the vessel to its destination. The owners of the vessel would then pay the Corporation for these services. This was a charitable organisation set up by Henry VIII in 1514 for the safety, welfare and training of mariners and relief of those in financial distress. Frost must have used his boat to carry the coprolites across to Colchester's manure works in Harwich or up the Orwell to Ipswich.

There were only two coprolite labourers recorded in Walton, whose population had increased by 28 to 1016. They were 45-year old William and 14-year old Thomas Smith, who lived on the High Street. Thomas Woodgate, mentioned earlier, still farmed Gulpher Farm but there was no mention of him employing coprolite diggers. Over the decade he had purchased a further 25 acres. Only employing 13 men and one boy, a reduction of 29 labourers over ten years, suggests increased mechanisation or that any diggings on his land were on a small scale.

PLAN OF CORALLINE CRAG HILL.
AT SUTTON, SUFFOLK.

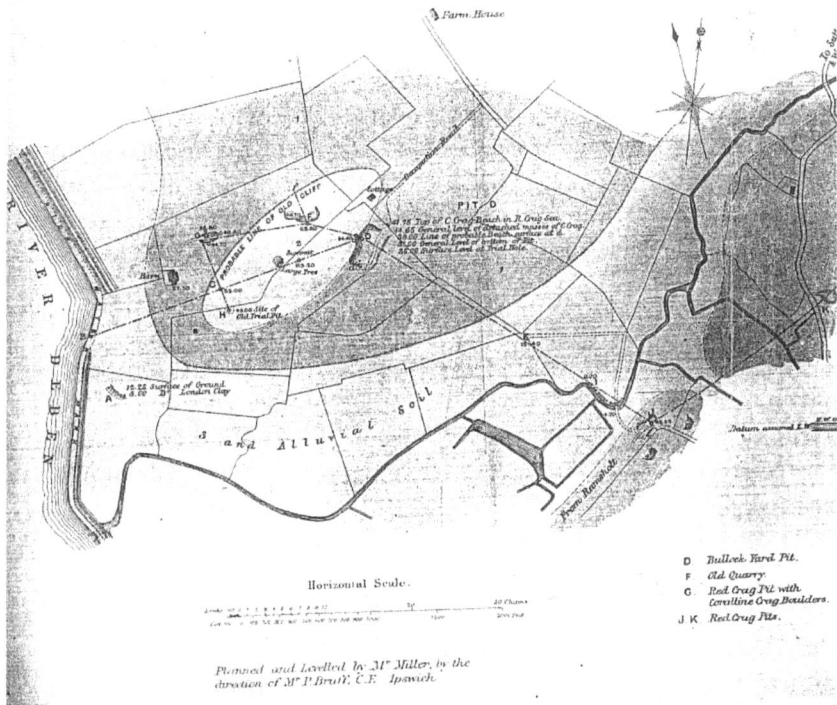

Whitaker, W. (1885), 'The Geology of the Country around Ipswich,
Hadleigh and Felixstow', *Memoirs of the Geological Society*,
London, p.67

Bucklesham's numbers had fallen by 41 to 321, an 11% drop. Only two 12-year old *"boys in coprolite pit"*, James Lewis and Henry Gardner, were described as involved. Clearly others must have been but did not describe themselves as coprolite labourers.

The largest recorded number of diggers was in Foxhall. Its population had increased by twenty-one to 213, a 12% change over the decade. 45-year old Frederick Wainwright was described as *a "farmer of 1150 acres employing 13 men and 27 boys also 23 men and 15 boys in Coprolite Pit".* Yet none of the villagers described themselves as coprolite diggers. Wainwright was benefiting from the sale of the coprolites as, living with his wife, two daughters and two sons, he had two servants. How long he had been working in the parish is uncertain but he was still involved in the late 1870s. His company was included in several entries of the government's statistics of Suffolk coprolite production (Mineral Statistics, *Mem. Geol. Soc.* 1876, p.132; 1877, p.145; 1878, p.147).

Boyton's population had increased by sixteen to 270 but there was no reference to anyone as being involved. 77-year John Lucock was recorded as a farmer but made no mention of employing any coprolite labourers. Maybe he had purchased land with his coprolite revenue as the census showed that he farmed an extra two acres whilst still employing five labourers. 68-year old James Stebbing farmed an additional eight acres yet still employed four men.

Whilst there were workings in Newbourn during the 1870s, the census gave no indication of any diggers. Its population had fallen by seven to 161. 37-year old Horace Walton of Newbourn Hall (TM 274428) described himself *as "Farmer of 851 acres employing 23 men and 13 boys".* Subsequent evidence shows that he had these labourers work the coprolite pits on his land. In 1873 the local trade directory mentioned that *"Coprolites are found here in considerable quantities among the marine deposits".* Another Newbourn farmer who may have had his labourers work the coprolites was John Hunt. He advertised as a *"coprolite raiser"* but no records of any his agreements have come to light. Perhaps the papers of Sir C. R. Rowley, the lord of the manor, may show that he allowed his tenants the right to raise them (*K.P.O.D.* 1873).

By 1871 70-year old Thomas Waller had expanded his holdings to become one of the leading figures in Sutton. He was described as a *"Landowner and Occupier of 1025 acres employing 70 men and 17 boys"*. Again none of the locals were described as coprolite or fossil labourers. Its population continued its fall since its peak in 1851 of 732, falling by fifty-eight to 600.

Waldringfield's returns showed 23 men involved under 18-year old William Kersey of White Farm. This is probably White Hall Farm (TM 286438). He was described as a *"Farmer of 310 acres employing 9 labours, 1 boy. Worker of Coprolite employing 13 men, 10 boys"*. This could not have been the earlier contractor. Most likely he was his son. The family would have been considered as one of the new gentry as, living with his wife Mary, were two young girls, a governess, a cook and a housemaid. There was no evidence of any other contractors. None of the men in the parish described their work as coprolite labour. As in the other parishes the vast majority described themselves as agricultural labourers.

With the huge demand for artificial manures in the early 1870s, Messrs. Clark and Ganham, two corn millers, set up their own manure manufacturing works by Darsham railway station, about five miles north-northeast of Saxmundham. They converted their mill for crushing bones and coprolites (S.C.R.O. HA 38/2/76-90). A. W. Pashley set up the Waveney Valley Chemical Works at Haddiscoe near Lowestoft in 1872 selling phosphate, superphosphate, sulphuric acid, sulphate of ammonia, bones and turnip and mangold manure. No records have emerged which showed where they were making their purchases (*East Anglian Handbook,* 1872).

Production would not have been on the same scale as the Ipswich works. An observation made by a frequent traveller on the Great Eastern Railway in 1872 noted Packard's extensive works: *"Acid chambers produce enough sulphuric acid for the manufacture of 800 tons of manure a week... Two new engines started at Bramford...."* (*ibid.*).

LAWES SELLS HIS MANURE BUSINESS

In 1872, after thirty years in the manure and coprolite business, John Bennet Lawes decided to sell up. Maybe his dealings in the international side of the business made him realise that there would be problems ahead? The profits from his patent, his manure business and coprolite contracts made him an extremely wealthy man - a typical Victorian entrepreneur. From 1869 to 1872 his company had a growth rate of 10%. On 1st July he sold his *"valuable and extensive business"* for £300,000, the present day equivalent of about £13.7 million! (Valence House Museum, Dagenham, (VHM), Lawes Chemical Manure Co. Minute Books, 16th November 1880). A third of the sale price was used to establish an agricultural trust and Rothamsted became the world's first agricultural research station.

William Colchester was appointed the deputy chairman of the new company which kept its original name to maintain custom and he managed the Barking manure works. He moved from Springfield House in Ipswich into Burwell Hall in Cambridgeshire. This he restored and rebuilt on the lines of his former residence. He also acquired land at Raynham in Essex on which he erected yet another large chemical works. It is said in his obituary that he was the originator of the Manganese Bronze Company and the inventor of steamship propellers but this is not borne out by the company's official history or the propeller display in the London Science Museum (Suffolk Chronicle, 26th November 1898; *Geological Magazine*, March 1899; Author's correspondence with Giles Colchester, London).

One of his first tasks was to double the salary of his coprolite manager to £300 per annum. Maybe his promotion also explained the company's increased prices for Suffolk coprolites in the first half of the 1870s. He certainly could have influenced purchase contracts. Average

154

prices rose from fifty-two shillings and sixpence (£2.65) per ton in 1873 to sixty shillings (£3.00) in 1875 (Valence House Museum, Dagenham, Lawes Chemical Manure Co. Minute Book, 1872 - 5).

By 1875 Packard had formed a limited company with his two sons. Maybe he left them to manage the business and became the company's representative at meetings started that year with the directors of Colchester's, Fison's, Prentices and the other major manure companies. They agreed to meet regularly to discuss issues like prices, supplies, production and competition. So was born the Fertiliser Manufacturers Association. It acted rather like a triad to control prices and regulate the industry.

INTEREST IN OVERSEAS PHOSPHATE

The exhaustion of the South American guano deposits by 1872 provided a further stimulus to the British coprolite industry but also invigorated overseas exploration for phosphates. The mid-1870s was the peak of Great Britain's trade and industrial development in the 19th century and it coincided with the 'boom years' of the coprolite industry. Given the huge demand for fertilisers at home and abroad, some of the entrepreneurial manure manufacturers started to invest in the extraction and import of overseas phosphate. Packard won concessions to import French phosphates from the newly discovered beds in the Somme and Bordeaux and American phosphate found at the mouth of the Ashley River in Charleston, South Carolina.

COPROLITE DIGGINGS IN IPSWICH

It was mentioned earlier that the coprolite bed was worked in Ipswich in the 1850s. The location of the pits was not recorded until 1885 when Whitaker detailed the outcrops of Crag deposits. In Holywells Park in 1875 there was an old brickyard where the London Clay was worked. Close by, the fossil bed was exposed at the foot of seven feet (2.59 m) of Crag. There were pits to the south, just east of

Greenwich Farm (TM 173427). South of the farm, *"on the slope facing the river the phosphatic nodules have been worked"* (TM 168424). They were also found in Piper's Valley close to the river (TM 178413). This was probably the pit marked on the map, immediately north of the footings of Orwell Bridge in Orwell Country Park. The most extensive operations were stated to have been on Ipswich Racecourse *"In the middle of this the nodule bed has been worked more than anywhere else"*. They would have been north of the rifle range and now probably lie under the Recreation Ground immediately north of Holywells High School (TM 184434) and south of the Old Trolleybus Depot on Cobham Road. As this area is on sand and gravel above the coprolite bed, other workings may have been found lower down the slope towards the river. Horse and tumbrils carried the coprolites from these pits, and possibly many others, along the riverbank to Packard's manure works on the south side of Coprolite Street and at Bramford (Whitaker, (1885), op. cit. pp.50 - 51, 59; 25" Suffolk 75.12).

Phosphate workers at Charleston, South Carolina, United States

Packard and Co. expanded their works in Bramford, Dock Side and New Cut East in the early 1870s. They had offices on Princes Street and at 55 Corn Exchange. They also had a factory in Cambridge, Dublin, Derry, owned pyrites mines in Norway, phosphate mines in France and a complete manufacturing works at Limburg and a concentrated superphosphate works in Wetzlar in Germany. Clearly it had quickly become a successful international company in the search for, production and marketing of phosphates. Their investment in the Tarne et Garonne, Aveyront and Lot departments in France allowed them to import high quality Ardennes phosphates with yields of 70% in 1874. Their products were good enough to win the gold medal for manures and the silver medal for phosphate in the World's Great Show in Paris in 1878 (Mark Lane Express, 27th April 1874; 'How Chemical Manures are manufactured?' undated article in Norwich Argus, Suffolk County Record Office, Bury St Edmunds; East Anglian Handbook, 1878; Oxford Dictionary of National Biographies).

NEW DEPOSITS FOUND ON THE SOUTH COAST

Charles Bidwell, an experienced coprolite surveyor from Cambridgeshire, considered the reported phosphate content of 70% as not being permanent and that exploitation of the French deposits had not been such a profitable investment. In a talk to the Institute of Surveyors in 1874 he commented that:

Phosphate mill at Charleston Mining Company's works
(Frank Leslie's Illustrated Newspaper June 30th 1877)

"Considerable sums of money had been launched by men who had tried to import coprolites from abroad - especially from France, where extensive beds exist in the Ardennes - but they did not bear the expense of importation, for the reason that the French phosphatic nodules were, frequently, too poor in phosphate of lime, containing as a rule, not more than 40 or 45 per cent., and comparatively much carbonate of lime. Recently an extensive deposit of chalk coprolites has been found opposite to Dover, and in the neighbourhood of Dover itself coprolites had also been found - evidently the same bed extending under the Channel to Calais."

It was the autumn of 1870 when the Folkestone Chronicle provided the first evidence of their exploitation in Kent:

*"**A SPECULATION.** - During the past week much curiosity has been excited in this town and neighbourhood at the sight of between thirty and forty men in a field adjoining Sandgate and Shorncliffe Railway*

Station, digging and sifting the soil. Various rumours have been afloat in reference to the object of this excavating process, and many credulous people have reputed that a gold mine has been sprung in the neighbourhood. Such a statement, and the report of the work going on at this place, has drawn a large number of people to inspect the ground, and who have tried to discover, what seems like one of the wonders of Folkestone. The men at work have been forbidden to impart any information, and this has increased the curiosity of spectators. The facts, we believe, are these. Some speculators have undertaken this work, and they are the pioneers, for this part of the country, of a new branch of industry, yclept (sic) coprolite digging. The great resemblance between the geographical character of this part of the country, to that of other places where these lucrative diggings flourish, induced one or two speculators to test the soil for this valuable production, the result of which is so far satisfactory. For the benefit of the uninitiated, it may be observed that coprolite is generally supposed to be the fossil excreta of an extinct race of animals (although some learned men say otherwise). After being operated upon by vitriol, or other powerful acids, it forms the most potent and valuable manure. We hope success will attend the efforts of those who are trying to discover such a valuable produce beneath our soil."

Phosphate mill at Charleston Mining Company's works
(*Frank Leslie's Illustrated Newspaper* ,June 30th 1877)

The article stimulated considerable local interest. The rumours of what was going on must have been interesting. The following week, further light was shed on the operation:

*"**COPROLITE.** - The search after this valuable remains of a bygone period, which has been going on near the Shorncliffe Station during this past week, is now brought to a conclusion. A large quantity of coprolite has been discovered, and the excavations have extended ten feet below the surface. Further down than this, in the part of the land where the digging has been confined, this substance does not extend, and the vein appears to terminate, and is succeeded by strata of another substance. The probability is, however, that there is a considerable deposit in the neighbourhood, but whether sufficient to undertake erecting manure works here is another question. There can be no doubt the land presented a promising aspect, or the speculator would not have gone to the considerable expense he has done in making discoveries. The large pit, or trench, which has been dug, is now filled in, and yesterday boys*

and men were engaged in sifting, and sorting the coprolite which will be carted away to the railway station, and sent to a destination for the purpose of chemical analysis. Many tons have been set apart for this purpose, with what result time only will reveal."

Documents show that Colchester was involved but its success, as shall be seen, was short-lived. The deposit found in the neighbourhood of Boulogne proved more remunerative. Packard, Colchester and Fison's bought large quantities. France further supplied English manure manufacturers with phosphorite, large deposits of which were discovered in the Departments of the Loire and Garonne (Voelcker, Dr. A. (1875), 'On the Chemical Composition of Phosphatic Materials used for Agricultural Purposes', *Journ. Agric. Soc.* p.399). These imports brought valuable business to Ipswich docks.

ATTEMPTED SINKING OF THE ZELIA

One of Packard's ships laden with 'super' was nearly sunk before it reached the Channel. *The Times* reported in April 1874 that Henry *Luscombe,* one of the crew members, was charged

with feloniously and maliciously damaging a certain ship called the Zelia with intent to destroy her. Mr Bulwer QC and Mr Graham appeared for the prosecution; Mr Reeve defended the prisoner. The vessel in question was the property of Messrs Packard, and at the time of this occurrence was laden with artificial manure for the Mauritius. She left Ipswich on the 20th of March, and dropped down to Harwich harbour, where she remained at anchor till the morning of the 24th. At about 9 on that morning the captain went on shore, leaving the vessel all safe but in about two hours he heard of a distress signal being hoist, and on going aboard he found that a hole had been bored in the side of the vessel about 5ft below the water line, this hole having apparently been made with an auger about seven eights bore, and the captain stated that he had seen an auger of this description at the foot of the companion ladder shortly before he left the ship, but his auger could not be found after the occurrence. To connect the prisoner with this act it was proved that he had been below a short time previous, and suggested that his motive for committing the act was his desire to escape from going the voyage.

At the close of the case of the prosecution, the learned Judge said that, although it was a case of strong suspicion against he prisoner, there was not sufficient evidence to convict him of so serious a charge, and a verdict of not Guilty was returned

(*The Times,* **6 April 1874** page 9)

FURTHER EXPANSION IN THE 1870s

Such was the expansion in the 1870s that Fison, unable to develop the site of his Eastern Union Mills in Bridge Street, Ipswich, established his own sulphuric acid plant on land by the river at Bramford. The Halifax Mills site was developed with new docks constructed partly on reclaimed land from the sandbanks in the river (Author's Communication with Eileen Adkins).

Demand for chemical fertilisers was so great that there was room for another chemical manure business. A. Noble and Co. started advertising from offices at 6 Corn Exchange in Ipswich. According to the government mineral statistics for 1875 they were based at Needham Market, just south of Stowmarket. There was no further mention of them and, as yet, none of their records have come to light (*K.P.O.D.* 1874, White, (1874), op.cit; *East Anglia Handbook* 1872 - 1874; Mineral Statistics, *Mem. Geol. Surv.* London, 1875, p.182). Packard was involved in the area as the Ipswich Journal of October 25th 1884 noted:

Mr Waller of the Swan Inn, Needham Market, applied for an hour's extension of time on Wednesday evening on the occasion of Mr Packard's annual treat to his customers and farmers in the neighbourhood. The Magistrates granted the application.

This expansion in chemical manure production was accompanied by increased demand for Suffolk coprolites. There was considerable expansion of the diggings during the early 1870s with many new pits opened and older ones dug down to twenty feet (7.4 m) and more. White's Directory for 1874 gave another detailed account:

"Immense quantities of coprolite, fossilized excreta and bones of antediluvian animals, chiefly marine, are got in all the parishes on or near the coast from Bawdsey to Boyton. It has fetched upwards of £3 a ton, and is used as manure and in the manufacture of fine earthenware etc. Thousands of tons of it are shipped yearly from the Deben to various parts of the Kingdom. Its fertilising properties are procured by trituration and treatment with sulphuric acid. Veins of it at various depths from two to twenty feet and thousands of pounds worth have been got out of a single small field. It is mostly found near springs of water, and the strata of the Suffolk Crag, chalk, etc. are very interesting. When dug up, it is carefully sorted, washed through sieves, and laid in heaps for carting. It employs hundreds of men, women and children daily between Bawdsey and Woodbridge. The parish is rich in antediluvian shells and fossils, numerous in the Crag deposits, copperas used in the manufacture of sulphuric acid; and cement stones along the coast."

These hundreds of people had not been recorded in the census. It was also 1874 when the Shotley Brick, Lime and Cement Works started under the management of Edward Gibbons. It was located at the end of the road used as a public footpath on the banks of Cockle Creek (TM 235342) on the Stour estuary. It is now the site of Rose Farm Cottages and the caravan park. There was no indication, however, that they were also selling coprolites (ibid.). These large works by the river may well have developed from the early coprolite workings that had exposed the London Clay at the base of the Crag. Like many other villages on the coprolite belt, these works took on the 'owd coproliters' once their industry had finished (Whitaker, op.cit. p.48; Suff. 83NW, 1891).

Searles Wood and Frederick Harmer's 1877 geological paper on the Crag revealed details of numerous workings on or near the southeast Suffolk coast. Wood was a Woodbridge palaeontologist who specialised in crag molluscs and Harmer was a Cambridge geologist who specialised in the glacial geology of Norfolk. They referred to a coprolite pit at Cowton Bottom, just northwest of Shotley village (TM 228356). No other documentation for this parish has emerged. There were references to several Crag pits from which the coprolites could have been exploited about three-quarters of a mile northwest of Kirton Hall (TM 269399). No evidence of the landowners' financial arrangements with farmers or coprolite contractors for these workings has come to light (Wood, S.V. and Harmer, F. W., (1877), 'Later Tertiary Geology of East Anglia', *Q.J.G.S.* vol. XXXIII, p.75).

White's trade directory for 1874, in its description of Sutton, included the comment that *"Large quantities of coprolites are found in this parish"*. Waller by this time had bought the manorial rights from Charles Austin of Fen Hall (TM 307460). Other landowners possibly involved were Lord Rendlesham, who had earlier arranged the coprolites to be raised from his estates in Boyton, Butley, Bawdsey, Capel St. Andrew and Ramsholt. Whether they continued during the 1860s and 70s is not documented. W.T. Phillips, Horace Weston, R. V. Edwards and C. Walker were other Sutton landowners. The one most likely involved was Charles Girling who was described as *"Farmer and Manure Agent of Pettistree Hall"* (TM 303448) (White, (1874), op.cit.).

However, as Charlesworth had suggested back in 1868, the Crag was in danger of being exhausted. By the middle of the 1870s many of the original pits had ceased operations. More than twenty years of digging had exhausted most of the shallow deposits. Whilst some were left open to the elements, others were considered worth restoring for agricultural use. Whitaker noted:

"About half a mile northward of Falkenham Church there was a nodule working in 1874 on the eastern side of the track but the work was finished as it was "then being filled up" [OS. 294395].

Following Tye's interviews with old coproliters, all sorts of fascinating tales about Falkenham were revealed. Mr Utteridge recalled how *"he used to have a lot of the funny shapes they found on our dresser. One of them was a fossilised pig's snout. They had some real good times at the "Dog" in the coproliting days"*. Later in the article, James Rivett recalled how:

"The pits were just stopping when I was leaving school. My father was a coproliter. I was a little, doddy old boy in them days. I remember times when the coproliters never did a stroke of work, but stayed in the "Dog" all day. It was open from six in the morning till ten at night then. They said that the wind was in the north and it was going to rain, so they couldn't work. But they were hard-working people. They had to run a solid square yard of coprolite across planks to the barges. A square yard weighs more than a ton. The coprolite sometimes lay 20 to 25 feet deep and they had to dig all that earth away to get it out. That shows you it was valuable stuff. But sometimes that only ran a foot deep beneath the surface."

In Brightwell there were a number of coprolite pits located west of St. John the Baptist Church. These were about a quarter of a mile south of the A12 roundabout at Brightwell Corner (TM 247436). The pit is still marked on today's Ordnance Survey map. In Trimley there was a newly opened coprolite working in 1874 *"at the top end of the little wood about a mile NW of Trimley churches, and close to the railway"*. This must be Broomhill Grove, a small wood in which a spring emerges and several ponds appear to be flooded coprolite workings (TM 264380). The overlying Crag was from four to six feet (1.48 m - 2.1 m) thick. As the phosphate bed was up to three feet (1.05 m) thick, it would have been a very profitable venture, especially when the railway opened in 1877. The same seam was worked in a pit at the back of a cottage about three quarters of a mile west-northwest of St. Martin and St. Mary Church and in pits just to the northeast and southeast. This sounds like they were in the fields between Flory Farm and Goslings Farm (TM 266374). Here it was only six inches (18.5 cm) thick below cover of up to seven feet (2.59 m) (Whitaker, op.cit. p.63.).

About a quarter of a mile to the south "*round Grimston Hall, half a mile west of Trimley, coprolites have been largely worked*". In 1874 there were still four workings in which the seam was exposed. The first, between seven and nine feet (2.59 m - 3.15 m) deep, was just southwest of the Hall (TM 267365). Several ponds in the valley look like they might be flooded coprolite pits. The second, up to sixteen feet (5.8 m) deep, was *"a little north of the farm, on the western side of the lane to Trimley"*. This would be in the field behind the back gardens of Grimston Hall Cottages (TM 268367). A third, six feet (2.1 m) deep, was on the opposite side of the lane and a little to the south (TM260367) and the fourth *"in full work"*, just northeast of the Farm, was about twenty-two feet (8.1 m) deep (TM 269366). A little to the southeast, close to Fagbury Cliff, the bed was worked again (TM 270346) (ibid. pp.52 - 53). Nowadays the container park has been built on reclaimed land just below the cliff. The 1881 25" map of the area showed a number of crag pits further north in Trimley. The largest was Hanging Crag Pit, just west of Loompit Grove, overlooking what is now Loompit Lake (TM 256278).

The only documented record of a coprolite working in Kesgrave was in 1874 when reference was made to a pit in Wood and Harmer's geological paper. It was three quarters of a mile northeast of All Saint's Church (TM 226465). It may have been George Ling of Bedfield, who was advertising in 1874 as a *"Coprolite Raiser"* from Great Bealings, less than two miles away (Wood and Harmer, op. cit. p.75). The three large ponds you can see today may well be the evidence of flooded coprolite workings but the sand continued to be excavated into the 20th century.

Being so close to the rivers was of great commercial advantage for the transporting of the coprolites to Ipswich. *"Waldringfield had its ferry crossing to Stonner Point...*[OS. 292447] *which came into very frequent use when the coprolite trade was in full swing"* (Arnott, op.cit. p.83). Not far from the coprolite pits at Waldringfield, the same bed was found in the vicinity of Martlesham. When they started is unknown but Wood and Harmer's geological report suggests that they were in operation in the 1870s. A coprolite works was noted about a mile south of the church (TM 263455). Whether it was St. Mary the Virgin or St. Michael & All Angels is uncertain but they included a sketch. (Wood and Harmer, op.cit. p.75). On the west of the Newbourn Road, about three quarters of a mile south of the Church, another coprolite working was noted (TM 262458). The large pond in the Moon and Sixpence caravan park may well be a flooded coprolite pit (Whitaker, op. cit. p.65).

There were several coprolite workings near Kirton. They were worked at the Lower Farm by the edge of Falkenham Marshes, a mile and a quarter east of the village (TM 201397) as well as from a 20-feet (7.4 m) deep pit a quarter of a mile northeast of St. Mary and St. Martin Church (TM 285400). There was a pit, about a mile north-northeast of the church and west of Corporation Farm (TM 283412), which was in work in 1877. Maybe it was the disused pit marked on the present-day map near Sluice Farm. Another, closed by then, was a fifth of a mile to the west (TM 279410). There were also several workings on the north and south slopes of the ridge near Corporation Farm (TM 285402) (Whitaker, op.cit. pp.59 - 60.).

Bucklesham's parish records reveal that Packard had one of his coprolite works on Church Farm, tenanted by Mrs Reeve. They were *"in full operation"* in 1874 when the parish authorities rated them with a value of £120. This revenue was added to the parish's Poor Relief, a fund to help the less well-off members of the local community (S.C.R.O. FC47.A1/1). How long they were worked is uncertain. A pit was marked on the 1881 map. ((25" Suffolk, 1881, 83.3; Armstrong, P. *'The Changing Landscape'*, p.106).

RATING THE COPROLITE WORKS

Over the first few decades of the industry those members of the gentry responsible for setting the parish Poor Rates became aware that landowners, coprolite contractors and merchants were making veritable fortunes whilst paying nothing in rates for their coprolite works. There was disagreement over whether only temporary diggings like coprolite pits should be included in the rating and many contractors refused to pay. It was 1867 when this matter came before the courts. Over the next four years there was a legal battle in which many coprolite merchants felt justified in contesting the rates. In Cambridgeshire some combined to hire a firm of solicitors to fight their case. The Cambridge Chronicle reported the appeal meeting:

*"**TRUMPINGTON COPROLITE ASSESSMENT**. At an appeal meeting of the assessment committee, Rev. W. Smith in the chair, held on Tuesday last, Mr. Nayler, the barrister, instructed by Messrs. Nash & Thurnall of Royston, appeared to support the appeals of nearly all the coprolite merchants round Cambridge against their being rated in the respective parishes in which they have works. Mr. Nayler contended that the Act of Elizabeth (Poor Law) gave no power to rate any but the occupiers, they merely had a license from the landlord to get out the coprolite, making compensation to the tenant. The law only contemplated rating what made an annual return, not taking out which could never be repeated. He cited numerous cases, showing that the thing was uncertain, and averred that no officer could make a rate that would enable a magistrate to issue a distress if the rates were not paid. The Committee took time to consider."*

They considered it for over three years. In some parishes horse-powered wash mills were rated at £50 and steam-powered mills at £100. When brick works were only rated at £20 it helps one appreciate the differences in profit that the operators were making (C.C.R.O. Little Eversden Parish Vestry Minutes; C.C.R.O. Cambridge Session Orders 1869 - 1874 pp.26, 69-70, 91, 118-121, 133-8, 187-195, 235-244; Cambridge Independent Press, 7th January 1871 p.5; Cambridge Chronicle, 7th January 1871 pp.8 - 9; Leighton Buzzard Observer, 17th January 1871).

The Assessment Committee appealed for help in fighting the case but the Board of Guardians of Cambridge Union felt unable to contribute to the legal costs. They were *"not of sufficient extent and value in this Union as to justify the Guardians acceding to this application"* (C.C.R.O. Guardians of Cambridge Annals. Annual Minutes 9th December 1868). It was not until early 1871 when a decision was made which had important implications for all the parishes on the coprolite belt. The Leighton Buzzard Observer reported on the:

COPROLITE RATING - A case of considerable interest to the owners of Coprolite property and contractors for coprolite excavations came in for hearing at the Cambs. Epiphany quarter sessions on Friday in the form of an appeal by Mr. Charles Roads v the Churchwardens and Overseers of the parish of Trumpington. Mr. Naylor and Mr. Mills supported the appeal and Mr. Peland (specially retained) with Mr. Mayd and Mr. Horace Browne were for the respondents. The parties had agreed upon a special case for the court of the Queen's Bench, and last November Mr. Justice Blackburn and Mr. Justice Melor decided that the appellant was liable to be rated in respect of the increased value of the land upon the commencement of the excavations. The question in the appeal at the sessions was the basis upon which the rate was confirmed, and the court decided that the whole land was liable for rates until it was actually restored to agricultural use and dismissed the appeal with costs. This decision will govern more appeals which have been entered."

MORE ON THE BOYTON DIGGINGS

Only a little evidence of the Suffolk Relief Boards rating coprolite works has come to light. Mr Ling of Boyton was asked to make a contribution. However, he successfully managed to persuade the Trustees of the Mary Warner Charities that they should pay half the rate, as they were also benefiting from the revenues! (S.C.R.O. GB412: 4125, Box 2, Minute Book 21/9/1867 - 6/8/1941). Although Bucklesham and Boyton were the only Suffolk parishes where evidence has emerged of coprolite rating, further analysis of other coprolite parish records ought to reveal how they too benefited from the ratings over the next few decades.

The renewed demand for coprolite, the higher sale prices and accompanying profits led Ling to comment that there had been a *'great increase in cost of labour, coals etc.'.* Others wanted a share of the money being made. Coprolite diggers went on strike in Ashwell in Hertfordshire and were successful in getting higher wages. These factors prompted Ling to ask the trustees for a reduction in his terms. In March 1873 the Trustees of the Charity allowed him:

"... to take Coprolite on the expiration of his present agreement at 18/- per ton. The quantity not to exceed 1000 tons yearly and openings not to be made on other parts of the farm without Trustees' permission."

This new rate was two shillings (£0.10) less than Packard had paid initially but it kept the trustees a steady income coming in. Although the work had come to a temporary halt in January 1874, Miller had sold a further 1,455 tons. By this time the most accessible seams had been exhausted.

In May that same year, George Ling put in an advanced request for the lease of Miller's farm when it was due to expire in 1877. As there were very few entries in the records until then, his diggings appeared to have ceased. This is evidenced from the account books of Emma Clouting, the local blacksmith. Ling was described as a *"Coperliter"* for whom she did shoeing work, repairs to axles, carts, traps, wheels, tool repairs, housing and the laying of pumps. Over the period 1870 - 1875 his costs were quite small, totalling only £6 12s.5d. Emma and her husband, William, before her did a lot more work for Alfred Chambers, another *"coprolite raiser"*. He paid £21 for work from 1859 - 1876 but *was "one of the worst payers"*. The Cloutings also sold *"irons, rivets and sives"* to William Ely, a Sutton *"coprolite miner"* (Strong, B. op.cit. pp.55, 63).

The diggings continued on other Boyton farms. Several local farmers were advertising in the 1874 trade directory. Horace Miller, presumably a relative of William Miller, was working Walk Farm (sic). Exactly where this farm was is uncertain. It could be Walk Barn between Red House and Hollesley Grove (TM 366453). Robert Johnson farmed land at Hollesley as well as (probably Boyton) Hall Farm (TM 383464), in front of which large, water-filled pits can be seen today. Frederick Johnson, possibly a relative of Robert, was working Dock Farm, on the northern end of the low northeast of Boyton village (TM 383477). A disused pit is marked on the map at the end of a farm track (TM 384479). Mr. Bennington had died earlier and his executors allowed Johnson to take over the tenancy. Thomas Pettit was a farm steward and James South was a *"brewer and victualler"* at 'The Bell' (White, (1874), op.cit.).

SPENDING THE COPROLITE ROYALTIES

Lord Rendlesham became one of the Boyton Trustees in 1875. They used their coprolite revenue to add six more out-pensioners, increase the in-pensions to ten shillings (£0.50) per week and the out-pensions to nine shillings (£0.45) a week. Two new cottages were built on Miller's and Johnson's farms. They bought Ransom's four copyhold cottages and, for £250, a further six cottages on Mill Lane. The Marsh Wall, near Flybury Point (TM 397464), was constructed, quite likely to provide extra security for the diggings that were taking place down in the marshes near the sea.

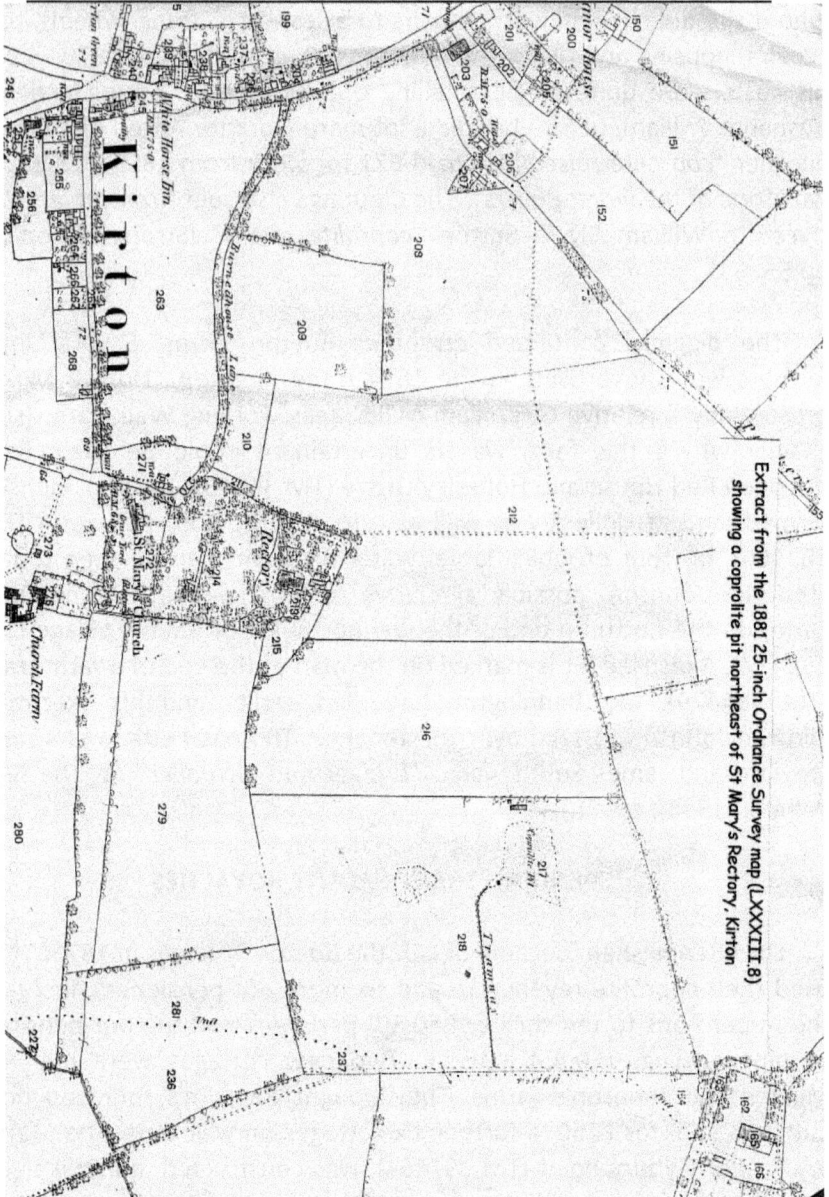

Extract from the 1881 25-inch Ordnance Survey map (LXXXIII.8) showing a coprolite pit northeast of St Mary's Rectory, Kirton

Thanks to the efforts of Rev. Hoste, the new vicar, a subscription of £400 was raised to erect the Village School; to pay for a schoolmaster's house and to contribute £20 a year towards expenses. A similar sum was raised, contributed to by the coprolite royalties, towards the renovation of St. Andrew's Church. Maycock quoted from the 1879 Terrier that:

"...the Parish Church has been entirely rebuilt in the years 1869 – 70 with the exception of the steeple on the thorough repair of which one hundred and twenty pounds was expended - twelve feet in length was added to the church with a proportionate increase in breadth. A new and handsome font with cover has been provided. The great Door and the communion table have been repaired and improved. The Norman Door formerly more than half hidden has been carefully and sparingly restored and placed where it now stands."

MORE PITS IN THE 1870s

The discovery of a new coprolite deposit at West Dereham in Norfolk in 1873 led James Fison and Son of Thetford to join Colchester and Thomas Thwaites Ball, the Burwell manure manufacturer, to make arrangements with Hugh Aylmer, the sheep breeding landowner. This reduced their dependency on other coprolite merchants for their supplies (*K.P.O.D.*, Norfolk, 1879,1883,1892). They experienced keen competition from the West Norfolk Farmers' Co-operative of King's Lynn (The Early Fertiliser Years', *Fison's Journal* no.77, December 1963).

Wainwright's pit in Foxhall was one of several described by Whitaker. He stated that the bed was worked about a quarter of a mile east of Foxhall Lodge (TM 224434). In 1875 there were two pits in operation at the southern end of the plantation. One of these could be the pit marked on the present-day Ordnance Survey map on the east side of the minor road going through Brookshill Wood (TM 223435). Opposite and east of Lodge Farm there was a pit that had been worked out by 1874. A pond remains in the northeast corner of the field which may have been it (OS 229433). Just to the south of Foxhall Hall a new pit was opened in 1875 which was 27 feet (9.45 m) deep (TM 230435).

Further east of the Hall another coprolite working showed a foot (0.37 m) thick bed at 33 to 36 feet (12.21 - 12.6 m), a section of which was included in his paper (TM 232436). On the west side of the lane, about a quarter of a mile west of Foxton Lodge, there was another coprolite pit in operation in 1876 (TM 228434). It was 25 feet (9.25 m) deep and on the opposite side of the lane was another 27 feet (9.45 m) deep (TM 224434). About a third of a mile to the east, on the northern side of the little valley, there was a pit reported in 1877 with another just east of it (TM 226434) (Whitaker, (1885), op. cit. pp.61 - 63; Wood and Harmer, op. cit. p.81).

Although they did not mention their involvement in the industry, many of the Bawdsey farmers advertising in 1874 would have profited from the trade. These included Edward Cavall at Bawdsey Hall (TM 347394), William Gobitt at the Red House (TM 349404), Samuel Gross of the Manor House (TM 339404) and William Turner of High House (TM 347397). Ransby could have acted as the middleman, purchasing the coprolite and then selling them on to the manure manufacturers (White, (1874, 1877), op.cit.).

Over the years the 'celebrated' cliffs at Felixstowe and Bawdsey attracted many geologists in their search for fossils and Whitaker recorded:

"I believe that the nodule bed has been worked just SE of Manor House, Bawdsey [OS. 342403] and in 1874, there was a small working in a field about a third of a mile SW of the church [OS. 342397]. At the spot where the bed was shown it was about three feet down, and capped by Shelly Crag."

COLONEL GEORGE TOMLINE IN FELIXSTOWE

The Felixstowe workings were still in operation in 1874. There were pits close to the western part of the cliff. Others were further up the coast *"close to the cliff edge, in the field east of Martello Place"* (Whitaker, (1885), op. cit. pp.56 - 58). In the summer of 1874, the 51a.2r.20p. Cottage Farm on the Walton Road was up for sale and its sale particulars revealed that:

"...Much of the valuable property is suitable for building land, being situated on the road between the increasing Watering Places of Felixstowe and Walton, and a railway is in contemplation from Ipswich to Felixstowe. The land has not been examined for Coprolite but it is believed it may be found to some considerable extent on the property."

(S.C.R.O.HA 119 50/3/2.Walton Papers)

As the farm was almost completely surrounded by George Tomline's Orwell Park estate, he took the opportunity to consolidate his holding and purchased it for £8,350. This was the equivalent of £160 an acre, considerably more than its agricultural value (Ibid.). As he had an arrangement with Packard dating back to at least 1874 which allowed him to work all the coprolites on his estate, there is every likelihood this property was also worked. The *Ipswich Journal* detailed Tomline's land acquisitions, possibly paid for from his coprolite royalties:
:
"The Orwell Park estate comprises 18,479 acres, not one single part of which was inherited by the late owner. It was all accumulated by purchase, and the result of his continuous acquisition was that he became the owner, with the exception of a few small holdings, of nearly all the Colneis Hundred[13], having a frontage to the sea of about six miles, and there are few properties in England which combine so many attractions and advantages. The Colonel's Suffolk possessions also include a pretty little estate at Bacton and Old Newton, the home of his

175

ancestors. Col. Tomline obtained his extensive proprietary interest in the soil of Felixstowe and the neighbourhood by purchasing in 1867 three thousand acres of copyhold land, one thousand acres of shore and saltings, quit rents, rights of common, and 2,400 acres of unenclosed lands, &c., with six farms, cottages, Walton Ferry Inn, and woods, known as the Trimley estate, the property of his Grace the Duke of Hamilton. This was bought privately from Messrs. Fairbrother, Clark and Co., who had successfully offered the estate to public competition at Tokenhouse Yard on July 23rd 1887. Before this (in 1862) he had purchased the Old Hall Farm, at Felixstowe, now in the occupation of Messrs. Hyem, then the property of the representatives of Capt. Montague R.N., deceased, and about 210 acres in extent. Earlier still (in 1856) he had bought the Peewit Farm of Mr. Abraham Abbott, of Walton (father of Mrs. Shuckforth Downing, whose husband was himself Colonel Tomline's confidential agent from 1872 to 1876) for £6,500. This was 152 acres in extent. Another purchase, even earlier, was the Wadgate Farm, at Felixstowe, 434 acres, bought from Mr. John Jakes Steele; and further acquisitions were the East End Farm (now, as regards the farmhouse, the head-quarters of the Felixstowe Golf Club), almost 500 acres; and Mr. William Fulcher's estate, the Grange Farm, of 365 acres. Indeed, every farm in the Colneis Hundred which came into the market, and was added to the already large land possession of Colonel Tomline. He did not stand for price when he had made up his mind to have an estate, as proved by his purchase at public auction (through Mr. Shuckforth Downing, then his agent) on the 14th July, 1874, of the Cottage Farm at Walton – commonage – for £8,350. Whilst Mr. Downing was his agent Col. Tomline bought through him no less that £156,000 worth of property in Walton, Felixstowe and Harwich, besides constructing the railway to Felixstowe at a cost of over £140,000. The Riby Grove estate in Lincolnshire, comprising, 8,439 acres, with a rental of £11,534.2s., were entailed upon the Colonel and his brother William. He acquired his brother's interest in the property by purchase about the year 1875. In addition to the Riby estate, Colonel Tomline owned, amongst other property at Grimsby, a large piece of valuable land extending from Riby Square to Humber Street.

"...Colonel Tomline was at one time said to have been the largest fundholder in England, and it was understood, by those who transacted business for him, that a certain portion of his income was always set apart for the addition of field to field and house to house, and that from this source he had ample means to meet all expenses. One story is told, upon pretty good authority, which affords some idea of his vast pecuniary resources, as well as a glimpse of family history. The Riby Grove estates in Lincolnshire, comprising 8,439 acres, with a rental of £11,534. 2s., were entailed upon the Colonel and his brother William. At the dinner table one night, about the year 1875, when William Tomline was staying at Orwell Park, there was something of a quarrel between the two, the upshot of which was that the Colonel purchased his brother's interest in the property there and then. "I want so much money", he said directly afterwards to his business agent, "go and mortgage the whole of my estates." When the Colonel said "go", those who knew him went. The estates were mortgaged accordingly, and the money raised. When the amount for the first six months' interest was presented, however, the Colonel was so enraged at the amount that he communicated instantly with his brokers, obtained the ready cash, and paid off the mortgage at once."

(*Ipswich Journal*, 30th August 1889)

Tomline was responsible for the Port of Felixstowe and its rail connection. His Felixstowe Railway and Pier Company was built in 1875 and the branch line from the Eastern Union Railway at Westerfield opened in May 1877. There were stations at Derby Road, Orwell, Trimley, the Beach and the Pier. Two years later the Great Eastern Railway took it over and by 1887, confident that Felixstowe had a bright prospect, purchased the whole undertaking from Tomline's company. Eventually it was renamed the Felixstowe Dock & Railway Company. In 1884 Tomline's firm was authorised by parliament to construct a dock basin at Felixstowe, the start of a development of international importance what was to make the town a world famous container port.

Roy Gooding reported how, following Tomline purchasing the Manor of Walton-cum-Trimley, a long legal wrangle started with the War Office. They owned about 100 acres of land adjacent to Tomline's, upon which they held a 999-year lease, at a rent of £10 a year. On January 6th 1875 Tomline received a notice that he would be offered 10/- (50p) per acre for his land with an option towards future purchase. His reply to the War Office stated that he would be prepared to sell the property for £360,000. This offer was rejected immediately and:

"An arbitration court was convened in January 1876 in Ipswich, to assess the value of the land under question under the compulsory powers of the Defence Act. Tomline's new assessment for the Manor was £40,000, this included items for wreckage, seaweed, minerals and bathing machines. An additional £22,000 was asked for Langer Common. The Jury assessed the value of Tomline's 200 acres at £11,039. This amount was refused by Tomline and he took it to appeal to the London Law Courts. The outcome of the appeal was to increase the value to £15,000, and was accepted. A local paper dubbed this protracted case "The Civil War". In subsequent years George Tomline had several more legal tussles with the War Office concerning the extraction of coprolites, shingle and water supply. Only a person with Tomline's financial resources could have taken on a government department in this way. He must have taken much pleasure in doing battle with such a strong opponent."

(http://www.ast.cam.ac.uk/~ipswich/Observatory/Tomline.htm)

One such squabble was detailed in the *East Anglia Daily Times*. As the then Lord of Felixstowe Manor, Colonel Tomline had allowed Packard's men to work a large pit just behind Tower Hill Cottage. It was just to the southeast of what was called '2 Tower' in some papers and 'Q Tower' in others (TM 300342), adjacent to the Battery under Bulls Cliff. Today it is under the Leisure Centre and Tourist Information Office on the seafront. The tenant, John Chevallier Cobbold, was MP for

Ipswich and a man of considerable influence in the Eastern Counties. He was unhappy about the interference with his grazing and took Tomline to court. According to *the East Anglia Daily Times* of 2nd June 1880 the area in dispute was land:

"... on which a Martello Tower, known as the Q Tower, was situated. On the Tower land, which the Secretary of State for War, as copyholder, had left to Mr. Cobbold for grazing purposes, Colonel Tomline had dug for coprolites ...".

Cobbold sued Colonel Tomline for trespass and the illegal raising of the coprolite. His argument was that Tomline's men had:

"...broke and entered Q Tower Land, broke, damaged and removed the fences whereof and by his servants, Workmen and Agents had dug trenches and holes therein and damaged and destroyed the herbage growing on the said land and dug up and removed from the said land and converted to his own use large quantities of coprolites and other minerals and soil and hindered and prevented the water from using and percolating in through and under the said lands."

(S.C.R.O.HA 119 50/3/209)

Colonel Tomline, a man of considerable means and influence, took legal advice. A lengthy court case ensued which revealed how:

"In about the month of November last the Defendant gave permission to Mr. Edward Packard (who has an agreement with him the Defendant for the taking of coprolites from his Suffolk Estates) to enter upon the portion of the licensed land now in dispute for the purpose of taking the coprolites therefrom. The land was accordingly entered by Mr Packard's men and a large quantity of coprolites were extracted from the land which are now lying at Walton Ferry and have not been mixed with the coprolites taken from other portions of Colonel Tomline's Estate. On the 12th December 1874 an Information and Bill

was filed on behalf of the Attorney General, The Principal Secretary of State for War and Prince Arthur against Colonel Tomline for the purpose of restraining the latter from continuing the digging of the coprolites and from continuing the alleged trespass..."

With such powers ranged against him, Tomline undertook not to allow the workmen to dig for more coprolites on the east side of the Tower. Many witnesses vouched that the fences had in fact been breached for years and that cattle, sheep and ponies had grazed on the land without hindrance for many years, drinking *"at a spring which came out of the spot where coprolites have recently been dug"*.

Tomline's legal wrangling with the War Office over the coastal diggings ended the same month The case was reported in an article in *The Times* of June 1880 which stated:

"To this land the Crown, claimed title on the ground that it has been vested in the Secretary of State for the War Department on behalf of Her Majesty from a remote period down to the present time. In 1874 the defendant in order to assert his right to the land as lord of the manor, granted a licence to Messrs Packard of Ipswich to enter upon the land and dig for coprolites. In December of that year information was filed on behalf of the Crown seeking an injunction to restrain Colonel Tomline from digging in or continuing to trespass upon the land in Question, and praying an account and payment of the profits made by him form the sale of coprolites taken from the land and relief in damages. At the hearing in May, 1877, Mr Justice Fry granted an injunction and an account against the defendant on the footing that the proper measure of damage was the gross amount produced by the sale of the coprolites less the expenses of the working, and such a sum of money as would induce a third person to undertake the enterprise. His Lordship also held that he locus in quo to which only a possessory title was shown by the Crown, was originally an encroachment upon the waste and that the successive tenants had acquired by adverse possession only a copyhold title to the encroached land. In assessing the

damages under this decree, the Chief Clerk had certified that the defendant was liable for the full amount of the royalties (12s per ton) which he had received from Messrs Packard for his licence so them to work the coprolites."

(*The Times*, 5th June 1880, page 6)

Although Tomline tried to reduce the amount of damages, Mr Justice Fry refused, arguing that, as a wrongdoer, he was in no position to insist on any division of the royalty between himself and the Crown. In another of Tomline's documents he revealed that::

"As a matter of fact the supply of coprolites lying under the spot in question was then exhausted, and no further excavations have been made thereon. In fact the excavations have been filled in and the ground restored to its original state save and except that the herbage thereon is of course to some extent damaged."

Evidence suggests that Packard's men transferred their operations to another part of Tomline's estate to the north, in the meadow east of St. Peter and St. Paul Church (TM 302344). Here the coprolite bed was up to two feet (0.74 m) thick beneath twelve feet (4.44 m) of overlying crag. This working now lies underneath housing development. Whitaker's paper revealed that there were also workings, presumably Packard's, about half a mile northwest of Felixstowe Church just south of junction of the line to Felixstowe railway station and the line to the port. It is probably buried under hundreds of Felixstowe and Walton bodies that now lie in Walton cemetery (TM 294348). Another pit was noted in the field in the angle of the roads half a mile north of St. Mary the Virgin Church in Walton (TM 298365) (Whitaker, (1885), op. cit. pp.56 - 58).

WOODBRIDGE FOSSIL COLLECTORS

Woodbridge itself was becoming an important port, trading in salt, timber and agricultural produce with Hull, Liverpool, Holland and Baltic ports. Shipbuilding took place on the banks of the Deben along with rope making, malting and brick-making. The Saturday market attracted large crowds. The diggers had a ready market for interesting specimens at the fossil stall. Several fossil collectors lived in the town. They included James Baker, the watchmaker, William Whincopp, the wine merchant, Percy Boswell, a geology professor, and Major Edward Moore.

When Baker died in 1873 his Suffolk Crag collection was advertised in the *Athenum* for £250 and consisted of over 4,000 specimens, including teeth of Mastodon, Rhinoceros, Hipparion, Tapir, Hyaena and Deer, and shells, fish and reptile remains. They were bought by Edward Charlesworth and moved to London. Here further study was done on them before some were sold to William Reed for the York Museum. Some went to the Geological Museum and others Charlesworth made into smaller series and 'dispersed' them.

William Whincopp was a collector of geological and antiquarian objects and began his Crag collection in about 1845. Falling into debt forced him to sell part of his collection to Joseph Prestwich, a fellow wine merchant and geologist from London. Unable to raise enough money he passed his collection to Messrs. Alexander's Bank as security on a £400 overdraft. He was made bankrupt on 2nd June 1871 and Charlesworth, then a London fossil dealer, acquired the collection. Slightly different to Baker's collection, most were sold to the geological Museum and the rest to William Reed and the York Museum. Amongst them were beaver, walrus and dolphin.

Percy Boswell was born in Woodbridge but was not a contemporary of the fossil diggers. His interest started in the early 20th century as a demonstrator and later professor of geology at the Royal School of

Mines and then the University of Liverpool. Major Moore was born in Woodbridge and lived at the Gate House. His collection included rostrum of whale and shells which were given to Ipswich Museum when he died in 1939. His grandson, also Major Edward Moor, was a keen ornithologist and Crag collector. His collection was given to the Ipswich Museum in 1935 (Markham, R., coprolite notes in Ipswich Museum).

ORFORD CASTLE FOSSIL EXPLORATION

Edward Charlesworth, a local geologist and entrepreneurial fossil trader was employed as honorary curator of Ipswich Museum between 1835–7, the Zoological Museum between 1837–40 and the Museum of the Yorkshire Philosophical Society in York between 1844–58. He brought out the London Geological Journal in 1847 and published numerous papers on his finds and set up a small business in buying and selling fossils.

There were new workings opened near Boyton between 1875 and 1878. To capitalise on the new source of supply, Charlesworth set up what he called the *"Orford Castle Fossil Exploration"*. He advertised a *"Crag Exploration Fund"* to which people were invited to subscribe. This allowed them to purchase good specimens from the fossil diggers who had opened a cutting in the River Marshes near Orford Castle (TM 419498). This cutting must have been the pit marked on the map at Boyton (TM 386468) but he probably included the castle as a selling point. Each specimen, unless it was too large, was sent in one of his well-known circular glass-topped boxes that could be returned, or kept for a small additional payment. Included with each purchase was a list of his thirteen papers and a *"List of Fossils found in the Orford Castle (Boyton) Cutting"*.

Over 150 collections of these fossils were sent to subscribers, an indication not only of the commercialisation of the fossil industry but also of the quality of the material being raised. Typical prices were seven shillings and sixpence (£0.37) for 35 specimens of 20 species. Over the years he acquired several Crag fossil collections from local people. They included those of William Whincopp and James Baker of Woodbridge and Mr Amey of Felixstowe. Many of these he sold to Edward Grimwade, the shipping merchant and mayor of Ipswich after Edward Packard, and also to William Reed of York. Visitors to museums in Ipswich, London, Oxford, York, Liverpool, Dublin and elsewhere can find specimens of the Crag fossils on display which they bought or had donated. Others went to private collections (Markham, R. Notes on Edward Charlesworth, 1813 - 1893, in Ipswich Museum).

THOMAS WALLER IN SUTTON

Kersey was advertising in the 1874 trade directory for Waldringfield as a coprolite raiser and coprolite merchant (White, (1874), op.cit.). His men had completed the diggings on Garden Field by summer 1876, paying only thirty shillings (£1.50). In June that year he sold his planks and tools and purchased clay pipes to drain the land.

The new tenant of Church Farm was Thomas Waller of Sutton. He probably bought Kersey's plant and machinery to work the remaining deposit. Isaac Stollery, the landlord of the 'Maybush Inn' was taken on as foreman. Able-bodied labourers would have been hired to do the heavy and back breaking work in the pits, the washing and then loading onto barges. Probably they were regulars at the pub. Stollery combined these two businesses with operating the ferry. Not only were goods carried across the river but also workmen from Sutton (Thursk and Imray, op.cit. p.81; Arnott, op.cit. p.84).

The expenses of raising the coprolite had risen by well over 100% since the earlier operations to between twenty-eight and thirty shillings (£1.40 - £1.50) per ton. However, with the increase in phosphate imports, coprolite prices had dropped to only forty-five shillings (£2.25) a ton. Despite increased costs and falling profits, fifteen to seventeen shillings a ton would still have been a welcome addition to Waller's income. The labourers and their families would have appreciated the higher wages (S.C.R.O. GB412: 4125, Box 2, Minute Book 21/9/1867 - 6/8/1941). There was business for the blacksmiths, coal merchants, wheelwrights, carpenters, and engineers with a knock-on effect on trade for other traders and retailers. In Arnott's book on the Deben estuary he comments that:

"The industry gave employment to hundreds of men, women and children between Bawdsey and Woodbridge, and there were men living in Waldringfield now who were earning 6d. a day "coproliting" and sleeping on benches in the bar of the Maybush Inn on a Saturday night because they were too tired to go home."

By September 1876, Waller's men had raised 100 tons. They were washed on the banks of the estuary. Photographs of the washing operations, taken in about 1887 outside what is now Waldringfield Sailing Club (TM 286444, Suffolk Photographic Survey, Abbot's Hall Museum) show a straw fence erected to protect the men washing the fossils from the icy winds that blew in from across the North Sea. From here, Stollery barrowed them onto barges himself for three pence (£0.015) per ton. He also put in claims for beer money. Only fourteen labourers were engaged and on the 22nd December he gave them a Christmas bonus of two shillings (£0.10) each for the five men and one shilling (£0.05) each for the nine boys.

Whitaker's geological account of the county included references to Waldringfield. He hinted that Stollery's labourers must have worked the seam at great depths to get at the four-foot (1.48 m) thick seam. This must have increased both the danger to the men and also the costs. Despite the high yield, such deep workings became uneconomic with the higher wages, increased costs and lower prices.

"The large coprolite working NE. of Waldringfield Church... [OS. 284444] was almost given up by 1876, except close to the road... Mr. Stollery, the foreman, who had a large collection of shells from the

Crag, told me that the working had been carried to a depth of about 40 feet."

Map evidence shows that south of the village, by the crossroads, there was a long, deep trench which was probably a coprolite pit (283437). There was a smaller working on the slopes going down to the river. Whitaker also referred to another working in 1877, seventeen feet (6.29 m) deep, just south-southeast of All Saints' Church, where a new three-foot (1.05 m) thick seam was being worked (TM 284441) (Whitaker, op. cit. p.64). Another working was noted the same year a mile and a half northwest of the church. A pit is marked on the present day Ordnance Survey map at the hawthorns (TM 268457) (Wood and Harmer, op. cit. p.81).

In the Spring of 1877 a further 120 tons were raised and sold for forty-five shillings (£2.25) a ton giving Waller £340. This almost doubled to £603 by June when Packard paid the same price for a shipment of 118 tons.

Later that year Whitaker took two well-known geologists, Messrs. Taylor and Charlesworth, on a trip to examine the fossil pits, *"...the party now made their way over the steep escarpment of the cliffs, and across the fields beyond, to one of Messrs. Packard's "coprolite" workings"* (*Proc. Geol. Soc.* Vol. V. 1877, p.112).

Waller's lease of Church Farm was with the Ecclesiastical Commissioners. In 1858 they had to introduce the Ecclesiastical Leasing Act because a number of parish glebes in Cambridgeshire had been worked for the coprolites without their permission. The vicar or rector who farmed the glebe often pocketed the royalties. As part of the farm was Waldringfield's parish glebe, the commissioners kept two thirds of the sum received and invested the rest, allowing the rector the interest. Their regulations stipulated that this money could not be spent on a new vicarage or rectory, only on improving existing buildings.

From the accounts, All Saints Church in Boyton was considerably refurbished during this period of coprolite digging. The bulk of the royalties was spent on repainting the walls and buying new pews but a new stained glass window was installed in the east end of the church. What was not revealed was by how much the rector's living had increased (Parish Book in possession of Rev. Trevor Waller, Waldringfield Rectory, Woodbridge; Thursk and Imray, op.cit. p.81).

Rev. H. Canham, one of the earlier rectors of Waldringfield, built up a notable collection of the fossils over the years. These he donated to the Ipswich Museum where they can be seen today. Edward Packard donated his collection when he rose in the gentry to become mayor of Ipswich (White, op.cit; Flower, W.H. (1877), 'On Occurrence of Remains of Hyaenarctos in Red Crag of Suffolk', *Q.J.G.S.* p.534; Markham, R. Notes on Edward Charlesworth in Ipswich Museum). William Colchester collection eventually went to Imperial College, London. (Communication with Giles Colchester)

The trustees of Mary Warner Charity had a valuation done of the Boyton Charity estate in 1876. Their surveyor, Charles Lenny, revealed details of what was considered a short-term operation at Valley Farm (TM 367469) (S.C.R.O. GB412, 4125):

"The extent of the Fen and Pasture land near the House is limited, not exceeding 26 acres and the distant Marshes, (on certain parts of which considerable quantities of coporolites (sic) have been raised) contain, with the Saltings and the Wall 143a.0r.39p..."
(The 12 year lease for £450 included) *"an allowance for waste of surface soil by digging for coporolites on the same may occur, and also for inconvenience and injury to roads by carting and for the use of the Quay Headings, the sum of 6 shillings per ton on the gross quantity raised, subject also to the usual reservations and contracts contained in the leases of the Boyton Trust Estate..."*

"Two other questions only appear to remain for the Trustees consideration... As to the best method of temporarily housing the Persons, say some ten or fifteen hands, engaged in coproliting which can at best be deemed only a temporary industry..."

It is interesting that it was termed a temporary industry as by this time the Boyton diggings had been in operation for twenty-three years.

THE SOCIAL AND ECONOMIC IMPACT OF THE DIGGINGS

Whether the 'persons' were given lodgings was not stated but there must have been some social problems created, especially in terms of overcrowding, potential drunkenness and brawling. These were hinted at later in Lenny's report:

"It ought to be added that although no great future may be in store for the parish - which must always remain an obscure agricultural village - nevertheless strenuous and laudable exertions have recently been made on all sides, to improve the morals and add to the comforts and conveniences of the labouring population."

Deep concern about the diggers' poor morals was expressed in some coprolite parishes. Their social life led Samuel Hopkins, grocer, postmaster and deacon to the Bassingbourn Congregational Church, to report how:

"...the discovery of coprolites... brought together a large influx of persons from all parts who were employed in digging them out of the earth. These persons were the refuse of society, and with few exceptions, were extravagant, intemperate, licentious, depraved and atheistical in their conduct. One of the principal employers was an avowed Infidel. By his example, by his distribution of pernicious writings and tracts, the minds of many became infected.
"The employment of these men (who are called Diggers) was lucrative. They earned much money, they required lodgings.

Consequently they were spread all over the village and neighbourhood. Whenever they lodged, with a few exceptions, they caused a spiritual blight, the people became indifferent, careless in their attendances and unconcerned about their state; many who were hopeful characters fell away and gave evidence that an increase in riches is destructive of spiritual life.

"To meet this gigantic evil, fresh evangelistic efforts were put forth, with the aid of surrounding friends, a large room was built for the use of these people for reading and instruction on week days and for divine service on the Sunday evenings, an evangelist was also employed to converse with them, or preach, distribute tracts and endeavour to restrain them, but drunkenness and immorality so awfully and universally prevailed that these efforts for their salvation were fruitless. Some of these characters would occasionally attend our services, one or two were brought under the power of the word and were added to the church.

"To prevent the spread of infidelity Mr. Harrison gave lecture series with the assistance of other visiting ministers. The increase of population by the opening of the coprolite pits and the widespread wickedness caused thereby made his position more trying than any of his predecessors experienced yet he ceased not to warn the wicked."

Rev. Leonard Jenyns, was born in Bottisham, a small village six miles east of Cambridge where he went to University and became fascinated in the natural sciences. He published numerous papers on the subject and, as mentioned earlier, was invited on the trip round South America by Captain Fitzroy on HMS Beagle. As he had been appointed vicar of Swaffham Bulbeck, a nearby village that was extensively worked for coprolites, he stayed to serve his parishioners. His colleague at Cambridge, Rev. Henslow, married his sister. When Jenyns moved to Bath in 1850 he founded and became the first president of the Bath Natural History and Antiquarian Field Club. When he returned to his family home and previous parish he took great interest in the fossil discoveries being made along the edge of the Cambridgeshire fens. He was also concerned about the social and economic issues arising from the diggings. Over the years he developed a keen interest in the industry and in 1866 gave a talk on the subject to the Club. His notes read as if he was giving a sermon.

"...The consideration of the subject impresses us with a sense of the vast an important results following in some cases from most trifling incidents - Here in this case vast mines of wealth discovered so to speak from a man of science handling and observing in his walks what to others was but an ordinary stone - It teaches us how all observation and learning may lead to most important practical results - but it teaches a far higher lesson too. - As we look at these shapeless stones they seem to have a voice which leads our thoughts above the world to its One great Ruler - even the stones cry out and speak to us how through countless ages He prepared the world for man - His greatest and last creation - how for man He hid beneath the surface of the earth treasure houses of precious things which from time to time he brings forth for their welfare and provision. Yes in these little stones let us see the tracings of the fingers of God - and evidence of His mighty power - and evidence of his care for man - one of the countless proofs of His lowing Providence with which the earth is filled - and so to Him be all the glory."

His speech acknowledged the immense wealth that the diggings brought to the area but made some observations on the social consequences. He argued that they had:

"... led to a manifest improvement in their condition in some respects, while it has had an unfavourable influence upon it in others. The introduction of a new kind of labour, which may be carried on all through the winter, brings the men plenty of work, and from the nature of that work, higher wages than they were formerly used to. And this is greatly of the advantage of those men who are steady and provident. Earning from 15s. to 20s. a week, - even young boys of fourteen years getting 10s. for barrow work, - they not only live better, and are visibly better clothed on Sundays, but they are able to save. Further, some of

the more intelligent labourers have become good mechanics, and have got to having the charge of steam-engines and other machinery; while the genius of the men generally has been much stimulated by endeavouring from time to time to discover the best and most advantageous methods of digging out the nodules, washing them, and carrying on other operations. The unfavourable result of these diggings is that drinking has increased. The men work very regularly their own time, and have their allotted beer - two or three pints a day - whilst engaged in it, which is not much more than the labour requires. But leaving work every day at four in the afternoon, and on Saturdays always at twelve at noon, they have much time at their disposal, inducing idle habits, and tempting them to sit long at public houses on their way home.

"...The diggings have also, to a certain degree, operated unfavourably for ordinary farm work. The labour is considerably affected in some places, though the scarcity of the men, at first much felt, has been partly corrected by immigration, families coming in from the woodland parts of the county to settle where the hands are most wanted. Formerly the price of labour was regulated by the price of wheat, now in the neighbourhood in which my informant lives, he tells me, for the last six or eight years, it has been affected simply by the supply and demand for labour, a principle before unknown in this part of the country. All the able-bodied men go "a-fossillising" as it is called; and they scarcely ever go back to their former employments. The farmers, consequently, are obliged not only to pay a higher rate of wage than formerly, but to put up, in many instances, with the old and very young, the latter being taken away from school at proportionately early age, and thereby receiving detriment to their education. Boys of fourteen years get to consider themselves men in all their habits, and to assume an air of independence, not favourable either to their manners or morals, before they are much more than half grown up."

As gangs of up to 600 men descended into some of the coprolite villages as new pits were opened there was an urgent need for accommodation. Some got lodgings in local cottages. Others slept in the pubs, in farmers' barns, in tents by the roadside or in mobile barracks brought in and hired out for the purpose. Beer shops opened and other services were provided to tap into their increased spending power. Little evidence of large gangs has emerged in Suffolk. It was more common for the landowner or tenant farmer to take on their own labourers.

In Cambridgeshire a group of concerned church members established the Cambridge University and District Coprolite Visiting Society (C.C.R.O. Rev. Conybeare's diaries, March 9th 1875). This group raised funds to print and distribute religious tracts among the diggers, hold prayer meetings, set up Temperance Societies and open coffee houses, reading rooms and 'schools' where moral and religious instruction was given. College professors and students came from Cambridge University to give talks to the men and win quiet influence over them.

Lillian Birt's 1931 biography of Annie Macpherson in '*The Children's Home Finder*' shows that she met with a measure of success in her evangelical work amongst the coprolite diggers.

"*It was not easy for a timid woman to approach these rough characters... at first her efforts were received with sneers and scoffing. Often she would spend hours in prayer before she could get enough courage to approach a gang of men or even say a word apart... Gradually she won a hearing and a quiet influence among them...* "

During her time in Cambridgeshire she occasionally went down to London to attend a Church mission. This provided her with new resources for:

"*...a new power was soon evidenced in Annie Macpherson's work among the coprolite diggers. Clubs, coffee rooms, evening classes, prayer meetings and mission services were carried on, not only in the evenings but at the dinner times in barns if no other place was* *available, or in the open fields. Many Cambridge undergraduates took part. At first the speakers were always men; it was unthought of that a woman should speak publicly... Miss Ellice Hopkins, whose father was a distinguished mathematical tutor at Cambridge, came over to address the gatherings of coprolite diggers and villagers. Ere Annie Macpherson left Cambridgeshire the fossil strata had been almost worked out in that immediate neighbourhood so that only the labour of the regular population was required but the result of her efforts were far reaching. A temperate, united band of pious young men had been gathered out, full of simple earnestness each seeking to work for God according to his measure of light time and talents."*

It would be fascinating to discover details of the "*strenuous and laudable exertions*" undertaken in Waldringfield and other Suffolk parishes. Reverends Canham and Waller were probably much involved in this work.

When the Boyton farm leases were renewed in 1877, Frederick Johnson continued on Dock Farm (TM 383477). His lease stipulated that it was *"subject to (him) having control over the coprolite labourers"*. This shows not only that the diggings had not finished but that there was concern about the diggers' behaviour. Ling took over the tenancy of Valley Farm from Miller and was allowed to work whatever coprolites he could still find for the same eighteen shillings (£0.90) a ton as in 1873.

The completion of the railway line from Ipswich via Westerfield to Felixstowe that year ought to have been a tremendous boost for the industry but it was not to be. Between 1875 - 1878, according to government statistics, about ten thousand tons of coprolite were dispatched annually from the quaysides of the Deben and the Orwell to various parts of the United Kingdom. Those involved were Packard and Co., Wainwright and Co. and Smith and Co. Maybe the latter company was William and Thomas Smith of Walton. No other references for them have come to light. Production in Cambridgeshire fell from

55,000 tons in 1877 to 40,000 in 1878. In comparison, over the same period, 4,000 tons were raised from Bedfordshire. Over those four years, their value fell from £627,000 to £150,000, a 32% drop! (Mineral Statistics, *Mem. Geol. Surv.* London 1875, p.182; 1876, p.132; 1877, p.145; 1878, p.147). The cause was partly the exhaustion of the deposit but also overseas competition.

"The manure manufacturers now depend chiefly upon Foreign supplies. The port of Charleston, America, is supposed to supply 170,000 tons yearly, of the value of 500,000l.; and other places, quantities to the value of nearly 200,000l. Consequently the English production is become of small importance, and returns are obtained with great difficulty."

THE BEGINNING OF THE END?

As the demand for phosphates rose during the 1860s and more especially during the mid-1870s, manure manufacturers imported increasing quantities of cheaper and often better quality rock phosphate from many parts of our trading area. Ship-owners were bringing in supplies from mining operations in Germany, the Netherlands, Spain, France, Norway, Sweden, Denmark, Algeria, Morocco, the West Indies, Canada and, most importantly, the United States.

Deposits were exploited in Florida and Tennessee in the 1860s but the most abundant source was a natural rock phosphate deposit found on the banks and in the river beds around Charleston, South Carolina. Packard's first order was in the early-1870s and by 1878 the American supplies exceeded British coprolite production. To capitalise on these new supplies he made a milestone in the fertiliser business in 1878 by erecting England's first phosphoric acid and concentrated superphosphate plant ('The Early Fertiliser Years 1843 - 1929', *Fison's Journal*, December 1963). The East Anglian Handbook for 1878 included a detailed description of Packard's Works:

THE MILLS AND STORES AT IPSWICH

"The Wet Dock at Ipswich, although spoilt by clumsy engineering, is still a noble piece of water. Ships of heavy tonnage line its sides, giving to the old river town quite a maritime appearance. Great manufactories succeed each other along its banks. Close to the Custom House it stands noticeable amongst the rest by a large wooden gabled frontage supported on pillars over the road and railway. At right angles to this a series of low flat buildings extend back for a considerable distance. At the top of these are lines of tramways. At the western end are situated the mills, from which towers a solitary chimney, seeming all the more tall by the lowness and flatness of its surroundings. The great blocks of phosphate brought up the river by the ships are being hauled from the hold by means of a huge crane. This, by ingenious contrivance, not only lifts the block to a necessary height, but draws it into a room and empties it into a truck which immediately it has received it, runs along a slightly inclined tramway to the mouth of a gigantic hopper, down which it falls into the first crushing mills. The mill itself is in a lower chamber. As we descend the roar of the mighty machinery and the whirlwind of the tremendous stones which crush to the softest powder stones almost as hard as themselves, are most bewildering, and the effect is not lessened by the clouds of grey-green dust which rendered everything dim and indistinct. The room itself looks like a vast corridor, the further extremity being veiled in obscurity. The wear and tear which go on here are terrible. It is no soft grain that has to be ground, but massive blocks of rock have to be rent asunder and 'scrunched' into powder, and it will be useless to comment on the necessary excellence of the machinery and the awful speed of the revolving stones. Every ounce of the phosphate has to go between three series of stones, each regulated according to the desired fineness of the substance. By the first process it is merely crushed, then it is carried by a series of elevators from one set of stones to another till it emerges at the further end as a soft velvet violet powder which is fast becoming a necessary adjunct to the lady's toilet. The firm being exclusively wholesale dealers, ship to various parts of the world considerable quantities of ground

phosphate, and vast stores extend beyond the mill where mounds of its different varieties await the orders which shall consign them to the retail producers or the farmer who prefers his own preparations. These phosphate mills and stores occupy an area of 1.75 acres.

"On the other side of the docks are other stores, to which the superphosphates made at the Bramford works are carried and whence they are shipped to all parts of the globe. These are even more extensive than those devoted to the raw materials already described, and the thousands of tons which each of the numerous sheds contains, give one some idea of the enormous production of the famous works at Bramford. Mr. Packard pointed out to me a curious fact respecting the storage of these manures. Noticing that the partitions between the stores were of wood not brick, he told me that only wood was suitable, the brickwork always bursting outwards from the absorption of acid by the mortar or cement whenever superphosphates were in any quantity brought into contact with it.

"The Bramford Works.

"It is a pleasant drive from the good town of Ipswich to the village of Bramford. The traveller passes through 3 miles of flat meadows and fertile fallows by a straight road, along which a private telegraph runs, erected by our energetic friends the Packards, so as to have all their places of business in communication. It was a warm moist afternoon, one of those days when yeomen love to button hole you and point out the beauties of the turnips. During the morning a heavy rain had fallen, and now the sun was shining it seemed to draw out fragrance from everything. Even when the great Bramford manufactory and its surrounding village loomed in the north with its wide range of flat leaden chambers, its picturesque Gay Lussac towers and its great chimneys towering up to reach the sky, no symptoms of the nauseous fumes I had expected reached me, and whose house was situated but half a mile from the works, assured me that only when the wind was due north did the irritant gases trouble them, and then only in slight degree. It would be impossible from my brief visit to give any definite plan of the buildings which spread out on every side. The most prominent objects are eight Gay Lussac towers and the seventeen mysterious leaden chambers where the acid is stored and manufactured. And noticing these, I cannot do better than commence my description by a slight sketch of the difficulties which have to be surmounted before this sulphuric acid is captured.

"The Making of Sulphuric Acid

"Accompany me therefore through the works towards the railway and the banks of the river. There on a great uncovered space with lines of rail running round it in every direction and piles of wood and coal towering on either side, you see a large engine at work, a group of men busy shovelling into a machine attached to it vast pieces of green-coloured stone, from, a heap fed by steam cranes from a barge below. These stones are pyrites or sulphur ore just shipped from Spain or Norway. As the great pieces are thrown into the engine they are nipped by its powerful jaws instantaneously, and broken into minute particles. These are now carried by a tramway into the works to be burnt. The sulphur contained in this ore (about 45%) renders the pyrites sufficiently flammable, and these fires never go out night or day. The heat itself liberates the sulphur in fumes, and when all, save about 4%, has been extracted, the movable bars of the burners are turned around, the cinders fall into a pan below, and the smelting furnaces in the north. These burners are built in sets, to each of which are attached two receptacles, containing nitrate of soda and acid. The sulphur fumes evoked pass over these receptacles and the moment they do so nitrous acid is given off and sulphate of soda settles at the bottom. This latter is allowed to run out of the receptacle into vessels placed to receive it, and on coming into contact with the atmosphere crystallises, and is known as nitre-cake. When, as already explained, the sulphuric acid acts upon the nitrate of soda, the thick glaring fumes which arise are conducted, with the sulphurous fumes, to the leaden chambers. Terrible looking chambers are these, 17 in number, each one containing acid of a given strength. When the fumes are comfortably settled in these chambers their harmony is dissipated by an injection of steam. The sulphurous acid immediately absorbs oxygen from the nitrous acid and falls to the bottom in the form of a liquid, known as sulphuric acid or oil of vitriol, throwing off nitrous oxide which absorbs oxygen from the steam, and again as it passes along the chamber forms fresh sulphuric acid, the process going on so long as there remain sulphurous fumes in connection with the nitrous gases. To collect the fumes which have not been condensed in these chambers, the best means at present known are Gay Lussac absorbing towers. A hollow leaden column runs to the top of the tower, this column is filled with coke, and the escaped fumes are carried through it. At the top of the column is a supply of concentrated sulphuric acid. When this nitro-sulphuric acid has reached the bottom of the tower again it has to be released, and since only absorption and not chemical combination has taken place, this may be done by mixing it with weak sulphuric acid. The nitro-sulphuric acid is conducted to the summit of another tower, called the denigrating column. Here are two tanks, it flows into one, the other contains weak sulphuric acid. The two liquids run down parallel pipes to the next storey, and thence into gigantic leaden structures, known as the denitrating and concentrating tower, in which the nitric acid is liberated sand passes to the chambers, while the sulphuric acid, concentrated by the heat, runs out at the bottom.

"THE MAKING OF SUPERPHOSPHATE

"I have now explained how the two essential ingredients of superphosphate are obtained. The chief phosphate mills, as I have already pointed out, are at Ipswich. In these works, however, the mills are almost as extensive and quite as perfect. There is also a wonderful oven, in which the guano or phosphate is dried by merely passing through it. Cambridge coprolites, a fossil manure first introduced by this firm, is crushed and then ground. The mixing of the phosphate and the sulphuric acid has now to be explained. Hitherto my progress had been by no means an unpleasant one, and only when I climbed the Gay Lussac towers to the open acid tanks had my olfactory nerves been met with the stinging and irritant smell of flouric and silicic acid. Now, however, I could boast no longer. The ground phosphate is brought direct from the mill, where it has been carefully weighed, and is drawn up an inclined plane to the mixer, down the hopper of which it is thrown together with a given portion of sulphuric acid. The shaft of the mixer rotates rapidly for two or three minutes. During this time the mass is thoroughly incorporated; the phosphate of lime has become soluble and the semi-liquid mass falls into the dens below. Meanwhile the gearing of the truck has been reversed and it has gone back to the mill for more phosphate. Only the very brave would venture near this mixing apparatus. Flouric and silicic acids are given off in great quantities, and as you approach, it is as if a cleverly manipulated mixture of snuff and pepper was making its way up your nose, down your throat, through your ears and into your eyes. The mixers themselves, used to it perhaps from their boyhood, have to work with covered mouths and nostrils. Although the fumes are only a irritant smell and not poisonous, it is necessary to destroy them before they find their way into the atmosphere. A powerful fan drives the fumes along a flue 500 feet in length along a stream of water runs, which condenses them so thoroughly that large deposits of pure silica are continually collected from the water. I have already stated that the superphosphate goes through the mixers into the 'dens' - and dens they are unmistakably. I visited during the evening, and on my way had to traverse a series of extensive and dimly lit stores. Suddenly a broad red glare seemed to burst from an obscure corner. Within this cavernous opening I saw, as it were, the shadowy forms of men with muffled faces filling a wagon with the steamy superphosphate, just fallen from the mixing apparatus over their heads. The hot vapour filled with silicic acid reached me where I stood, and I did not care to enter the vault. As soon as the wagon was filled it was drawn up the incline by machinery and run down a tram line over a weighing machine to the river where a barge waits to receive it. Then it returns for another load; for nothing is stored in these premises, and this goes on night and day the whole year through.

The tramway just mentioned passes the rooms where the special manures are mixed. I saw several of these mixing operations going forward. These several ingredients are carefully weighed and thrown together in a heap, where they undergo a preliminary mixing by hand. They are then passed through specially constructed machines, while so *thoroughly does it work that the powder which it throws out has not only a most uniform appearance, but not a trace of a single ingredient can be found even after the most minute investigation.*

"Of course the advantage of such excellent mixing need not be dwelt upon. As I have still to say something of the Dublin and Derry Works I can merely mention here the apparatus for preparing ammonia, the Smith's and Joiner's shops, the gas works, the bag stores, the three pairs of magnificent engines, one of which is by far the largest and most beautiful I have ever seen, steam cranes and hoists, and several engines all doing their several parts in completing the productions of the largest works of the kind I know of; the plumber's workshop, where all the lead work is done, old lead remelted, and cylinders, and the spacious laboratory, with its pair of Dertlings balancings and its Bunsen filter pump, the chemical fire engine, and last but not least, the workman's hall, comfortable, handsome, and spacious, to which a kitchen, reading room, and library are attached."

William Packard said in a talk to the Fertiliser Society that the mills made so much noise that you could not hear yourself speak within five yards (1.65 m) of them and that they were very heavy on repairs (Packard, W.G.T. (1952) 'The History of the Fertiliser Industry in Britain', The Fertiliser Society, p.10).

THE AGRICULTURAL DEPRESSION IN THE LATE-1870s

With all the foreign competition, the prospects for Great Britain's coprolite industry were not good. They were further intensified by natural factors. The latter half of the 1870s was dominated by bad weather. Four consecutive years of heavy rain ruined many crops and reduced harvests. As a result, farmers' demand for fertilisers fell. Manure manufacturers could not sell their superphosphate at the same prices. Competition led some to reduce prices to only thirty shillings (£1.50) a ton. As a result, many companies reduced or stopped their coprolite purchases.

Average prices for Cambridgeshire coprolites dropped from sixty shillings (£3) a ton in 1875 to fifty-six shillings and sixpence (£2.83) a ton in 1877. Over the same period Suffolk prices dropped from an average fifty to thirty shillings (£2.50 - £1.50) a ton. Colchester's price for Butley coprolites dropped to only thirty-two shillings and sixpence (£1.63) per ton for a 500-ton contract. Lawes Manure Company records show that they made no further purchases of Suffolk coprolites for the next four years (Valence House Museum, Dagenham, Lawes Chem. Man. Co. Minute Book, 1877 - 81).

With the fall in demand, those farmers working their own pits and the coprolite contractors suffered too. Increased rainfall made the work in the pits dangerous. It also increased pumping costs with the additional water and made it difficult to properly dry out the slurry. As a result many curtailed their operations. Some closed down altogether. Plant and machinery were sold. Labourers were laid off which, coupled with the decline in agriculture, resulted in many families suffering distress. Many of the younger people left the area to find work in the industrial towns and cities.

Another contributory factor to the industry's decline was Henry Bessemer's discovery in 1878 that basic slag, the by-product of his improved iron-smelting furnace, proved an effective and cheaper manure than superphosphate. Joseph Fison, of Stoke House, Ipswich, died the same year, aged 58. He was highly respected by a large body of agriculturalists. This probably reduced his company's involvement in the industry until a new family member took over (*East Anglian Handbook*, 1878).

Farmers' economic problems were further exacerbated by the then Tory government's introduction of Free Trade. This allowed entrepreneurs to capitalise on the newly developed refrigerated shipping and import vast quantities of cheap meat and grain surpluses from the American Prairies and South American Pampas into Great Britain. Home prices plummeted. Wheat prices fell to a half of what they were in the 1860s. With lower food prices, many farmers went out of business. Some managed to arrange rent reductions of up to 30% but others were evicted. Many farms went untenanted and there was a knock on effect on other local businesses. Huge numbers of agricultural and other labourers were forced to accept lower wages or were laid off.

The effects of this downturn were evidenced in Boyton. Ling's coprolite royalties in 1878 were £704. The following year they had dropped over 50% to £324. By May that year the Boyton Trustees had received well over £1,000 from Valley Farm. Aware of Ling's financial difficulties, they reduced his royalty 30% from eighteen to twelve shillings (£0.90 to £0.60) a ton *"plus half the selling price if he sells over 38/- a ton OR 14/- fixed (£1.90 or £0.70)"*.

Raising coprolites brought in more revenue than farming and Ling managed to continue his operation. However, in 1880, on account of *"the extreme depression"* the Trustees agreed to reduce his rate by a further 10%. Despite this, he felt it was no longer economic to work the deposit and gave notice he was terminating his agreement. Humanitarian concern for those involved rather than a potential loss of revenue led the Trustees to further reduce the royalty to only ten shillings (£0.50) a ton. However, they added that this was *"to last until the present marsh is worked out or not exceeding 14 months.* In the circumstances Ling agreed to continue (S.C.R.O. GB412: 4125, Box 2, Minute Book 21/9/1867 - 6/8/194; Maycock, op. cit. p.39).

Whilst the Charity documents gave details of May's and Valley Farm, little is known about whether other landowners made reductions. It helps to explain why the industry managed to continue during otherwise very difficult times. As well as Packard and Co., the other Suffolk manure manufacturers were still making purchases, albeit at lower prices. Given the revenue to be made, some landowners and farmers in other parishes continued to cash in on the work. Evidence shows that John and Elizabeth Barthorp and Mary Tweed near

Cauldwell Hall allowed their land to be worked. Maybe it was philanthropic, providing employment for local villagers during difficult times.

AMERICAN COMPETITION

The rock phosphate brought into Ipswich and other ports from Charleston, South Carolina, was very similar to the East Anglian coprolites. But, in true American fashion, they were on a far greater scale and variety. The *Industrial Issue* of the Charleston News and Courier of 1880 reported that:

"These deposits consist of nodules of phosphate of lime, thickly interspersed with the huge bones and teeth of antediluvian mammalian and marine mammoths of stupendous and gigantic proportions; the chrysonicocrisides, ichthyosauri, hadrosauri, stupendous giant baboons, prodigious mammoth gorillas, lizards 33 feet long, and other huge graminovorous and carnivorous quadrupeds; also the squaladons, phocodons, dinotherinons, and members of the ichthaurian, saurian and cetacean families, whales 500 feet long, sharks 200 feet long, briny leviathons, voracious marine vultures and other monster, rapacious denizens of the mighty deep - land and water animals lying in the same bed. These wonderful and awe-inspiring skeleton remains, styled by Professor Agassiz "the greatest cemetery in the world", constitute by far the most valuable fertiliser known to man since the exhaustion of the Peruvian guano deposits; and are an inexhaustible source of wealth to the State and people of South Carolina, and thence to the whole world."

There were twenty-two contractors working just over sixteen thousand acres (6,464 hectares)! However, with the decline in demand for superphosphate on the other side of the Atlantic, its sale declined dramatically. British and European farmers could not afford to purchase expensive fertilisers. As a result production fell and no new contracts for overseas purchases of phosphate were made. This caused almost identical problems for the American suppliers as those involved in the British coprolite industry. The South Carolina Ministry of Agriculture described the problem in early 1880 as being:

"...a very general and widespread depression prevailing in the production of river rock. As is generally known, the great bulk of this rock is shipped to foreign countries. The short crops, and general agricultural distress which has for some years past spread over the whole of Europe, had most seriously affected the capacity of the farmer to purchase and pay for fertilisers, and consequently diminished to a very large degree the demand for the Carolina rock. Thus not only was the market lost, to a great extent, but the prices at which the rock could be sold were very greatly diminished. In consequence of this, river mining became unprofitable. A large number of the smaller companies ceased work entirely, and even the larger ones were compelled very greatly to curtail their operations and to continue with a much reduced force and at great loss."

THE RESULT OF COBBOLD'S LAWSUIT

In the early summer of 1880 Cobbold's case was heard. *The East Anglian Daily Times* reported that Tomline had wrongfully trespassed for which he was fined £200. He agreed, through his counsel, to pay Cobbold a sum per ton for the coprolites raised. Although he had received £222 from Messrs. Packard, half their gross value, he had only offered Cobbold £150. This was refused. The Colonel considered that this decision was unfair and appealed to the higher court. The Lords Justice of Appeal decision did not find in his favour and the case was dismissed with costs (*East Anglia Daily Times*, 5th June, 1880).

EVIDENCE FROM THE 1881 CENSUS

Evidence of the decline in the coprolite industry's fortune came from the 1881 census. It shows a 24% reduction in numbers engaged in Suffolk, fifty-three compared to the sixty-nine in 1871. Yet there were still six parishes where people were described as involved, including four that were not mentioned in the 1871 census. The six were Boyton, Falkenham, Hollesley, Kirton, Trimley St Martin and Waldringfield. The decline was also evidenced in Cambridgeshire which saw a 65% drop in numbers, down to 714. Bedfordshire's numbers dropped 87% to 45. Only one was recorded in Hertfordshire and one in Buckinghamshire.

Fourteen of the thirty coprolite parishes experienced population loss, five of them with % losses into double figures. Bucklesham's numbers remained the same but the rest saw increases ranging from less than 1% in Boyton, Falkenham and Shottisham to over 20% in Hemley and Woolverstone.

In Boyton, for example, there were 271 in the parish, one more than in 1871. 44-year old Robert Johnson was the only one who admitted his involvement in the industry. He was presumably William's son. Living at the Hall he was described as a *"farmer of 700 acres employing 37 men and 12 boys of whom 10 men and 6 boys are employed in Coprolite Raising"*. However, none of the men and boys in the census described their work as coprolite raising. The business had been lucrative, as in 1871 William only farmed 520 acres employing thirty men, women and boys.

Two men who were engaged in the diggings in the 1870s made no mention of their involvement. 37-year old Frederick Johnson lived at the Farm House on Dock Farm and was described as a *"farmer of 435 acres employing 13 men 3 women and 3 boys"*. 60-year old Ling was described as a *"farmer of 700 acres including 200 on Heathland employing 12 men and 1 boy"*. He could afford two servants who lived with him, his wife Sarah, and a grandson (S.C.R.O. 1881 census).

Falkenham's population had increased by two to 272. Five were recorded as coprolite labourers. 20-year old Frederick and 11-year old Arthur Stevenson lived on Kirton Road. 26-year old William Pace, 29-year old James Wright and 33-year old John Chapman lived on Dover

Street. Only Chapman was born in the parish. The others came from nearby villages which confirms an influx of labour to work the pits.

Kirton's population had increased by twelve over the decade to 627. Nobody was described as involved apart from George Hines who was recorded as a *"carrier and Coprolite Raiser employing 16 men and 7 boys"*. This was the largest number reported that year. Another Kirton man who may have been involved was Henry Laws. He was described as a *"farmer of 1085 acres employing 31 men and 7 boys"*. Maybe he was related to Frederick Laws of Foxhall Hall, the coprolite contractor in the late-1850s.

Trimley St Martin's population had increased over the decade by twenty-three to 611. Five local men were described as fossil diggers, all living on Lower Street. 40-year old Daniel Brown was the eldest with 22-year old Henry Collins the youngest. Their average age was 31, showing that it now tended to be the work of older men.

Stollery died in 1880 but the census returns for Waldringfield gave no indication that anyone else had taken over as foreman. George Hunt was the landlord of 'The Maybush' but it is unknown if he acted as coprolite foreman. The population had increased forty-two to 270. This was the third successive decade of growth with 21%, 11% and 18% respectively. One wonders whether it was linked to the diggings. Only 14-year old George Moles was described as a *"coprolite labourer"*. There were a considerable number of cement labourers however.

In Hollesley ,59-year old Robert Ling from Sutton lived on the Main Road. He was described as a *"coprolite raiser"*. Whether he was the employer or a digger is uncertain but there was no mention of anyone else.

CHEMICAL MANURE WORKERS

37-year old Edward Packard was still living in The Grove House, Bramford, describing himself as a *"Chemical Manufacturer employing 320 hands"*. Living with him was his wife, five daughters and three sons, two house maids, an under nurse, an upper nurse, a cook and a coachman driver with his wife, two children, five other children and a retired blind organist. Analysis of the census returns only revealed 89 chemical manure workers recorded in 24 different parishes in Suffolk. 75 of them were in the area around Ipswich. David Palgrave's article 'Employees in the Suffolk Phosphate Industry in 1881 in *Suffolk Roots* commented that

"Bearing in mind that large tonnages of raw materials including imported mineral phosphates together with finished products needed to be handled and that substantial volumes could be transported by barge along the River Orwell up to Ipswich, the selection of the county town as a manufacturing centre was very practical".

James and Charles Fison described themselves as Ipswich cornmillers, merchants and chemical manure manufacturers employing 82 men and 2 boys. As well as William Colchester, other Ipswich manure manufacturers were Henry and William Chapman and Henry Read. The Prentices advertised as chemical manufacturers in Stowmarket. Walton Burrell, a farmer from Fornham St martin and his brother, Robert, from Honey Hill, Bury St Edmunds, ran a chemical manure manufactory employing 8 men and 2 boys. The foreman was William Mingay who lived in Manure Works Cottages in nearby Westley with Henry Hayward, a sulphur burner. In Yaxley, farmer George Barnes was a manure manufacturer and in Elmswell, Robert Durrant did it as well as making harnesses.

Suffolk Chemical Manure Workers in 1881

Bramford	2
Bures St Mary	1
Bury St Edmunds	1

Claydon	10	
Combs		2
Dunwich		1
Elmswell		1
Fornham St Martin		1
Framlingham		1
Ipswich Clement		7
Ipswich Margaret		2
Ipswich St Mary Elms		1
Ipswich Peter		4
Ipswich St Mary Stoke		5
Ipswich St Mary Tower		1
Ipswich Matthew	14	
Little Blakenham		8
Long Melford		1
Somersham		2
Sproughton		2
Stowmarket		2
Westley		2
Whitton	16	
Yaxley		1
Total	98	

THE REVIVAL IN THE 1880s

With his investments overseas Packard saw the benefit of expanding the company's Bramford works. According to a report in the *Norwich Argus*:

"A fourth powerful steam crane was fixed for hoisting bones, phosphates and other goods out of the barges on to trucks running on an overhead high-level tramway, by which they are conveyed evenly and expeditiously to their respective stores, a distance of from three to six hundred yards. At the end of this tramway new and extensive bone stores, in close proximity to the bone mills have been built. At the

discharge point, a powerful stone breaker, with steam engine and elevators, has been placed so that the raw phosphate brought up by the barges, after it has been filled into the crane bucket, it is not touched by hand until it has been ground fine in the mill, four hundred yards distant. It is passed through the stone breaker and crushed, then elevated on to trucks which run down the tramway to the mill, are tipped out into other elevators which again carry it up to the stones, again it is crushed, and again a third time elevated to the finishing stones; and after having passed through them it is weighed by hand, and again machinery takes possession of it till the finished manure is produced, ready for the land or exportation. More complete grinding and crushing appliances from beginning to end it has never been my privilege to see.

"Three months only have passed since I visited the great Bramford Chemical Manure Works, and yet in that short space of time, what things have taken place. Can it be that the honour and distinction achieved by the firm of Edward Packard and Co. at Paris can be the cause of this activity? In very truth I think that it has something to do with it; but I am assured that the great building which I am about to describe is chiefly the outcome of the increase in the home department of retail trade, which has taken place in the last few years; but it was naively admitted by the works manager that the foreign trade of the firm has so increased that it was sorely taxing the energies of those who direct the works; and so after all there is practical proof that exhibitions are of some good. On the south side of the works, where I last saw a heap (thousands of tons) of accumulating debris of years, I now find a level space on which there is an erection, unique of its kind, two hundred feet long by seventy feet wide, with a lattice girder roof extending from side to side without support of any kind. This may certainly claim to be the largest warehouse in the eastern counties, covering as it does quite one third of an acre. The object of this building is solely the extension of the retail manufacturing and forwarding department. An inclined tramway communicates with those uninviting 'dens' I described on a former visit, and a system of overhead trams and *steam hoists conveys the stock manures to any desired position within the building.*

"There is one of Turners new powerful Gyppeswick engines, and a large Carr's Disintegrator, by which the manures are thoroughly pulverised, and prepared for use by the farmer.

"These stocks of material, both phosphatic and nitrogenous are conveniently placed between timber bulkheads, and by means of tramways are conveyed to the disintegrator to be pulverised, and after this process the finished manure is passed on to the other end of the building to await bagging, and it is then conveniently placed so that the utmost expedition can be insured upon receipt of orders from head office.

"The Great Eastern Railway evidently appreciate the efforts of the Firm to extend their business, for they have laid down for the exclusive use of the department a new siding with turntable and tramway, running the whole length of this building; and the Company, no doubt, will benefit by the additional traffic which the enterprise of the Firm may be expected to put upon their system of railway.

"Other improvements and additions were pointed out to me, but neither time nor space enables me to do more than allude to them.

"It is said that nothing succeeds like success; so then indeed success should succeed and attend the efforts of Edward Packard and Co."

('*How Chemical Manures are manufactured?*' undated article in Norwich Argus ,Suffolk County Record Office, Bury St Edmunds)

By the middle of 1881 the slump in trade bottomed out. The weather had improved but more importantly for the coprolite industry, William Colchester took over the chair of Lawes Chemical Manure Company. Unable to secure supplies of the American phosphate, he revived demand for local supplies and started making contracts for large quantities. Between March and August the Company purchased over 2,000 tons of Suffolk coprolites including 500 tons from A. Forbes of Butley. Whether he was the local landowner, farmer or a coprolite agent is uncertain. He was paid thirty-three shillings (£1.65) per ton for them. Later in the year prices had improved to forty-six shillings and sixpence (£2.325) a ton (Valence House Museum, Dagenham, Lawes Chemical Manure Co. Minute Book, 21st June, 29th August, 1881). However, prices were about 25% lower than during the 1870s. The fluctuations in the trade can be seen on the table on the following page.

Whether these purchases put business his colleagues' way cannot be determined. The improved economic situation in the early-1880s saw Packard, Fison, Prentice and the Cambridgeshire manure companies increasing their purchases of Suffolk coprolites as they were cheaper than those being raised in Cambridgeshire. The inland manure manufacturers, particularly those in Cambridgeshire, were keen to continue their demand for coprolite. One factor was the high rail transport costs incurred in bringing in the new rock phosphate from the ports of Ipswich, London and elsewhere.

Fred Cornwell, the agent for Lawes Chemical Manure Company, was supplying Cambridgeshire coprolites at prices averaging fifty-seven shillings and sixpence (£2.87) per ton and Suffolk coprolites at forty-three shillings (£2.15) a ton. Workable deposits of the poorer quality Bedfordshire coprolites were still available from where Lawes' company bought increasing quantities. Their prices were cheaper than the Suffolk coprolites, only thirty shillings (£1.50) a ton in 1882. They fell to twenty-eight shillings (£1.40) per ton in 1883 and down to nineteen shillings (£0.95) in 1888 (Ibid. 14th August, 1883, 7th December, 1888; *K.P.O.D.* 1883). Although there was still a demand for the Suffolk coprolites it was not on the same scale as in earlier years (Valence House Museum, Dagenham, Lawes Chemical Manure Co. Minute Books, 1880 - 81).

Lawes Chemical Manure Co. Contract Purchases of Suffolk Coprolites, 1873 - 1882

Year	Tons	Price	Condition	Agent

1873	500	52/6	Ed. Packard
1875	200	60/-	Packard & Co.
13/12/1875	200-250	55/-	Packard & Co.
13/12/1875	250	55/-	Joseph Fison
13/12/1875	70	50/-	Smart, Snell & Co.
1/12/1876	500	52/6 whole	
1877	Whole cargo	52/6	G.H. Wilson
11/03/1881	300	42/6	J. I. Cornwell
21/04/1881	200-240	42/6 whole	J. I. Cornwell
21/06/1881	500	32/6	A. Forbes, Butley
16/07/1881	500	45/- clean	
29/08/1881	120	46/6	Fred Cornwell
29/08/1881	420	46/-	G. Bennett
26/05/1882	20	40/-	F. I. Cornwell

(Lawes Chem. Man. Co. Minute Book, 1873 - 82)

The increased demand for the lower priced Suffolk coprolites allowed the diggings to continue into the 1880s. Although wages were reduced and many of the younger men had left to find alternative work, the diggings provided welcome employment for the older men who had been through the depression. Some landowners continued to allow tenants reduced coprolite royalties. For philanthropic reasons, as happened in parts of Cambridgeshire, some local landowners may have allowed their farm labourers to raise the deposit for no royalty at all. This was to keep the men and their families in the parish rather than cause the social upheaval of out-migration (O'Connor, B. (2000), 'The Dinosaurs of Fen Ditton', Bernard O'Connor; Arnott, op.cit. p.84).

Two 'coprolite pits' were marked on the 1881 geological map a quarter of a mile north of Aleston (sic) Hall at the end of Common Lane in Trimley St Martin (TM 264374) (25" 1881 map 83.15). There were also two Crag pits near Milford Cottage half a mile east-northeast of the village. These were a continuation of the diggings referred to in 1874 and appear to be under the A154 bypass. As no records of agreements have come to light, it is most probable that Packard's men were still raising them from Tomline's estate.

With intense competition during the early-1880s Packard and Co. made every effort to capture as much of the European market as they could. 50% of all Ipswich's exports of artificial manure and crushed coprolite went to Holland and Russia. Supplies of overseas phosphates returned to normal in 1882. 199,428 tons were imported with a value of £613,198. The future of the coprolite industry was under threat: *"A great deal of these imports were made into superphosphate and then re-exported to Hamburg in Germany and to other European countries"* (Aikman, C.M. (1894), *'Manures and Manuring'*).

The 1883 trade directory confirmed the continuation of the industry in Waldringfield. *"Coprolites are dug from the Crag in this parish, specimens of animals have been found"* (*K.P.O.D.* 1883). John Henry Waller, presumably a son or close relation, advertised himself as farming both Church Farm (TM 282442) and Whitehall Farm (286437). Perhaps confirming the philanthropic reasons for the industry's survival, White's directory for 1885 stated that *"Coprolites are raised in this parish by Rev. T. H. Waller"* (White, (1885), op.cit.).

Ling had not finished his Boyton diggings by October 1881 and was given an extension until harvest 1882 but at an increased royalty of twelve shillings (£0.60) a ton. This confirms an upturn in the market. The change in fortune continued which led to the royalty being raised a further shilling in July. The seam had clearly not been exhausted. The rent on Johnson's Dock Farm was reduced 30% by 1882 with a further 10% in 1883 and 1884. Despite another reduction to ten shillings (£0.50) a ton Ling's labourers eventually finished in 1885. When Whitaker's account of the geology of Suffolk was published that year it noted that:

"Coprolite has been raised in the fields E. and SE. of Caldwell (sic) Hall, SE. of Boyton, and pockets of it have been found under the alluvium thereabouts... Near Caldwell Hall Coralline Crag phosphate is worked, below the alluvium and therefore generally under water which is kept down by pumping. Only about 18" of Coralline Crag are overlain by Red Crag, and... in working the labourers mix the two together."

These pits must have been on the southern side of the low hill (TM 380457) and accessed by the footpath running from the Hall towards the River Ore and Flybury Point. The article went on to say that the coprolites had also been worked to the north of Stonebridge Marshes, northeast of the Hall (TM 384489), where the two Capel St. Andrew farmers had worked. They were still being worked in that area in 1883 as Alfred Chambers from Capel St. Andrew was advertising in the trade directory for Butley as a *"Coprolite Raiser"* (*K.P.O.D.* 1883). It would be interesting to ascertain whether the Johnsons in Boyton were related to Packard's coprolite agent in Cambridgeshire. This was Nathaniel Warren Johnson who was born in Wickhambrook.

Over this thirty-five year period Boyton charity received at least £4,722 which today would have been worth about £150,000. It was an extremely valuable addition to the Charity coffers (S.C.R.O. GB412: 4125, Box 2, Minute Book 21/9/1867 - 6/8/1941; Communication with Colin Maycock, Chesterfield Lodge, Boyton). With other farms being worked over the same period, there must have been a real boost to the economy compared to those villages away from the coprolite belt.

Map evidence shows considerable coprolite workings in a field just east of Coulton Farm in Butley Low Corner (TM 383497; 25" Suffolk 1881, 68.16). A mile to the east was also a large Crag pit, half a mile south-southwest of Church Farm, Chillesford. The geological map locates these and several other coprolite workings in the area.

Some farmers and contractors were unable to afford to continue when the fall in prices made the diggings uneconomic. Many pits were abandoned. Some filled up with rainwater and the sides eventually became overgrown with weeds and bushes. Whitaker's geological account of the area evidenced the changing fortunes of the industry:

"Much of the ground between Nettle Hill Cliff and Sutton Hall [OS. 298455] has been found productive of phosphate, and some of the abandoned pits are still open."

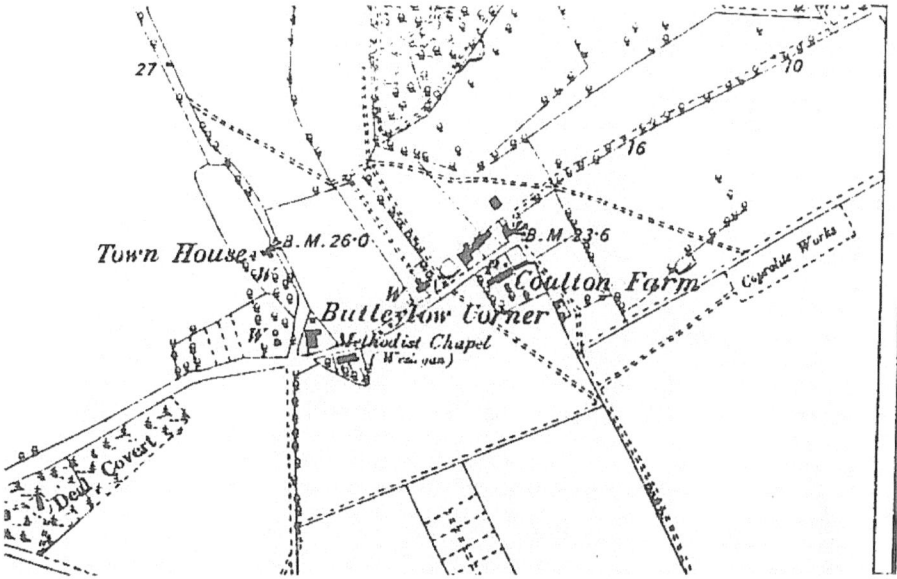

Extract from the 1881 25-inch Ordnance Survey map (LXVIII.16) of Butley showing the coprolite works east of Coulton Farm. Note the tracks leading to it.

Sections of several of these pits, including Bullock Yard pit on the north side of the hill, just south east of the Hall were included in the journal. A disused pit is marked on the present-day map, just northeast of the Hall (TM 306453). Those contractors who managed to get lower royalties, paid lower wages and generally employed older men. Tye mentioned that:

"In those days the Orwell would have been a very busy river, with barges ran by the Wards, Quantrils and Fred Strange, who brought in coprolite to the Griffin, Flint and Neptune wharves, and to Fison's, of Wherstead Road. People who lived near the docks must have seen and heard a good deal of the coprolite industry in the 1880s when, almost every day, coprolite laden barges would have been seen on the river and tumbrils brimming with them would have rumbled along "Coprolite Street" on their way to the manure mills."

SUDBURY MANURE WORKS CLOSE

The decline in farmers' demand for fertilisers hit many of the smaller manure works badly, especially when they were distant from coprolite supplies. Sudbury's works closed in 1883 and the *Bury and Norwich Post* detailed their auction on February 27th:

"The Great Cornard Soap and Manure Works were offered for sale at the Mart, Token House Yard. The property is described as extensive and valuable and is sited on the river Stour abutting onto the Great Eastern Railway about two miles from Sudbury, in the centre of an agricultural district where artificial manure is extensively used. The soap works and bone boiling business has long been established and profitable. Offers were made but the reserve of £ 7000 was not reached."

Extract from W. Whitaker and W. H. Dalton's 1882 1-inch Geological map of Suffolk (XLVIIINE) showing several PHOSPHATE references

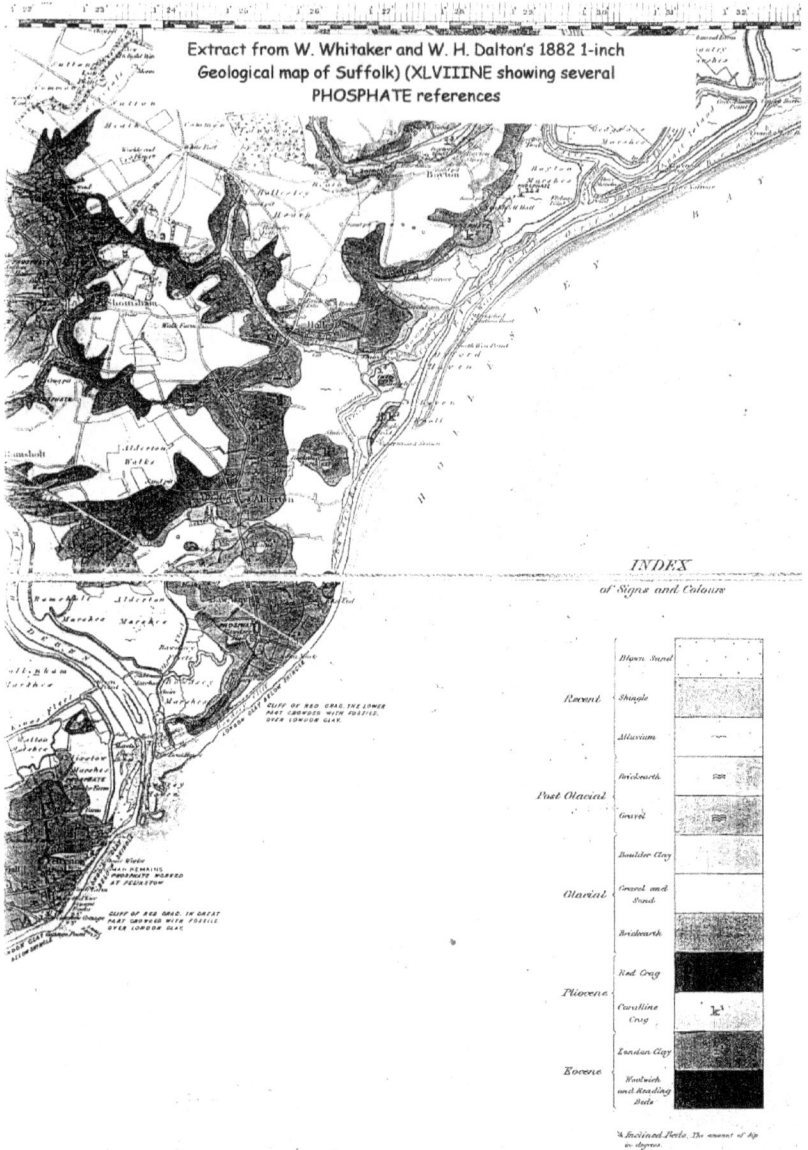

Extract from W. Whitaker and W. H. Dalton's 1882 1-inch Geological map of Suffolk) (XLVIIINE showing several PHOSPHATE references

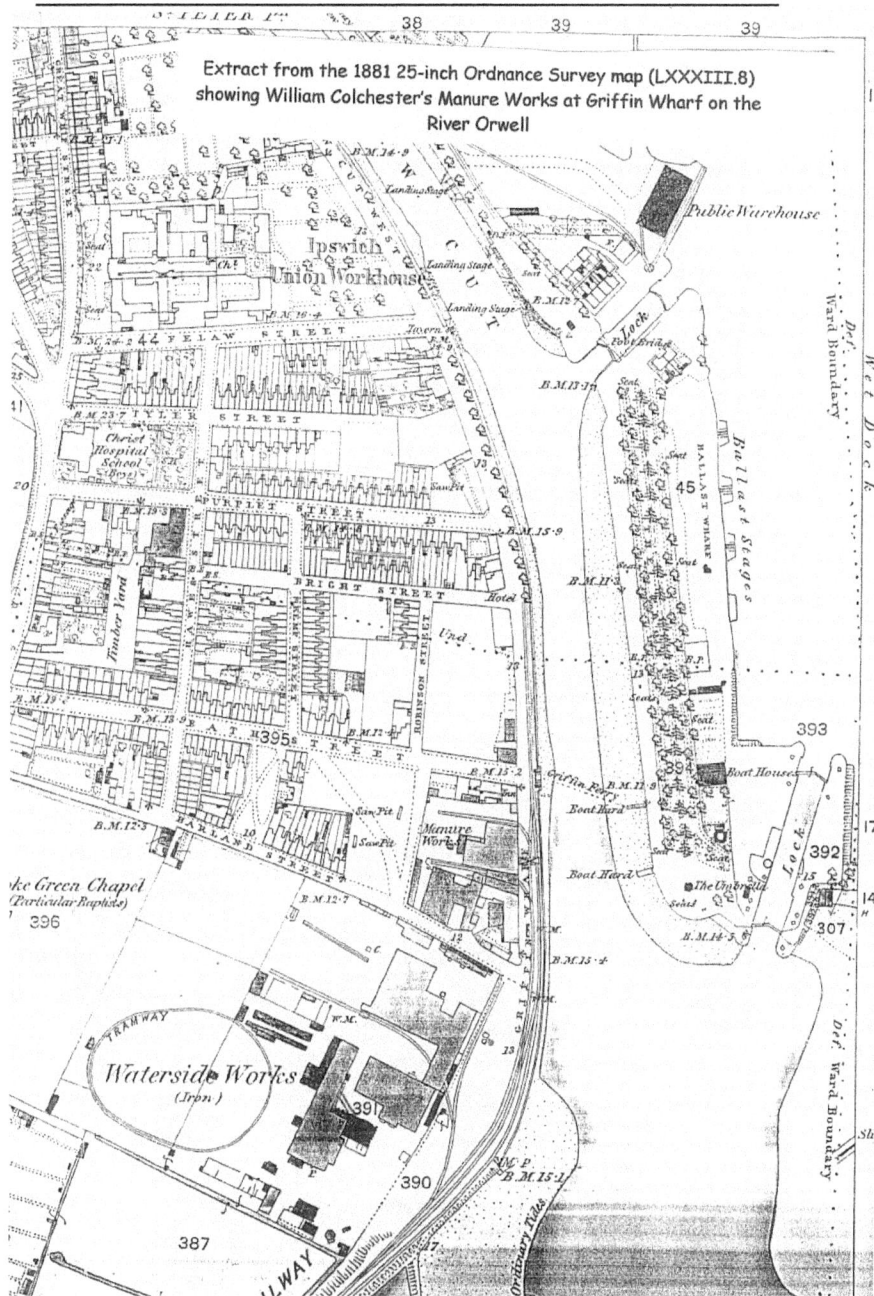

Extract from the 1881 25-inch Ordnance Survey map (LXXXIII.8) showing William Colchester's Manure Works at Griffin Wharf on the River Orwell

THE DEMISE OF THE STOWMARKET NAVIGATION

The renewal of the lease of Stowmarket Navigation came up in 1888, by which time the coprolite trade had dramatically diminished. The Great Eastern Railway refused to enter a new agreement as they received such little income from it. Instead they paid the Navigation Company compensation for the bad state of repair of the navigation. Although trade with Stowmarket then ceased barges were still supplying Fison's & Packard's at Bramford.

THE 'OWD' COPROLITERS

Tye's interviews with some of the 'owd coproliters' who worked in Waldringfield during the 1880s and 90s provide fascinating details of all aspects of their work. There had not been the improvements in technology as in Cambridgeshire and Bedfordshire. Much of the work used the cheaper methods employed in the early years.

"The main jobs connected with the industry were digging, sifting, washing, sorting, carting and loading. The younger and stronger men did the digging and loading. Older men, often past their prime, had the job of washing. Small boys, often not more than ten, did the sorting, for which they were paid about three shillings a week. When strong enough to carry a four stone tin of coprolite they were promoted to sifters and carriers, getting an increase of two shillings in their weekly pay packet. Men could earn then as much as 16 shillings a week in the pits - a good wage in the nineties. Men in other jobs were jealous of the coproliters, who had a comparatively high wage and a short-houred day. They started at 8 am and finished at 4 pm, with a break of an hour for dinner. But they had to work hard, usually taking all jobs at 'stint' prices. Everything was paid for by the yard, hod or load. No time there for idle gossip or 'go slow'.

"The opening of a new pit was no small job in the days when everything was done by hand. Shovels and picks were the order of the day, mechanical excavators and cranes were unknown by the

coproliters. So for days and days they had to dig and dig until they struck the seam. Whilst small pockets were sometimes found near the surface, they usually had to dig down from thirty to forty feet before striking the main seam, which generally lay at the bottom of the Crag and on top of the clay. The Foxhall pit is said to have been the deepest in the country, varying from forty to sixty feet.

"A coprolite pit was roughly V-shaped in pattern, with shelves from three to six feet wide running along the 'face' side where the extension was taking place. As all work was taken by the yard, everything was measured in that dimension. The men worked in gangs of four, each gang keeping to its own 'kench' as the shelf was usually called. A gang was expected to move fourteen loads a day, each load weighing a quarter of a ton. The boy sifters and carriers helped the men at the bottom of the pit, where they had reached the coprolite. Two boys were allocated to each man, spending all their time sifting and carrying. Taking a four stone tin of coprolite shoulder high to the top of the pit was not a bad performance for a boy in his early teens.

"Inexperienced men, when first entering the pits were kept to the lower 'kenches' where they'd little fear of falling from the planks when shifting the soil. Planks were laid, supported on 'horses', from one side of the pit to the other, and over these the soil had to be moved, in wheel-barrows. As men got accustomed to work in the pits they were allowed to work on the higher 'kenches' where the task was naturally more risky. Wheeling a barrow load of soil on a nine-inch plank, over a pit some thirty to fifty feet deep, was no easy task, needing strong arms, a sure foot, and a steady nerve.

"Experience, however, soon begot confidence. Accidents did occur, but not often. On frosty mornings all the planks were turned and fastened securely before the 'roads' were used. Occasionally, the barrow was known to slip off the planks and crash to the bottom, leaving the 'man on top' with nothing to balance by. In such a predicament, anyone could be forgiven for getting down and hugging the plank, which some were said to have done.

"'The men at the top', as they were called, usually walked the planks as if they were out for a brisk morning's walk. Only the best planks, measuring 20ft. by 9ins. by 2ins. were used, and they were securely fastened from 'horse' to 'horse'. "As long as she bends, she's all right" they used to say, but they'd strong suspicions of the safety of the 'road' on hearing a crack. So gradually those 'tight-rope' men got quite used to the job well able to time their steps to the bend and 'whip' of the planks. As for the boys working below, especially the beginner, they were not too happy when the 'men on top' were passing over.

"For all that, once they became fully accustomed to the pits, they had their fun when the older men were otherwise engaged. Those of gymnastic turn of mind are reputed to have stood on their heads on the topmost plank. This explains their keenness for joining the Navy after the pits were closed!

"Never a day passed but what the foreman made a visit to each pit on the farm. His was a responsible job. In addition to general supervision, he had to assess each man's work for the day and fix his pay. He also had to keep a special eye to the 'men on top', who were expected to keep the topsoil on top when filling in the pits. Failure to do that was responsible for thin crops for many years afterwards. Then he would turn his attention to the men below, wondering how near they were to striking the seam.

"To test the depth of the coprolite he made use of a tool like a giant corkscrew, called a 'dipper', which shuddered in his hands when striking the mineral. Local cottagers always knew what the foreman was after when he came into their gardens carrying his 'dipper'. Naturally, they strongly objected to their gardens being turned topsy-turvy, however much coprolite he might find there, and they were always delighted to see him go. Old residents today say that a sixpenny tip usually had the desired effect.

"The nearer the diggers got to the seam, the greater the quantity of water found, which had to be drained away, or pumped out at intervals. What a dirty job the old coproliters must have had! What with the red Crag around them and slush underfoot, they must have looked like bedraggled Red Indians when emerging from the pit at night. Anyhow, they seemed to have liked their job. The pay was comparatively good, the hours short, and the ambitious could afford to emulate those men above, who made a difficult job look so easy. By way of practice, the boy sifters often ran over the top planks during the dinner hour, or when work was held up on a wet day.

"As soon as the coprolite was taken on top, washing began. That was an old man's job when he became too old for the pit. A long tank some thirty feet in length, was specially provided for the job. The coprolites, along with a certain amount of dirt and bones, were shovelled into sieves which, when full, were placed on a ledge in the tank, just under the surface of the water; to each sieve was fastened a long pole, which the washer pulled backwards and forwards until the stones were clean. When there was a shortage of water, in or near the pit, the washing was done at the quayside before loading.

"After washing, the coprolites etc. were tipped out on the sorting table, where small boys stood alongside ready for action. With a keen eye and deft fingers they picked out anything and everything that would not pass as coprolite with the manure merchant. To avoid cutting their hands on the sharp-edged shells, they used a wooden scraper to push the coprolite from side to side, whilst with their left hands they picked out the refuse and threw it over their shoulders.

"Those small boys, still of tender years, are reputed to have worked with extraordinary speed, only hesitating when they spotted a fossil worth keeping for the collectors. Evidently such finds as sharks teeth, double teeth, bits of ivory or an occasional ear of some huge extinct animal, all found a ready market those days. A two-penny sale meant a good deal to a small boy in the nineties. I'm told that an exceptionally large shark's tooth, as big as a man's hand, was sold to a local doctor for a guinea.

"Having been washed and sorted, the coprolites were then ready for dispatch to the manure factories. Where the pits were situated near the Deben or Orwell, the coprolite was carted to the nearest Quayside. Those further inland, such as the Foxhall pits, sent it direct by road to the Ipswich docks where the manure merchants had their grinding mills. [By 1869 Joseph Fison, Noble and Co. and William Colchester were advertising themselves as grinders of coprolite. Prentice Bros., of Stowmarket, ground coprolite in a mill on the Stowupland Street.]"

Shortly after Eustace Prentice's death in 1884, Manning Prentice took over the main running of the business. His first strategy was to buy out Colchester's manure and coprolite business. How much was paid is not known but probably not as much as Lawes received for his business. Colchester had just taken on the post of managing director of Lawes Chemical Manure Co. This may explain the boost to the Suffolk coprolite industry at this time. By 1882 Colchester had sold all his vessels and closed the shipyard two years later and retired to Burwell Hall, Cambridgeshire. Mr. Hubert, his manager, also retired. However, they still described themselves as ship-owners. As Colchester's holdings included a partnership with Ball in the manure works in Burwell, Manning appointed Colchester's son, George, to join Ball. According to White's 1885 trade directory, Prentice's provided *"employment to about 40 persons"* in Stowmarket.

The same directory made mention of another important company which would have been able to supply Prentice with his needs: *"Adam & Co. Coprolite Raisers, Stowupland, Stowmarket. Engineers, millwrights, machinists and manufacturers of bone and coprolite mills"* (Ibid.). None of this company's records have come to light.

The revival of the diggings was further evidenced that year when White's directory described it as:

"A department of industry which is now employing a good deal of capital as well as labour... There are extensive beds of coprolites in Suffolk, chiefly at Kirton, Trimley, Felixstowe, Bawdsey, Alderton and other places in the Colneis and Witchford Hundreds... Immense quantities are raised in Colnei Hundred. Whole fields have been regularly turned over, sometimes to the depth of 30 or 40 feet. It is usually undertaken by the tenant, who pays a royalty to the landlord of so much per ton. The work is carried on with more or less vigour, according to the season when labour is scarce or plentiful. The surface soil is carefully preserved at top, so that the land from which the

coprolite has been taken is not materially damaged. The tenant sells and carts to the nearest town or wharf at such times as his horses are most at liberty. The depression in agriculture has caused a corresponding slackness in the manufacture of artificial manures and the raw material which the coprolite furnishes has not now a very ready sale."

The slackness in domestic production continued throughout the 1880s and in time led to decreasing demand for the Suffolk coprolites.

OTHER DIGGINGS IN THE 1880s

The seam worked in Erwarton on the Shotley Peninsula was found to extend west into Harkstead where it was worked in the 1880s. No documentation relating to the diggings has come to light apart from references in geological literature. Pits were noted three-quarters of a mile east of St. Mary's Church on both sides of a small valley (TM 203352). They were also worked further down the valley where, according to the 1881 map, a pit was still in operation 270 yards south of Lower Houses, near Burnthouse Queach (TM 197352). The track nearby led down to Waterhouse Creek where they would have been washed and loaded onto shallow-draught lighters bound for Ipswich. Crag pits where the coprolites may have been extracted were noted just west of Erwarton Hall (TM 208354) and a third of a mile southeast in the valley to the south of Rence Park Farm (TM 228348) (1881 25" OS map 89.1; Whitaker, op. cit. p.48).

In the farmyard of Hemley Hall (TM 284429) the fossil bed was found in a sandpit nineteen feet (6.85 m) deep. Just to the north was a long coprolite trench running northwards down a little side valley in which the bed was found at ten feet (3.7 m). At the crossroads, south of All Saints Church, there was another working. A pond remains as evidence (TM 285423). Close by, south-southeast of the church, another pit was in operation in the early-1880s; it was seventeen feet

(6.29 m) deep where the coprolites were found in a bed three feet (1.05 m) thick (TM 286432) (Whitaker, op. cit. p.64).

This was confirmed in July 1884 when C. J. Cooper's 284a.1r.4p. Hemley estate was valued. Charles Bidwell, the Ely-based coprolite surveyor was called in. He reported that it was worth £7,560, *"There are said to be coprolites under part of the land, but it is doubtful and if there are any the Suffolk Coprolites are of little value"* (C.C.R.O. Bidwell 43, p.181).

Whitaker reported pits in Falkenham just southeast of the lane leading from St. Ethelbert's Church to Corporation Farm (TM 295394) and another in the small valley half a mile north-northwest of the Church (TM 288397), *"Here the workmen had to remove cover of 13 to 15 feet of sand and Crag before reaching a two feet thick seam"* (Whitaker, op.cit. pp.58 - 59). Records of these workings have not come to light but the local landowners would have been very keen to capitalise on what remained of the deposit. Probably as a result of Whitaker's publication, the local trade directory for 1885 included the comment that, *"Coprolites have been formerly obtained in this parish"* (White (1885), op.cit.).

Messrs Everett and Wainwright were not the only coprolite contractors involved in Foxhall. The local trade directories of the 1880s and 1890s revealed other coprolite raisers: Henry Clarke in 1885 and George Clarke in 1892. The latter lived at Foxhall Lodge (TM 230429). Whether James Fison who was farming Valley Farm in 1892 was a relative of the Fison manure manufacturing family is uncertain (White (1885, 1892), op.cit.).

Landowners in the parish during the time of the coprolite diggings included Captain Ernest Pretyman, the lord of the manor and one of J. C. Cobbold's executors. No records of them having made arrangements to have the coprolites worked have come to light but, if the deposit underlay their property, they too would have profited from the royalties being paid. Tye commented that:

"Veins and pockets were found on most farms in the district, and as much as £20 worth was often dug from a cottager's garden... On looking up old Suffolk directories, I find that Mr. Wainwright of Foxhall... had pits on his farm from which he extracted coprolites and continued working them until about 1893 when the industry petered out... The Foxhall pit is said to have been the deepest in the country, varying from forty to sixty feet... It is said that Wainwright's carters at Foxhall often had to do two journeys a day to the docks, and that in addition to loading and unloading."

From 1963 the Foxhall sand pits were used as a landfill site for Suffolk County Council. By 1982 800,000m³ of household and dry industrial waste had been disposed of. It is still being used more than twenty years later so perhaps several million tons have been compacted, an industry on a completely different scale from its 19th century origins.

The 1885 Post Office directory, in its account of Newbourn, included that *"Coprolites have for the last ten years been raised in this parish by Mr. Horace Walton of Newbourn Hall"* (K.P.O.D. 1885). Whitaker confirmed the Waltons' involvement. He described a valley running through the wood, about a quarter of a mile northwest of Newbourn. The stream had a few springs on its eastern side that had cut deep into the shelly Crag and exposed the coprolites. This is Newbourne Springs Nature Reserve (TM 269437). There was a reference to a large Crag pit 40 feet (14.8 m) deep, marked on the 1891 OS map nearly a quarter of a mile northeast of St. Mary the Virgin Church and just northeast of Brook Cottage. The coprolite bed was found at its base (TM 276435). They were also worked in a long cutting in the stackyard at Street Farm, about a quarter of a mile east of the church (TM 277431) (Whitaker, op. cit. pp.63 - 64; Suff. 76SE).

It is uncertain whether Johnson continued his coprolite operations throughout the 1880s but he was given a boost in 1887 when the Trustees of Boyton Charity agreed a further reduction in royalty to eight shillings a ton. This was about the same as the royalties offered in the 1850s but it indicates a philanthropic aspect of the trustees in providing local employment in difficult times. Maybe Rev. Clowes, the new vicar in 1886, felt it important to reduce further out-migration (Maycock, op. cit. p.39).

DISASTROUS FIRE IN 1889

The Illustrated Police News described an incident that may well have contributed to the industry's demise. Although the cause was not mentioned, there had been cases of arson reported in many areas as the result of disgruntled employees. Whether that happened at Packard's factory in Ipswich has not come to light.

A disastrous fire broke out at midnight at the large coprolite works of Messrs E Packard and Co at Ipswich, situate on the dock side and the flames spread so rapidly that it was impossible to do any thing beyond preventing the destruction of adjoining buildings. The Orwell Works, which are close by, were at one time in great danger, but there being a plentiful supply of water, both from the dock and from hydrants in adjoining streets, they were saved. Several ships in the dock were also in a perilous condition. They were removed from their moorings, and thus escaped any damage. Messrs. Packard's premises were entirely destroyed, and although the damage cannot at present be ascertained, it must amount to thousands of pounds.

(Illustrated Police News, 30th March 1889)

It was the same year when a Miss Browne presented a rostrum, the snout bone of a fossil bottle-nosed whale, to Ipswich Museum. She reported that it came from the coprolite works at Bucklesham but whether they were still in operation then is not known (R. Markham's

228

Coprolite file, Ipswich Museum). Coprolite production in the Suffolk area had declined to 5,000 tons a year by 1889. Whilst it could be attributed to the fire, there was reduced demand caused by the country's manure manufacturers importing increasing quantities of the cheaper, foreign phosphates. By this time much of the seam had already been worked out or beneath cover that was too deep to be economically viable (*Victoria County History*, 'Suffolk', pp.285 - 6; 25" Suff. 1889, 90.1, 90.2).

Tye's research included an interview with a Mr. Ford of Newbourn who helped shed more light on the social impact that the diggings had on the local community. He mentioned the Waltons of Newbourn who had coprolite pits on their farm. One of their largest workings was known as 'Newbourn Sink' that had a spring rushing out at the foot of the Crag.

"*From all accounts the men who worked in the pits were hefty and big, as most men were who lived in the Colneis and Carlford hundreds. Elderly people in this locality today (1930s) still talk about the Pages, Fosters and Stebbings, all men of big stature and strength. Who has not heard of Page, the Newbourn Giant, who left his native village to exhibit himself in shows all over the country?... It is said that Wainwright's carters at Foxhall often had to do two journeys a day to the docks (with their tumbrils full of coprolite) and that in addition to loading and unloading. What with the soft sandy roads, steep hills and slow moving tumbrils, those patient carters must have worked from sunrise to sunset. Places like Newbourn, Waldringfield and Hemley took full advantage of barges on the river.*

"*In those days barges were always coming and going, bringing in manure and cattle food from London, and taking away coprolite, farm produce and cement. Old inhabitants say that hardly a week went by but what Fred Strange in his 'Victoria', or Stebbings in the 'Kingfisher' or Fred Ducker in the 'Three Sisters' were seen making their way down the Deben.*

"Then, of course, there was Jimmy Quantril and his 'Azarias' then operating from Pin Mill, who was frequently seen in local waters, bringing back a load of 'eye powder' from Dunkirk to grind in with artificial manures... When loading from the Quayside, all work in the pit had to stop, for every available man and boy were required for the job. It was indeed a busy day, for 100 tons of coprolite had to be moved between morning and night. Boys did the 'felling' and men the running. To avoid stoppages, 'two-way' gangplanks were laid from beach to barge. The coprolite was shovelled into tins, each weighing one hundredweight when full. And so for all day long, except for a short break at noon, the boys were 'felling', while the men were running up and down the gang plank with their wheelbarrows.

"Fortunately for the coproliters, they never knew what it was like to go short of sustaining food. They, like local farm workers, usually had two pigs in the sty and a few hens in the backyard. Then they nearly all brewed their own beer, costing them about halfpenny a pint. The Dutch cheese, too, costing about sixpence, was a good standby when working far from home. So the housewife those days could easily make up a mid-day meal of salt pork, cheese, pickled onions, and good home-made bread. And these could be washed down with pints of good home brewed."

The 1890 map of Sudbourn showed Crag Farm had two old crag pits and in Sudbourn Park there was a very large pit over 200 feet (74 m) wide. This was just north of Fire Engine House and a quarter of a mile north-northeast of the Hall. Whether these were worked for coprolite was not stated. They were and still are Coralline Crag pits. There was another on the estate opposite the White Lodge and another by the roadside in Sudbourn Marshes. A mile to the east of the village there was one on the SW corner of the crossroads and there were others in the neighbourhood of All Saints Church (TM 25" Suff. 69SW, 1890; 69NW, 1891; Prestwich, J. (1871), 'Structure of the Crag Beds', *Q.J.G.S.* (read 1868) p.122).

How long the work carried on for is again uncertain but they were still extracted in the late 1880s and early 1890s as Kelly's Post Office Directory for Sudbourn pointed out that:

"Beds of oysters have been found in making excavation near the church. The strata of Crag is largely intermixed with shells and other fossil remains, so much so as to make them of considerable value as manure, when carted onto and mixed with the surface soil."

Following J.E. Taylor becoming the new president of the Ipswich Museum, his 1891 address on 'The Story of Felixstowe Cliffs' mentioned that *"at least a million pounds worth had been worked up in scientific agriculture since their discovery by Professor Henslow"* (*East Anglian Daily Times*, 23rd July 1891). There were still diggings in Felixstowe in 1889. Map evidence shows a coprolite pit at the top of the cliff about 60 feet (18 m) above the beach. It was at the end of Wilk's Lane, a few hundred yards southeast of St Peter and St Paul's Church (TM 317355), and is now built over. William Lawrence of Trimley St Mary told Walter Tye all sorts of stories about old Felixstowe, the opening of the golf course, Colonel Tomline's legal action about taking shingle and smuggling from Black Sal's caves half way along the cliffs from Cliff Hotel. He reported starting work in the Felixstowe pits when he was twelve:

"When the foreman first took a look at me he said: "I don't think he's quite man enough to do it". But the others said: "He'll do it after a time". So they took me on. I was there until I was 16. When I left I went for a year at the Docks. It was the same kind of work, and I was used to it. So I got on better than grown men who were working there. But they were all strong able-bodied men working in the coprolite pits, and the farmers couldn't do without them. So when harvest time came round, they closed the pits down, so that they could help the farmers with their corn. There were two coprolite works in Felixstowe. Down at Wilkes Lane and Dunkery Fort – that's where the old pits are. There's a park on each side of the lane, and one in each park. Mr. Gort, the boss, used to

come down to pay us and put up his pony and trap at the Old Felixstowe White Horse. That's where all the coproliters used to be paid too.

"Yes – we found some funny things in with the coprolite. Shark's teeth and the jaw bones of some strange animals. Some of them a foot long. But it wasn't once in a year that you would get a thing that size out without breaking it – because you had to pick. But we never found the biggest one of all – that was found up at Trimley. They had a rule that if we found anything special we had to show it to the owners. We used to keep some of the things we found, though, and sell them to gentlemen who came to see the coprolite pits. There wasn't a house where there was a coprolite man worked in the pits, where you wouldn't see some handsome thing taken from the pits, polished up and kept in there. They were so common we didn't think much to them...

"By the way, I don't think I told you that the coprolite used to be sent away from Walton Ferry up to Ipswich. Well then I went and worked in the Docks for a year, and then I worked on Cobbold's wall, down at Cobbold Point. That was done by a Harwich firm. Then I worked under a gardener, who came down from Holy Wells, at Ipswich, at Felixstowe Lodge...."

EVIDENCE FROM THE 1891 CENSUS

Analysis of the 1891 census returns for Suffolk confirmed the demise of the coprolite diggings. Nine people were recorded as involved in only two parishes, Kirton and Waldringfield. In comparison there were 247 in Cambridgeshire, a 65% drop in numbers over the decade. Bedfordshire's numbers had increased by one over the decade to 47 but there was only one reported in Hertfordshire and none in Buckinghamshire (S.C.R.O. 1891 census).

There was significant population decline in eighteen coprolite parishes, seven with percentages into double figures. However, eight showed increases in double figures. Felixstowe showed by far the largest increase, 88% to 1584, but there was no mention of any coprolite diggers.

Kirton's population dropped 26 to 472 yet three were described as coprolite labourers, 40-year old Frederick Rushbrook, 49-year old William Amy (sic) and his 19-year old son George. None of them were born in the parish. Two came from Trimley St Martin and the other from Chillesford. Waldringfield's population showed an increase of fourteen to 284. Six men and boys were involved. 29-year old Arthur Stollery of Cliff Road was the *"Manager at Coprolite Pit"*. The others were all teenagers, 15-year old Thomas Milligan, 14-year old Arthur Wardley and his two brothers, 13-year old James and 11-year old Henry. One would not have expected four teenagers and an eleven year-old to undertake all the work. Where were the others? The census recorded twenty-five cement labourers, twenty-four agricultural labourers and three general labourers. Could any of them have been involved? 32-year old John Waller was a farmer living with the Rev. Thomas Waller at the Rectory (S.C.R.O. 1891 census).

47-year old Edward Packard senior was still living at The Grove House, Bramford, with his wife, four daughters, the eldest a school governess, a son, cook, parlour maid, nurse and nursemaid and Hector Rose, a Scottish visitor. Packard was described as a *"J.P., Chemical Manufacturer"*. His father, 72-year old Edward Packard, was living at Pembridge House, Anglesea Road, Ipswich with his wife Anna, daughter, niece, parlour maid, housemaid, kitchen maid and cook. He was described as a *"Retired Chemical manufacturer, J.P, J.D. & D.I."*.

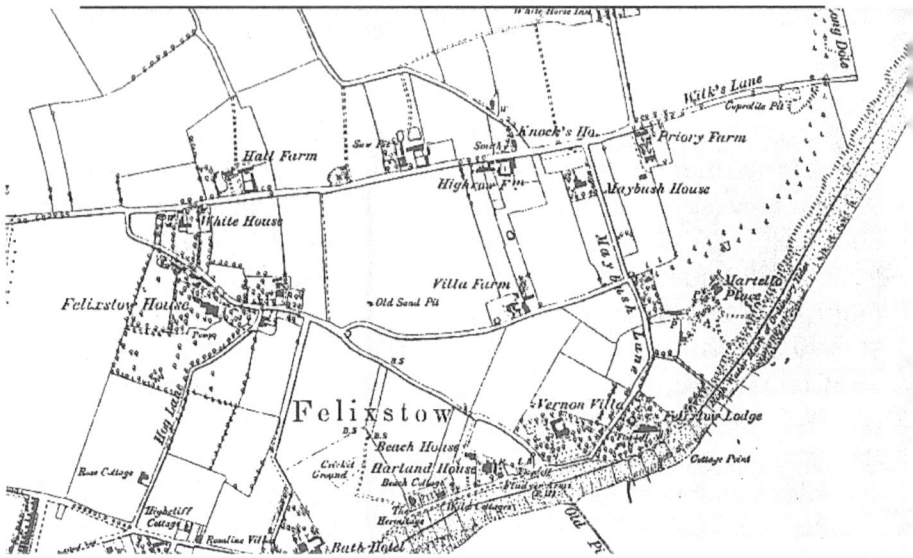

Extract from the 1881 25-inch Ordnance Survey Map of Felixstowe showing the coprolite pit at the end of Wilk's Lane.

SUFFOLK'S LAST COPROLITE PITS

The 1890 map showed several Crag pits in Sutton from which the coprolite may well have been worked. They were about half a mile northwest of Newshill Barn (TM 287475), in the same valley opposite Hemley Hall that had already been worked. The other was almost half a mile south-southeast of Broxted House, opposite the Oakhill Plantation (TM 317457) (Suff. 77NW). According to the 1892 trade directory there must have been a slight revival as the comment for Sutton was that *"The parish is rich in antediluvian shells and fossils, numerous in the Crag pits. There are also extensive diggings of coprolites"* (K.P.O.D. 1892).

The 1891 map (Suff. 76SE) showed several Crag pits about a half mile to the south of Whitehall Farm in Waldringfield which may have been worked. There were another two marked on the map just south of the cement works (TM 286445) and north of what is now the Sailing Club. The 1892 directory included that *"Coprolites are shipped from Waldringfield cliff and Portland cement is made here"* but there was no reference to Waller occupying Church Farm. Whether he had a special arrangement with Fison's and Packard and Co. has not been revealed.

His account books show that they made considerable purchases until 1894. There must have been a surplus, which Waller eventually managed to dispose of as late as 1897.

Fison's Purchases of Waldringfield Coprolites.

April 1890	460 tons
1891	386
1892	500
1894	567
1897	43

(S.C.R.O. FC54 A2/1 p52)

With such a thick deposit there was also a problem of unwanted stones. This provided employment for some of the younger villagers in separating them from the coprolites. In a poem written by 'Great Aunt Georgina Waller' and quoted in Tye's *Guide to Waldringfield and District* it confirms the view held in those days that the coprolite was actually fossilised droppings.

"My Village"

"...We'd "Pits" deep dug for raising
The coprolites they found;
In layers oft abundant,
Far down below ground.
An animal excretion,
As fossil shipped away;
Then ground for fertiliser,

Much used this time of day.
But ere it left our village
Carts moved it near the "shore";
Where cleared by hand of gravel,
Of stone, and what not more,
Then washed with river water
Taws duly put aboard
The pretty red sailed barges,
Our artists so adored.
I'd almost shrink from watching
Across that chasm deep,
On narrow planks, men wheeling
Their findings to the heap.
The load then safely landed,
How gaily back they run;
A sight to turn one dizzy.
Of fear those men had none,
Despite some obvious danger
The casualties were few.
As far as memory serves me,
No fatal one I knew."

When the diggings came to an end in Waldringfield there were two old barge posts left standing in front of the Club House and near the Quay. A gap in the cliffs was where Sam Mowles used to wash the coprolite (TM 286444) (Tye, W. (1950), *'Guide to Waldringfield and Newbourn'*, Norman Allard & Co. Ipswich, p.16).

"In Waldringfield today... no longer can tumbril loads of coprolite be seen and heard, rumbling slowly down the hill to the river and along the hard beach to the waiting barges.... There are still, however, one or two landmarks, and a few people to remind one of the early nineties and the coprolite industry. The gap in the cliff side, where the coprolite was dumped before loading, now shelters a few beach huts..., then in front of the Club House, still stands, or rather leans, the old post to which the

barges were tied during loading. The last pit to be worked can still be seen on the right of the road, opposite the village Post Office - it is now a caravan site.

"Yes, Waldringfield has seen vast changes since the days of the coproliters, but one thing remains constant, the hospitality of the Maybush Inn... From all accounts anyone would be guilty of a grave misunderstatement if they described pub-life in those days as 'gay'. 'Hectic' would certainly be a more suitable word to describe the evenings at the Maybush Inn, Waldringfield, where the coproliters, cement workers and bargees got together.

"This 'pub' was then their social centre, and, for some, board and lodgings - some dozen coproliters often stayed there for the night. Mrs. Hunt, the publican's wife had a reputation for strictness and cleanliness, and woe betide any miscreant who tried to sneak upstairs without removing his dirty boots, which had to be placed in a row under the high-backed kitchen settle. When would-be lodgers called late at night asking for a bed, all the reply they got from Mrs. Hunt was a curt 'Full-up', and a finger pointing to a long row of boots.

"This good lady must certainly have had her hands full, as in addition to looking after her lodgers, she had to serve drinks to numerous customers with a raging thirst. When her very mixed customers (coproliters, cement workers and bargees) got together, peace and quiet were short-lived, and sparks soon began to fly. Under such circumstances it's not difficult to picture the arguments and uproar which ensued, and it was the exception rather than the rule for the evening to end without a scrap.

"There was never any fear of giving a black eye to a pal, as each type of worker carried the colour of his trade. They could be classed as reds, whites and blues. As for the winners, whether in arguments or fisticuffs, I would fancy the bargees, who would most likely outclass their more hefty opponents through sheer agility. Whatever Mr. and Mrs. Hunt's difficulties may have been during those hectic days, they seem to have done very well financially, for he was often heard to say that he could show anyone, at any time, a half peck of sovereigns."

THE INDUSTRY'S DEMISE

Waldringfield's coprolite pits had been largely filled in by 1897. The last one to be worked was opposite the village Post Office, where the house, Stonner Point, was built. The impact the closure had on the village was intensified a few years later.

"Mason's Cement Works however managed to last a few years longer, being eventually closed down in 1907. The 'bottle-neck' kilns of Waldringfield stood little chance in competing against the rotary kilns of Germany. Hence Mr. Frank Mason's decision to close the factory, and start afresh at Claydon, where he installed modern machinery.

"For a year or so after its industries ceased Waldringfield felt very much like Oliver Goldsmith's 'Deserted Village', a village without a future. Accustomed to comparatively big wages, the old coproliters and cement workers could not possibly settle down on the land for ten shillings a week. Some left for the Army, Navy and Police, whilst several went north to the Burton breweries, where Suffolk men were always welcome. Many local tradesmen, too, feeling uncertain, left the village to try their fortune elsewhere. Old John Hill, for instance, closed down his brewery and coal business; and Jimmy Quantril, landlord of the Maybush, left for the Butt and Oyster, Pin Mill. A few, however, whatever the future, decided to remain. Amongst these were the two village shopkeepers, Mr. W.F. Spurgeon and Mrs. E. Stollery. Maybe they were influenced by the Rev Kervey, a yachting enthusiast, who is reputed to have said, "The men in red and the men in white have gone, but the men in peak caps will soon be here. Hang on, Spurgeon, the time is not far off when Waldringfield will become one of the leading yachting centres of East Anglia". How right he was is now generally accepted.

"'It's an ill wind that blows no good', says the old proverb. And so it was with Waldringfield after the cement factory was closed. For once again the Deben ran clear and unpolluted, and the local people were able to walk along its banks and bathe freely in its waters, enjoying to the full the fresh and invigorating air. The sailing men, too, the

Quantrils and the Rixes, were delighted to have both time and opportunity for trying out their eighteen footers. Then when winter came, the wildfowlers and fishermen were glad to resume their pleasant and profitable pastimes. But the greatest boon of all was the easing of the housing situation, for at last there were houses enough and to spare and, let it be placed on record, many old tenants were lucky enough to buy their houses on most generous terms."

(http://www.waldringfield.info/1850-1950.htm)

Many coastal manure manufacturers had been purchasing overseas phosphate supplies since the 1870s. Despite the fall in demand during the Agricultural Depression, imports rose dramatically during the 1880s. In 1890, 343,501 tons were imported with a value of £849,452. By this time, even the inland manure factories had a greater reliance on them. Algerian rock phosphates started arriving in Ipswich in 1889 and by 1894 had reached their peak of production.

In the 1890s many of the Suffolk manure manufacturers had expanded into alternative lines, including insecticides, disinfectants and sheep dips that, like superphosphate before, could be exported to all parts of the world.

Local transport costs had risen by the 1890s. Railway companies had been charging coprolite contractors and manure manufacturers one shilling and two pence (£0.06) for a ton of coprolite or rock phosphate to be taken ten miles. The government's introduction of the 1888 and 1892 Railway and Canal Acts led the railway companies to demand price increases of over 100%. They wanted two shillings (£0.10) per ton for the same ten miles but if it was to a large town they wanted five shillings and six pence (£0.28) per ton. A deputation from the Fertiliser Manufacturers Association petitioned Parliament to keep the transport price increases down, not only for British farmers but also for the nation's manure manufacturers. Rates were increased to half a crown (£0.12) per ton. This led to reduced profits for the manure manufacturers, especially since the superphosphate, by this time, was selling at only fifty-five shillings (£2.75) a ton. This was more than 50% lower than during the 1870s (Fertiliser Manufacturers Association, (F.M.A.) Peterborough, Railway Rates 1888-94; Commercial matters 1890 - 1898).

Packard retired in 1891 when he was 72. He left his sons Edward Junior and Henry to control the business and it seems that they saw little future for the coprolite industry. The only records of any subsequent purchases were from Waller's pits in Waldringfield. They had concentrated on the shipping side of their father's business purchasing a number of steam coasters, the *Dartmoor* (1882), *Sedgemoor* (1883), *Exmoor* (1885) and *Ringmoor* (1889) to carry their own goods and general cargo, mostly between Ipswich, Hull and Newcastle. Three of these 'moors' sunk within a few years of purchase so, instead of changing their names as they had done with the earlier boats, they bought Onyx (1891) and Winifred (1894). They set up the Ipswich Steam Shipping Company but, to maintain the superphosphate works, purchased several steam barges to operate on the Gipping and they became known after 1906 as 'Packard's dreadnoughts' (Moffatt, H. op.cit. pp.69 - 70).

Manning Prentice went on a tour of the largest American sulphuric acid plants in 1890 and visited the Florida phosphate workings in order to make himself aware of the developments in their industry. Aware of the increasing costs, the following year he used additional capital raised from local agricultural merchants and farmers to convert his business into a limited company. He was the managing director (*The Journal of the Society of the Chemical Industry*, November 30th 1898). It is thought that he had taken over the Cambridge Manure Company as his new directors had previously been on their board. This expansion included the 1893 take-over of the Norfolk coastal shipping business of Bailey, Sutton and Company of Great Yarmouth. Effectively he now controlled the local fertiliser industry, the coprolite industry, phosphate supplies, superphosphate manufacture and its distribution and sale. By this time however, supplies of coprolite had mostly been exhausted and increased labour costs had made the business less profitable.

Competition intensified with Robert and Walton Burrell developing a chemical manure works at Westley, near Bury St. Edmunds, on the railway line from Suffolk to Cambridge. This allowed them to market fertiliser to the predominantly agricultural area around the market town. They were advertising in 1892 as Artificial Manure Manufacturers (*K.P.O.D.* 1892).

In 1894 the introduction of the Quarries Act signed the death knell for the coprolite industry. It stated that any operations below 25 feet (8.25 m) had to comply with strict regulations about health and safety. These would have increased costs at a time when overseas supplies were increasing. By the mid-1890s Packard and Co.'s lack of capital forced Edward and Henry to form a limited liability company. With supplies of overseas phosphates reducing demand for the local supplies, the Suffolk coprolite industry came to an end. According to Jobson's account of Felixstowe:

"The pit closed, in common with all the rest, in 1893. It was said that through the discovery of these nodules a distinct race of men grew up in Suffolk, to be known as the "Owd Coproliters" or "the men in red". They toiled in slush and muck and became the colour of the medium in which they worked."

Tye found that the Waldringfield pits closed at the same time. Along with an improved rail network, the pit closures had a knock-on effect on the barging business.

"The coprolite pits ceased working during the late eighties and early nineties. Old coprolite workers in the Waldringfield area say that the local pits were closed down by the year 1893 - well before the Queen's Diamond Jubilee of 1897. For a year or two after the pits closed much

time was spent in trying to level out the pits and hollows, particularly those that lay in the middle of a field.

As to the cause of the industry petering out, opinion is divided. Some say the seams being practically worked out. Others, including agricultural experts, state that a more highly concentrated and cheaper form of phosphate was available elsewhere. It would appear that Mr. Walter Packard, (vice chairman of Fison's Ltd., and grandson of Edward Packard, the founder) is not far from the truth in saying, "The reason it ceased was that the shallow workings had been worked out and as deposits of phosphate on a very much larger scale were being opened up in many parts of the world, phosphate could be bought more cheaply abroad."

His interviews with some of the last coproliters showed how difficult it was for them and their families when they were laid off.

"The closing of the pits must have caused a certain degree of anxiety amongst those families whose livelihood had for many years depended on the industry. Having earned good wages, the coproliters had but little desire to return to agriculture, which was then passing through an acute depression (wheat was selling at seven shillings and sixpence a coomb). As a consequence, the younger and fitter men left to join the Army, Navy or Police. Some of the older men, who had accumulated a little saving, invested their capital in a small business rather than return to the soil. As for landowners and tenant farmers, they again settled down to routine agriculture, hoping for better days.

"Whatever adults may have thought about the old pits and their closing, the children seemed to have revelled in them before they were obliterated. They delighted to climb from "kench" to "kench" looking on the pits as their rightful playgrounds.

"I've no doubt they often vied with one another in their collections of fossils and souvenirs. Little did they realise in their childish fun that perchance they were playing with the remains of huge monsters, the like of which are never likely to roam this land again."

Arnott's book on the Deben estuary suggested that other pits closed a few years later:

"With the advent of new kinds of fertilisers and quicker means of transport by the railways, the industry waned and with it, the barge traffic up and down the river, and it finally died out about 1895."

Filling in the pits provided employment for those agricultural labourers still at work. Whilst they tended to fill in and level the pits in the middle of fields quite a number were left, filled with rainwater and today numerous overgrown coprolite and crag pits still dot the south-east Suffolk countryside.

The tremendous effort and energy used to build up Prentice's new company took its toll and Manning died in 1895, succeeded by W. Henry Prentice ('The Early Fertiliser Industry', *Fison's Journal*, December 1963). Packard and Co.'s sales of superphosphate expanded with trade with Russia and the West Indies.

William's son, Valentine D. Colchester, ran the Griffin Works in Ipswich from the 1870s and had a house in Belsize Square, London. He dealt in corn, fertilisers and coal and was an insurance agent for Scottish Widows' fund and Sun Fire Office. He owned the barge "Victoria" and a cutter called "Garson between 1884 – 1886. Prominent in Ipswich life he was commissioner of the Suffolk Boy Scouts, councillor for the Middle Ward and a member of the Ipswich Dock Commission, Deputy Chairman of the Ipswich Chamber of Commerce and later mayor. He advertised as selling fertiliser at the turn of the century but sales were down. The national production in 1901 was 20,000 tons with only 5,500 tons going to the home market.

CHARLES MAYNARD COLCHESTER'S OBITUARY

The importance of the Colchester family to Ipswich's commercial development was acknowledged in an undated Ipswich newspaper obituary of Charles Colchester. He lived at Fernleigh, Westerfield Road and worked for his father running the fertiliser factory at Ipswich producing superphosphate and Ichthemic guano.

"*The commercial community of Ipswich, in which very notable gaps have been made by death during the current year, suffered further loss on Monday by the demise of Mr C.M. Colchester, of Fernleigh, Westerfield Road, head of the firm of William Colchester and Co., chemical manure manufacturers, Griffin Wharf, New Cut E. Mr Colchester had suffered considerably for several years, indeed, he did not at any time give the impression of a particularly robust constitution. He was the youngest of the four sons of the late Mr William Colchester, a merchant, who, in the middle of the last century resided and carried on business in College Street, and was for a brief period a representative of the Bridge Ward on the Ipswich Corporation. Mr Charles Maynard Colchester, the gentleman now deceased, in his early business life took up the artificial manure business, establishing an extensive connection, both in England and abroad. The barley competition, for a gold cup and other prizes, every autumn in recent years brought out a large number of samples and attracted much attention. Mr Colchester took very little part in public affairs - one can only recall his membership of the Ipswich Dock Commission and this was scarcely more than nominal. He had a disposition for travel, and one very distinct trait in his character was his love for horses - he generally had in his possession one or two animals of exceptional quality; he was frequently seen out riding, and for many years he made a point of driving his waggonette on to the Ipswich racecourse when the races were in progress.*

"*The family has tolerably extensive ramifications with the business life of East Anglia. Mrs William Colchester migrated from Ipswich to Burwell, in Cambridgeshire, and the name still appears in the Burwell firm of Colchester and Ball, chemical manure manufacturers and brickmakers, the first-mentioned partner being Mr George Henry Colchester, one of the deceased gentleman's brothers. Another is Mr Valentine D. Colchester merchant of Ipswich. The deceased gentleman leaves a widow and two daughters, one of whom is married to Lieutenant Powell, RFA, son of the Rev John Powell, rector of St Clement's: this lady reached Ipswich from India on Sunday."*

To give you an indication of the Colchester family's wealth. when William died in 1898 his personal effects were valued at £21,726., the present day value of about £1.2 million. As he had already passed on his businesses to his children, this must have grossly underestimated his net worth. Valentine Colchester left £32,078 in his will when he died. His funeral cortege was a mile long. (Author's communication with Giles Colchester)

SUFFOLK IN 1901

In Bacon's 1901 Guide to Suffolk there was still reference made to the coprolite industry. The scenery was described as:

"Quiet and homely, picturesque and rich, but never wild or grand, and its landscapes have a park-like character, largely due to the custom of planting trees in the hedgerows. The estuary of the Orwell is well known, and offers, perhaps, the most pleasing views. The rivers afford chiefly bottom-fishing. The absence of any prominent hills makes Suffolk one of the driest counties in England....
"The mineral wealth of the county is small. The most important deposit is that of the phosphatic nodules, from which superphosphate of lime is obtained for artificial manure. These nodules or coprolites are partly the fossil excreta of animals of the Crag period, and partly concretions of mineral origin. Chalk is burnt for lime; some building stone is obtained; bricks, tiles, &c., are made from the clays; and the quartzose sands are used for glassmaking; while the shelly calcareous sands are sometimes used directly for manure."

When the last pit finished operations is unknown. Maybe farmers continued to use the unprocessed shells as a cheap fertiliser in the 20th century but all large-scale operations had ceased.

The Chemical Manure industry continued though. According to the 1901 census 42-year old Charles Colchester lived at Fernleigh, Westefield Road in Ipswich with two daughters, his sister-in-law, a German student, a German cook and a *'lady's maid domestic'*. He was described as a *'Chemical Manure Manufacturer'*. Next door at Brakefield lived 57-year old Edward Packard with his father-in-law, Walton Turner, a *'Tanner & Leather Merchant'*, his brother and sister-in-law, his son and daughter, a parlour maid, cook, housemaid and kitchen maid. He was described as a *'Chemical manufacturer, Fertiliser & chemical'*. (S.C.R.O. RG13/1780 f94 p.32) Not only did they live close together, they were very much involved in Ipswich's political life. They were all aldermen. Walton Turner and Edward Packard had been mayors and Valentine Colchester, William's son, later became mayor. (Author's communication with Giles Colchester)

REVIVAL OF THE INDUSTRY DURING THE FIRST WORLD WAR

During the First World War the coprolite diggings were revived. The German navy was attacking the merchant ships bringing in phosphates from across the Atlantic. With the country's dependence on overseas supplies being threatened, in 1916 the Ministry of Munitions, who had taken responsibility for the nation's shipping, commissioned the Fertiliser Manufacturers Association to investigate:

"... whether the possible cause of the abandonment of the use of the native source of phosphate was not due to foreign mineral phosphate having been obtainable at lower prices rather than by reason of the beds of coprolites becoming exhausted."

Given the urgency of the situation, it was not long before they reported to the committee that the industry's centre:

"... was practically the city of Cambridge itself, most of the colleges today standing upon beds of Coprolites within a few feet of the surface.

Within a radius of about five miles the yield was about 300 - 350 tons per acre. Further out, say from 5 to 10 - 13 miles, the deposits yielded about 200 - 250 tons per acre and the veins were thinner and usually at a greater depth... Undoubtedly considerable quantities of Coprolites have been won during the 45 years or so in which the industry has flourished... but it is the opinion of the few practical men now remaining who were connected with the industry that the cream was all worked out prior to 1885 and during the later years the "blocks" of Coprolites were in smaller areas, had to be worked at greater depths, say from 15 to 20 feet and the veins were much thinner. Mr E. C. Colchester, of Great Shelford, Cambs., who is recognised as the best authority, having had actual practical experience in raising Coprolites from between 2,000 to 3,000 acres in Cambridgeshire, Bedford, Bucks, Suffolk and even Norfolk, during the 25 years, 1871 to 1896, when he ceased operation, is of the opinion that... to his knowledge there is only one small area of about 18 to 20 acres near to Cambridge that has not been dug at all, for the simple reason that the owner wanted such an exorbitant sum for the right to dig, even in the palmy days, that no one would pay the price and the Coprolites have remained undisturbed."

Edward Packard, the son of the Suffolk manure manufacturer, had been responsible for pits in Grantchester, a few miles southwest of Cambridge. The remaining Suffolk deposit was not considered a viable proposition. He considered that there were only one or two possible sites and he estimated only 9,000 to 12,000 tons could be obtained in five or six years. This was an outside estimate but he agreed that there was the problem that *"nearly all the old workmen employed by his firm have either passed away or gone away and all records have been lost or destroyed"* (Ibid.).

Without losing much time, the major landowners in the area were contacted. What became known as the 'Hauxton Road Coprolite Works' got under way in Grantchester and Trumpington. Few local men were employed as most of them were in the forces and the farmers had to rely on women and children to get all their farm work done.

Most of the labour force, according to Mr Rogers, a Trumpington historian, was:

"Brought in by bus from Cambridge. Many were Irish labourers and their buses were covered in anti-British slogans. They were said to have been imported from Ireland as Government policy after the 1916 Rebellion."

The expense of the operation was excessive. Over £77,000 was spent on the Hauxton Road Works with 60.5% going on construction and equipment, 32.4% for materials and stores, with wages amounting to only 4.1%, or £70 per week. Whilst there has been no confirmation as to the numbers employed, one local farmer, glad not to have his fields excavated, reported that *"We hear of some erections and accommodation for 4,000 men near Cambridge for coprolite digging"* (Correspondence from Mr De Courcy-Ireland, Abington Pigotts, Sept. 2nd 1917). Local gossip had it that not even a ton of coprolite was raised before the Armistice was signed. Photographic evidence shows that it was certainly raised but in what quantities is unknown, nor whether any reached the Midlands. The contractors must have done exceptionally well out of it. Such a massive outlay for so little a return can only be seen as the Ministry's contribution to the local economy!

POST-WAR DEVELOPMENTS

Immediately after the war in 1919 the tradition of family-run manure companies was broken. Packard & Co. amalgamated with Messrs. James Fison's & Sons of Thetford. They expanded their manure and agricultural supplies business into Stowmarket and Thetford in Norfolk for the flourishing trade in foodstuffs from Ipswich and London. Shortly afterwards, Prentice Brothers absorbed Colchester and Ball's business in Burwell, and Colchester dropped out. The only other major competitor was the West Norfolk Farmers Manure Company at King's Lynn.

In 1929, under the pressures of international competition, Packard & Co. took over Prentice Bros. and Fison & Sons to form Fison, Packard and Prentice Ltd. One of their first activities was a programme of expansion. A new factory was built at Cliff Quay in Ipswich where deep water allowed the imported phosphates to be carried straight into the works and production was concentrated here.

First World War coprolite workings at Grantchester, near Cambridge. (Courtesy of the Cambridge Collection 93/31/12)

They formed a new company, Corby Basic Slag, in 1935 to exploit the waste product of the blast furnaces at Stewart and Lloyds Northamptonshire steel works. It was marketed as yet another fertiliser. The next year it opened works at Avonmouth, on the Severn estuary near Bristol, beside the National Smelting Corporation's works that supplied the acids for superphosphate manufacture. In 1937 they had an arrangement with the West Norfolk Farmers Manure and

Chemical Company to build a plant on the River Ouse at Flixborough, Lincolnshire, making sulphate of ammonia from nitrogen.

During the Second World War the company was renamed Fisons Ltd in 1942 and it focussed its attention on supplying the home market with superphosphate. By 1949 it was producing half the country's superphosphate and about half the country's compound fertiliser. Between 1946 and 1950 a new works was erected at Immingham, at the mouth of the Humber estuary, near Grimbsy, to make triple superphosphates and granular fertilisers. It started production in the following year. They also had a joint operation with the Imperial Chemical Industries (ICI) to work the potash deposits on the North Yorkshire coast, north of Whitby. ICI's Dulux paint plant evolved from Prentice's Chemical and Explosives works in Stowmarket.

As well as investment in Britain, Fison's also had interests in the Peruvian guano and Moroccan phosphate beds. Fison's (Chemicals) Ltd. was formed from British Chemicals and Biologicals with interest in gland supplies, chemists' supplies and specialist invalid products. With the ICI at Widnes they created the United Sulphuric Acid Corporation using anhydrite. Its international trade with the USA, Canada, South Africa and Zimbabwe made it a company of international importance but few will recall its early history exploiting the local coprolite deposits.

Levington remained a horticultural research station and has always been at the forefront of product innovation and development. It introduced the first growing bag and the first multi-purpose compost. It continued its operations in Suffolk until it was taken over by the Norwegian agrochemical firm Norsk Hydro, in 1994. Fison's Horticulture Division was bought by its management and commenced trading as Levington Horticulture Ltd.

ARCHAEOLOGICAL FINDS DURING THE COPROLITE DIGGINGS

Potentially thousands of acres were dug over during the fifty or so years of the Suffolk coprolite diggings. Throughout this period numerous archaeological finds were made, but only a selection of them have been reported in academic journals and can be seen in Ipswich and other Suffolk museums. As with the early geologists not giving exact locations of their finds in case of competition, the coproliters, and landowners who knew about the discoveries, often did the same when they found archaeological treasures. Even today, there are archaeological finds that go unreported for fear of trespass, robbery and unofficial metal detecting.

In 1853 what was considered a Roman burial ground was found in Felixstowe. Its location, according to contemporary map evidence, was on the beach, just north of the resort (TM 322357). Coprolite and septaria labourers digging on the beach and into the cliff must have been surprised by their discovery. One striking piece was a Samian vase over a foot (30 cm) high. Other finds included flue tiles, amphorae, a glass scent phial, bronze pins, tweezers, mirror fibulae, gold and silver rings, a gold chain and a bronze amulet. Numerous silver and bronze coins were uncovered dating back to the reigns of Victorianus, Constantine, Gordianus, Galienus, Arcadius, and Serverus. Many sepulchral urns and inhumations were found along with many shells which showed the Roman's taste for seafood. They included many mussels, periwinkle, cockles as well as snails.

The Suffolk Archaeology database describes some other finds made in the Felixstowe diggings. Whether they were from the beach, the cliff or cliff top was not reported. It specified a Bronze Age collared urn, a large number of other Roman finds and an interesting circular bronze brooch disc. It had an animal on it with traces of red enamel and was dated as from Saxon times. Some were sold and taken out of the country but others can be seen in the British Museum (Falconer, H. (1857), 'Mastodon', *Q.J.G.S.*, p.358; Lankester, R. (1865), 'Mammalian Fossils of the Red Crag', *Q.J.G.S.*, pp.221 - 32; Charlesworth, E. (1868), 'On the prospective Annihilation of the Suffolk Red Crag Phosphatic stones, 'Coprolite', Norwich Geol. Soc. Lecture, *Geol. Mag.* vol. v. p.577; 25" Suffolk, 1889, 90.2; Suffolk County Sites and Monuments Records, (S.C.S.M.R.), 03026, 03054).

In 1855 an interesting fossil was 'tipped out' at the Bramford works and enquiries were made as to its origin. It was reported that a coproliter working the fossil bed at sixteen feet (5.8 m) in a pit on Mr Law's Farm on the Foxhall Road (TM 229436), about four miles east of Ipswich, made a discovery that was subsequently to become of international importance. He found a mandible, the lower jaw, of a human (Vallois, Henri V., and Hallam L. Movius, eds., (1953), *Catalogue des Hommes Fossiles,* XIX Congres Geologique International, Algiers, p.210). It sparked enormous interest and became known as the Foxhall Jaw. George Busk, Thomas Huxley and Richard Owen, prominent British scientists and antagonists over the debate on Darwin's theory of evolution, examined it. A physician, Dr. Robert Collyer, wrote a brief article reporting the Foxhall fossil find. It is believed that he took the mandible with him when he returned to study in the United States in about 1878 *"after which all trace of its whereabouts was lost".*

Subsequent excavations by J. Reid Moir in 1919 found flint flakings and cracked flints at the 16-foot (5m) level of the fossil bed. They were presumed to be evidence of human action. Other bones found at the site were too fragmented to be identified (Roe, Derek A., (1981), *The Lower and Middle Palaeolithic Periods in Britain,* Routledge & Kegan Paul, pp.177 - 78; Blinderman, C. (1986), *'The Piltdown Inquest',* Prometheus Books, p.11; Forsythe, S. M. (1988) *'The Foxhall Peoples: An Encounter between Archaeology and The URANTIA Book,* Scientific Symposium I).

This jaw gave the name to a group now known as the Foxhall people. They were among those groups that travelled west from the continent and had settled in England by at least 900,000 BP. They are considered to be the first humans to inhabit England. They crossed from France to England by way of a land bridge now submerged beneath the North Sea and English Channel. The settlements or living sites of the Foxhall peoples were located along the banks of rivers or on the sea coast. The melting of the ice-age glaciers which once covered the north of Europe and the British Isles, caused the sea level to rise and inundate all but three or four of the Foxhall living sites.

Reid Moir recovered over seventy hand axes from the site that are now in the collections of the Ipswich Museum and the British Museum. They were described as being technologically the most advanced industry of the Foxhall people. The actual site of the pit represents the sedimentary remains of a small, ancient lake that formed in a hollow of chalky boulder clay. It is thought that it had one major lakeside occupation, followed by at least several other occupations of much shorter duration. The hand axes were found to be similar to those found at Hoxne, in Suffolk, which was occupied between 400,000 to 300,000 years ago. Whether the jaw was also from this period remains a mystery. The pit where the jaw was found was later used as a brick pit and is now built over (Roe, op. cit. pp.178, 198; Tattersall, I. Delson, E. and Van Couvering, J., eds., (1988), *Encyclopaedia of Human Evolution and Prehistory,* Garland Publishing, p.275).

Interest was sparked in Sutton in 1865 when the diggers uncovered what were thought to be the ends of some animal's tusks in a coprolite pit (Lankester, E. (1865), 'Mammalian Fossils of the Red Crag', *Q.J.G.S.,* pp.221 - 32; Prestwich, J. (1868), 'Structure of Crag Beds', *Q.J.G.S.,* p.460). According to the 25" map of 1889 a coin hoard was found in the diggings in 1870. The 1883 trade directory noted that *"Thomas Waller occupied the Sutton Hall Estate where two urns were dug up a few years ago, which contained copper coins of the reign of Constantine"*

(*K.P.O.D.* 1883; White, (1885), op.cit; TM.30624514). The archaeological records (S.C.S.M.R. 03678) omitted the date stating that:

"Two coin hoards were unearthed by the coprolite diggers during the diggings and they included nearly a bushel of mainly Constantinian bronze and copper coins from c.330 AD buried in a Saxon urn. Ten of them were donated to the Ipswich Museum."

As with the best fossil specimens, it is thought that many other interesting archaeological finds went unreported and were sold to the local gentry or taken to Ipswich or Woodbridge market to be sold at the Victorian equivalent of antiques stalls. William Whincopp of Woodbridge was reported as having a fine collection of British, Roman, and Saxon antiquities discovered in the neighbourhood.

CONCLUSION

During the fifty years or so of the Suffolk coprolite industry it has been estimated that about half a million tons were dug up and sold. Thousands of acres were dug over, an early form of open-cast agricultural mining, destroying millennia of the archaeological record along the banks of the Deben, Orwell and Stour estuaries. Much of southeast Suffolk's fossil record has been removed and destroyed, particularly the crag, although a small proportion has been saved in museums across the countries and in private collections. More than 2,000 years ago the cliffs stretched a further mile out to sea. The diggings assisted the further erosion of much of the coast by the sea and wind and prompted coastal defences like the stone wall at Felixstowe and the marsh wall at Boyton.

Entrepreneurial coprolite merchants made hundreds of thousands of pounds from selling the vast majority of the fossil deposit to local manure manufacturers like Colchester, Packard and Fison. They made their fortunes marketing superphosphate around the country but also overseas, thus contributing to a marked increase in food production and improved quality of life. These three small family-run firms eventually merged to become an industry of world importance.

Local landowners like Tomline, Rendlesham, Pretyman and Quilter, freehold and tenant farmers as well as coprolite contractors profited from the business. The business stimulated other trades. Local carpenters gained useful work in the erection and repair of coprolite sheds, making coprolite trucks and cutting timber for planks and supports. Coal merchants would have provided supplies to the coprolite and manure works. Local iron works were able to supply much of the plant and machinery in the works. Blacksmiths would have had work making and repairing tools and shoeing horses. Surveyors, solicitors and auctioneers made good business out of the arrangements between landowners and contractors. The diggings stimulated the development of the cement industry in Shotley and Waldringfield.

Bankers would have profited from the loans made to speculators in the industry. Brewers, inn-keepers, shopkeepers and other traders would have benefited from the increased spending power generated by the industry. Carters would have made a good trade taking coprolites to the washmills, the nearest wharf, railway station or manure factory. Sailing barge making was stimulated by the industry. Bargees got a good living plying the Deben, Stour, Orwell and Thames estuaries with coprolite. The railway companies gained additional revenue from coprolite traffic. Cottages were constructed, churches were renovated, chapels were built and much land improvement was done during this period. What was done with the money realised by the diggers is not known. Purchasing land, building houses and renovating property was common but probably a lot would have been spent on food, clothes and drink. The diggings brought many Suffolk parishes a level of prosperity never experienced before or since.

Documented Sale Prices of Suffolk Coprolites

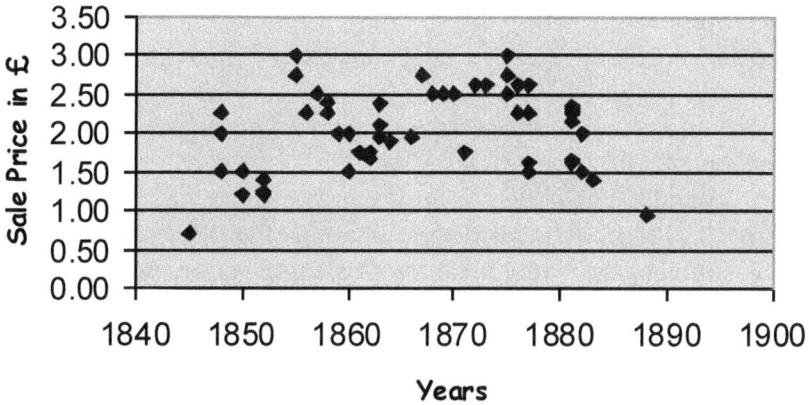

Fluctuations in Coprolite Sale Prices

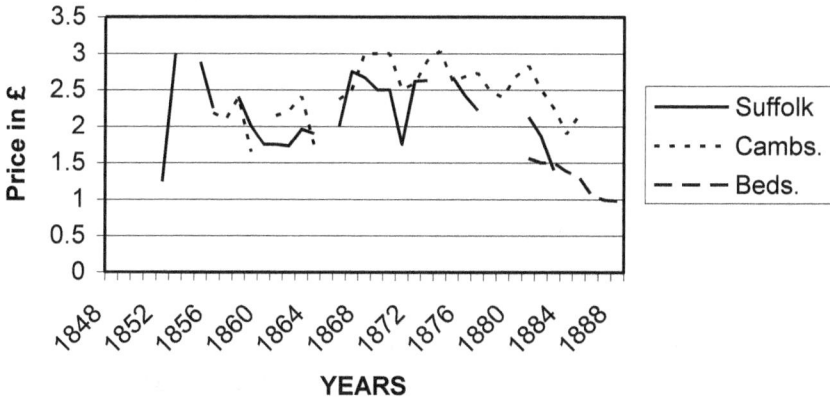

Bibliography and Suggested Reading

Aikman, C.M. (1894), 'Manures and Manuring'
Anonymous article, 'Reminiscence of a Scientific Suffolk Clergyman,'
Eastern Counties Magazine and Suffolk Handbook (in coprolite file at
Ipswich Museum)
Armstrong, P. (1975), 'The Changing Landscape - The Impact of Man on
East Anglia', Dalton, p.106
W.G. Arnott, (1950), 'Suffolk Estuary - the story of the Deben Estuary',
Adland, pp.84, 107
Bacon, G.W. (1901) 'Guide to Suffolk'
Balson, P.S. (1980), 'The Origin and Evolution of Tertiary phosphorites
from Eastern England', Journal of the Geological Society, Vol. 137,
pp.723-729
Balson, P.S. (1987), 'Authigenic phosphorite concretions in the Tertiary
of the southern North Sea Basin: an event stratigraphy', Contributions
to Tertiary and Quaternary Geology, Vol.xxiv, pp.1-2
Bell, A. (1915), 'A description of the sub-Crag detritus bed', Proceedings
of the Prehistorical Society of East Anglia, Vol. 2, pp.139-48
Bidwell, C. (1874), 'On Coprolites', Institute of Surveyors, 1874, p.312
Birt, L. (1931), 'The Children's Home Finder', London, pp.9-14
Blinderman, C. (1986). 'The Piltdown Inquest,' Prometheus Books, p.11
Brodie, Revd. P.B. (1872), 'On Phosphatic and Bone Bed Deposits in
British Strata, their Economical Uses, and Fossil Contents.' Transactions
of Warwickshire Natural History & Archaeology Society, p.58)
Buckland, W. (1849), 'On the Causes of Presence of Phosphates in the
Strata of the Earth and in all fertile soils; with observations on Pseudo-
Coprolites', Journal of the Royal Agricultural Society,. Vol. X, pp.520-1)
Charleston News and Courier, Industrial Issue, (1880)
Charlesworth, E. (1835), 'On the Crag of part of Essex and Suffolk',
Proceedings of the Geological Society,. Vol. ii, no. 41, p.195
Charlesworth, E. (1835), 'Observations on the Crag formation and its
Organic Remains with a view to establish a division of the Tertiary
Strata overlying the London Clay in Suffolk', Philosophical Magazine.

ser. 3, Vol. vii, p.81; abstract in *Proceedings of the Geological. Society.*
Vol. ii, no. 41, p.195

Charlesworth, E. (1835), 'Reply to Mr Woodward's remarks on the
Coralline Crag; with observations on Certain Errors which may affect
the determination of the age of Tertiary Deposits', *Philosophical
Magazine.* ser. 3, Vol. vii, p.464

Charlesworth, E. (1836), 'On the Crag of Suffolk, and on the Fallacies
connected with the Method now usually employed for ascertaining the
relative age of Tertiary Deposits', *Philosophical Magazine.* ser. 3, Vol.
viii, p.529; See also (under different title) *Edinburgh New Philosophical
Journal,.* Vol. XXII, p.110; *Rep. Brit. Assoc. for 1836; Mag. Nat. Hist.* Vol.
ix, p.537; Abstract in *Records of General Science,* Vol. iv, p.465

Charlesworth, E. (1837), 'A Notice of the Remains of Vertebrated
Animals found in the Tertiary Beds of Norfolk and Suffolk', *Report of the
British Association for 1836,* Sections, p.84 (in full in 1838)

Charlesworth, E. (1837), 'Observations on the Crag, and on the Fallacies
involved in the present system of Classification of Tertiary Deposits',
Philosophical Magazine, ser. 3, Vol. x. p.1

Charlesworth, E. (1837), 'Notice of the Occurrence of Voluta Lamberti
on the Suffolk coast; with Observations upon its claim to rank with
existing Species', *Magazine of Natural History,* Ser. 2, Vol. I, p.35

Charlesworth, E. (1837), 'Observations upon Voluta Lamberti, with a
Description of a Gigantic Species of Terebratula from the Coralline
Crag', *Magazine of Natural History,* Ser. 2, Vol. I, p.90

Charlesworth, E. (1837), 'Notice of a new Fossil Shell from the Coast of
Suffolk', *Magazine of Natural History,.* Ser. 2, Vol. I, p.218

Charlesworth, E. (1837), 'Notice of the Teeth of Carcharias megalodon
occurring in the Red Crag of Suffolk', *Magazine of Natural History,* Ser.
2, Vol. I, p.225

Charlesworth, E. (1838), 'Notice of the Vertebrate Animals occurring in
Tertiary Beds of Norfolk and Suffolk', *Magazine of Natural History*, Ser.
2, Vol. ii, p.40

Charlesworth, E. (1839), 'Illustrated Geological Notices, 1 On the
discovery of a portion of an Opossum's Jaw in the London Clay near

Woodbridge, Suffolk, 2 On some Fossil Teeth of the Genus Lamna from the same deposit', *Magazine of Natural History,* Ser. 2, Vol. iii, p.448

Charlesworth, E. (1845), 'On the Occurrence of the Genus Physter (or Sperm Whale) in the Red Crag at Felixstowe.' *Proceedings of the Geological Society,* Vol. iv. p.286; *Quarterly Journal of the Geological Society,* Vol. I. p.40

Charlesworth, E. (1868), 'On the prospective Annihilation of the Suffolk Red Crag Phosphatic stones, "Coprolite." Norwich Geol. Soc. Lecture, Norwich Mercury, 10th Oct. *Geological Magazine,* Vol. v. p.577

Charlesworth, E. (1872), 'Exhibition and description of some remarkable objects found in the Suffolk Crag Formation simulating human workmanship', *Journal of the Anthropological Institute,* Vol. ii, no. 1, p.51

Charlesworth, E. (1878), '*Fossil Exploration of Suffolk Crag (Orford Castle), and Hampshire Eocene Cliffs*', pp. 8, London Privately printed

Chatwin, C. P. (1961), '*East Anglia and Adjoining Areas,*' Her Majesty's Stationary Office

Clarke, W.B. (1838), 'Letter in reference to the alleged occurrence of the bones of terrestrial mammalia in the red and coralline Crag of Suffolk, *Magazine of Natural History,* Ser. 2, Vol. II, p.224

Clarke, W.B. (1851), 'A few remarks upon the Crag of Suffolk', *Annals of the Magazine of Natural History,* ser. 2, Vol. VIII, pp.205-11

Dalton, W.H. (1886), 'The Geology of the Country around Aldborough, Framlingham, Orford and Woodbridge', (Quarter Sheets 49S and 50 SE), *Memoirs of the Geological Survey.*

Desnoyers, J. (1838), 'Considerations upon the position of the tertiary System to which the Faluns of the Loire and the crag of England ought to be referred; and upon the difficulty of determining their relative age solely by the law of proportional number of fossil species analogous to species now in existence', *Magazine of Natural History,* Ser. 2, Vol. II, p.111 (partly translated from *Bulletin of Societe Geologique,.* France, t. viii, p.203, (1837)

Duncan, P.M. (1873), 'On Carophyllia Bredia, Milne-Edwards and Jules Haime, from the Red Crag of Woodbridge', *Quarterly Journal of the Geological Society,* Vol. XXIX, p.503

Dyke, G.V. (1993), *'John Lawes of Rothamsted - Pioneer of Science, Farming and Industry'*, Hoos Press, Harpenden, p.15

Eade, David, (18--), *'Rambles in Cambridgeshire'*, Soham, p.48

East Anglian Handbook, 1872-74; 1878-1879, pp.3ff

Ellison, D. 'Coprolites in the Orwell area,' *Orwell History Topics*

Falconer, H. (1857), 'Mastodon,' *Quarterly Journal of the Geological Society,* p.358;

'First Annual Report of the Commissioner of Agriculture of the State of South Carolina', Walker, Evans & Cogswell, (Charleston, 1880), pp.11-12.)

Fison's Journal, 'The Early Fertiliser years 1843-1929,' No.77, December 1963

Fison's News, 'Ipswich Firm's Remarkable Development,' S.C.R.O. 668.6

Flower, W.H. (1876), 'Description of the skull of a Species of Xiphodon, Cuvier', *Proceedings of the Zoological Society,* p.3

Flower, W.H. (1877), 'On Occurrence of Remains of Hyaenarctos in Red Crag of Suffolk,' *Quarterly Journal of the Geological Society,* p.534

Forsythe, S. M. (1988) *'The Foxhall Peoples: An Encounter between Archaeology and The URANTIA Book,* Scientific Symposium I

Fowle, K. (1992), *'Coton through the Ages'*, personal publication

Gathercole, A. F. (1959), 'Fenland Village,' *Fison's Journal,* No.64 Sept. pp.24-9

Geological Magazine, William Colchester's Obituary, March 1899

George, W. & Vincent, S. (1976), 'Some river exposures of London Clay in Suffolk and Essex', Tertiary Research, Vol. 1, pp.25-28

Goodwin, H. ("Humble Gumble") (1854) 'Letters from Felixstowe'

Graham, J. (1839), 'A Treatise on the Use and Value of Manure', London p.6; Pusey, P. (1840), Journal of the Royal Agricultural Society, England, p.1

Gray, A.N. (1930), *'Phosphate and Superphosphate'*, pp.110-111

Gray, A. N. (1944), *Phosphates and Superphosphates,* London

Grove, R. (1976), *'The Cambridgeshire Coprolite Mining Rush.'* (Oleander Press, Cambridge, 1976)

Gunn, Rev. J. (1868), Lecture to Norwich Geol. Soc.,' *Geological Magazine,* Vol. v. pp.578-9

Hailstone, Rev. J. (1816), 'Outlines of the Geology of Cambridgeshire', *Philosophical Transactions of the Royal Society*, pp.243-250

Hall, A. D. (1909) *'Fertilizers and Manures'*

Harrod's County Directory, *'Suffolk'*, 1858, 1873, 1877, 1883

Henslow, J.S. (1845), 'On Concretions in the Red Crag at Felixstowe, Suffolk,' *Proceedings of the Geological Society,* Vol iv, no. 99, p.281 and *Quarterly Journal of the Geological Society,* Vol.I.p.35

Henslow, J.S. (1846), 'On Nodules, apparently Coprolitic, from the Red Crag, etc.' *Report of the British. Association for the Advancement of Science, fo*r 1845, Sections, p.51

Henslow, J.S.(1846), 'Analysis of Crag nodules', *London Geological Journal,* No.1, September

Henslow, J.S. (1848), 'On Detritus derived from the London Clay and Deposited in the Red Crag,' *Report of the British Association for the Advancement of Science, fo*r 1847, Sections, p.64

Henslow, J.S.(1848), 'On Fossil Phosphates', *Gardeners' Chronicle and Agricultural Gazette*, p.180

Henslow, J.S.(1848), 'On the Phosphate Nodules of Felixstowe in Suffolk', *Gardeners' Chronicle and Agricultural Gazette*, p.764

Henslow, J.S.(1856), 'Phosphate of Lime', Report of an Ipswich museum Lecture, *Ipswich Journal,* 23rd February

Herapath, T.J. (1851), 'Some Observations on the Chemical Composition and Agricultural Value of the Fossil Bones and Pseudo-Coprolites of the Crag', *Journal of the Royal Agricultural Society,*. Vol. xii, pp.91-3

Hooker, J.J. (1979), 'Two new condylarths (Mammalia) from the early Eocene of Southern England', *Bulletin of the British Museum of Natural History, (Geol.)* Vol.32, pp.43-56

Hooker, J.J. (1979), 'The succession of Hyracotherium (Perissodactyla, Mammalia) from the early Eocene of Southern England', *Bulletin of the British Museum of Natural History, (Geol.)* Vol.33, pp.101-114

Hooker, J.J. (1984),'A primitive ceratomorph (Perissodactyla, Mammalia) from the early Tertiary of Europe', *Zoological Journal of the Linnean Society,* Vol. LXXXII, pp.229-244

Hopkins, S. Original MS in possession of Deacon of Bassingbourn Congregational Church, pp.210ff, Xerox copies in Cambs. Collection and C.U.L.)

Ipswich Borough Council, 'Artist's Views of Ipswich and its Waterfront over Two Centuries,'

Ipswich Dock Commission Report 1871

Jenyns, Rev. L. Bottisham, Lecture notes in C.C.R.O..

Jenyns, Rev. L (1866), 'On the Phosphatic Nodules obtained in the Eastern Counties, and used in Agriculture.' Proceedings of Bath Natural History Field Club, Vol. I, pp.9,17, 112

Jobson, A. (1968), 'The Felixstowe Story', Robert Hale

Jobson, A, (1967) 'In Suffolk's Border' Robert Hale

Johnson-Sollas, W. (1872), 'Upper Greensand Formation of Cambs.' Quarterly Journal of the Geological Society, p.402

Keatley, W. S. (1976), '100 Years of Fertiliser Manufacture,' Fertiliser Manufacturers Association)

Kelly's Post Office Directory, Norfolk, 1874, 1879, 1883, 1892

Kiln, A. (1969), 'The Coprolite Industry', Thesis for Putteridge Bury College, p.32

Kingston, A. (1889) 'Old and New Industries on the Cam.' Warren Press, Royston p.16

Kirby, J. (1764), 'Suffolk Traveller'

Knox and Ellison (1979) 'A Lower Eocene Ash Sequence in SE England', Journal of the Geological Society, London, Vol.136, pp.251-3

Kowallis, Gay P. (1970), 'To the Great Salt Lake from Litlington,' Bassingbourn

Lankester, E. (1864), 'On a new Species of Hyaena from the Red Crag of Suffolk, Annals of the Natural History Society, Ser. 3, Vol. xiii, p.56

Lankester, E. (1864), 'On New Mammalia from the Red Crag', Annals of the Natural History Society, Ser. 3, Vol. xiv, p.353

Lankester, E. (1865), 'On a Sources of the Mammalian Fossils of the Red Crag, and on the Discovery of a new Mammal in that Deposit, allied to the Walrus', Quarterly Journal of the Geological Society, Vol. xxi, pp.221-32

Lankester, (1868), 'On the Crags of Suffolk and Antwerp', *Geological Magazine*, Vol. 2 pp.103-6, 149-52; Lankester, (1868), 'The Suffolk Bone Bed and the Diestian or Black Crag in England', *Geological Magazine*, Vol. 5, pp.254-8

Lankester, E. (1870), 'Contributions to a knowledge of the Newer Tertiaries of Suffolk and their Fauna', *Quarterly Journal of the Geological Society,* Vol. XXVI, p.493

Liebig, J. (1840), *'Organic Chemistry in its Applications to Agriculture & Physiology*

Liebig, (1843) *'Familiar Letters of Chemistry'*

Lucas, C. (1930), *'The Fenman's World - Memories of a Fenland Physician,'* Norwich, p.25

Lydekker, R. (1885), *'Catalogue of the Fossil Mammalia in the British Museum* (Natural History), Cromwell Road, London S.W.

Lyell, C. (1840) 'On the occurrence of Fossil Quadrumanous Marsupial and other Mammalia in the London Clay near Woodbridge in Suffolk, *Annual Magazine of Natural History,* Vol. iv, p.186-189

Manwaring Paine, J. & Way, J. T. (1848), 'On the Phosphoric Strata of the Chalk Formation', *Journal of the Royal Agricultural Society,* Vol. IX, pp.78-9

Markham, R. J. (1976), 'Notes on Edward Charlesworth, 1813-1893', *Ipswich Geological Group Bulletin* no. XVIII, pp.14-16

Markham, R.J. (1982), 'Analysis of Phosphatic Nodules and bones from the Crags to determine Phosphate content', *Ipswich Geological Group Bulletin* no. XX, pp.16-19

Maycock, C. (1993), *'Charity, Clay and Coprolites – The Story of a Suffolk Almshouse Foundation,'* Mary Warner's Charity, Boyton

Mineral Statistics, *Memoirs of the Geological Survey,* HMSO, vol. I, 1850?, pp.40-1; 1860, p.375; 1876, p.132; 1877, p.145; 1878, p.147

Moffatt, H. (2002) *' Ships and Shipyards of Ipswich 1700 - 1970'*, Malthouse Press, Suffolk, p.132

Moir, J. R. (1918), 'The Kyson Monkey', *Geological Magazine*, Vol. LV, p.48

Moir, J.R. (1935), *'Prehistoric Archaeology and Sir Ray Lankester',* Norman Adlard, & Co. Ipswich

Morton, J.C. (1855), 'A Cyclopaedia of Agriculture,' Glasgow, p.545
Newton, E.T. (1891), 'The Vertebrata of the Pliocene Deposits of Britain, Memoirs of the Geological Survey,
Newton, E.T. (1890), 'On some new Mammals from the Red and Norwich Crags', Quarterly Journal of the Geological Society, Vol. XLVI, p.444
Oakley, K. (1941), 'British Phosphates', Wartime Pamphlets, Vol. VIII no.3
O'Connor, B. (1998), 'The Dinosaurs on Bassingbourn Fen', Bernard O'Connor, Everton
O'Connor, B. (1998), 'The Dinosaurs on Coldham's Common', Bernard O'Connor, Everton
O'Connor, B. (2000), 'The Dinosaurs of Fen Ditton', Bernard O'Connor, Everton
O'Dell, I. (1951), 'A Vanished Industry' (original MS in Luton Museum) pp.7-8
Owen, R. (1839), 'Description of the Fossil mentioned in the preceding letter', Annual Magazine of Natural History,. Ser. 2, Vol. iii, p.446
Owen, R. (1840), 'Description of the Mammalian Remains found at Kyson in Suffolk', Annual Magazine of Natural History Vol. iv, p.191
Owen, R. (1840), 'Description of some Molar Teeth from the Eocene Sand at Kyson in Suffolk, indicative of a new species of Hyracotherium', Annual Magazine of Natural History, Vol. viii, p.1
Owen, R. (1846), 'A History of British Fossil Mammals and Birds', London
Owen, R. (1856), Note in Quarterly Journal of the Geological Society, Vol. xii, p.217
Owen, R. (1862), 'On the Hyratherian Character of the Lower Molars of the supposed Macacus from the Eocene Sand of Kyson, Suffolk', Annual Magazine of Natural History, Ser.3, Vol. x, p.240
Packard, W.G.T. (1937), Superphosphate – its history and manufacture,' Transactions of the Institution of Chemical Engineers, xv, pp.21-2
Packard, W.G.T. (1952), 'The History of the Fertiliser Industry in Britain,' pp.8-10,14

Packard, W.G.T. (1952), *Proceedings of the Fertiliser Society,* London, p.19

Palgrave, D. (1991), Was your ancestor a coprolite digger? *Suffolk Roots,* Vol.17.No 3, pp.149-151

Palgrave, D.(2003), Employees in the Suffolk Phosphate Industry in 1881 *Suffolk Roots,* Vol.29. pp.175-178

Pickering Rev. R (1745) *Philosophical Transactions,* Vol. XLIII, No. 474, pp.191-2

Playfair, L.B. '(1850?), The Study of Abstract Science Essential to the Progress of Industry,' *Mem. Geol. Surv.* Mineral Statistics, Vol. I,

Prestwich, J. (1850), 'On the Structure of the strata between the London Clay and the Chalk. Pt. I The Basement-bed of the London Clay,' *Quarterly Journal of the Geological Society,* Vol. vi, pp. 252-281

Prestwich, J. (1868), 'Structure of Crag Beds,' *Quarterly Journal of the Geological Society,* p.460

Prestwich, J. (1871), 'Structure of the Crag Beds,' *Quarterly Journal of the Geological Society,* (read 1868) p.122)

Prestwich, J. (1871), 'Structure of the Red Crag,' *Quarterly Journal of the Geological Society,* Vol. XXVII, pp.326, 337

Proceedings of the British Association for the Advancement of Science, (1851), Ipswich

Pusey, P. (1840), *Journal of Royal Agricultural Society*, England, p.1

Reid, W.C. (1876), Mineral Phosphates and Superphosphate of Lime', *Chemical News,* Vol. XXXIV, pp.48, 55

Reid, W.C. (1890), 'Pliocene deposits of Britain', *Memoirs of the Geological Survey,* p.16

'Reminiscences of a Scientific Suffolk Clergyman,' *Eastern Counties Magazine & Suffolk Notebook*, Vol. I)

Roe, D. A. (1981). *The Lower and Middle Palaeolithic Periods in Britain,* Routledge & Kegan Paul, pp.177-78

Rogers, G. *The Parish Magazine,* (Grantchester) Oct. 1983

Slater's Directory, 1850

Special Report on Mineral Resources of Great Britain No.5, *M.G.S.* 1916

Spencer, H.E.P., '*A contribution to the History of Suffolk - Lowestoft,'* undated, pp.118-20

Strong, B. 'The Accounts of a Suffolk Blacksmith 1859 - 1881', *Journal of the Tools and Trades History Society*, Vol.9, pp. 55, 63

Tattersall, Ian, Eric Delson and John Van Couvering, eds. (1988). *Encyclopaedia of Human Evolution and Prehistory*, Garland Publishing, p.275

Taylor, J.E., (1880), 'Phosphates: Their Origins and Uses', *Nature's Bypaths*, pp.140-151

'The Farming of Cambridgeshire,' *Journal of the Royal Agricultural Society*, 1847, p.71

The Journal of the Society of the Chemical Industry, November 30th 1898

'The Study of Abstract Science Essential to the Progress of Industry,' *M.G.S.*, Mineral Statistics, Vol. I, (1850?), pp.40-1

Thorpe, *Dictionary of Applied Chemistry*, pp.507-10

Thursk and Imray, (1958), *'Suffolk Farming in the Nineteenth Century'*, Ipswich, p.81

Tye, W. (1930), 'Birth of the Fertilizer Industry, *Fison's Journal*, p.4

Tye, W. (1950), '*A Guide to Waldringfield and Newbourn*', Norman Allard & Co. Ipswich, p.16

Victoria County History, 'Suffolk,' Vol. ii p.286

Vallois, Henri V., and Hallam L. Movius, eds., (1953). *Catalogue des Hommes Fossiles*, XIX Congres Geologique International, Algiers, p.210

Victoria County History, 'Suffolk', pp.285-6

Voelcker, A. (1862), '*The International Exhibition at Paris*,' p.149

Voelcker, Dr. A. (1875), 'On the Chemical Composition and Commercial Value of Coprolites and other Phosphatic Materials used in England for Agricultural Purposes', *Journal of the Royal Agricultural Society*, pp.359-60, 399

Way, J. T. (1849), 'On the Composition and Value of Guano', *Journal of the Royal Agricultural Society*, Vol. x., p.215

Whitaker, W. (1877), *Proceedings of the Geological Society*, Vol. v. p.112

Whitaker, W. (1885), 'The Geology of the Country around Ipswich, Hadleigh and Felixstowe', *Memoirs of the Geological Society*, London

Whitaker, W. *(1921), 'Water Supply of Cambs.' Memoirs of the Geological Society, London, p.84*
White, (1844), 'History, Gazetteer and Directory of Suffolk', pp.31-34
Wiggins, J. *Quarterly Journal of the Geological Society,* Vol. iv, p.294
Wood, S.V. (1839), 'Letter announcing the discovery of Fossil Quadrumanous Remains near Woodbridge, Suffolk', *Magazine of Natural History,.* Ser. 2, Vol. iii, p.444
Wood, S.V. and Harmer, F. W., (1877), 'Later Tertiary Geology of East Anglia', *Quarterly Journal of the Geological Society,* Vol. XXXIII, p.75
Woodward, H. (1866), 'An Excursion to the Crag District,' *Intelligent Observer,* Vol. VIII, p.37, 39)
Yates, R. *'History of Potton,'* Unpublished paper, Potton History Society, p.44

Newspaper articles

Bedfordshire Times, May 18th 1962. from an original article in 1878
Cambridge Chronicle, 17th October 1863
Cambridge Chronicle, 30th November, 1867, p.8
Cambridge Chronicle, 7th January 1871 pp.8-9
Cambridge Independent Press, 18th January, 1851, p.3
Cambridge Independent Press, 7th January 1871 p.5
Charlesworth, E. (1868), 'Remarks on the prospective exhaustion of the phosphatic Crag stratum' Norwich Mercury, 10th October; also in reprint of Lankester, E.R. 1877 'The Crag Fossils in the Ipswich Museum, Suffolk Chronicle, August 4th 1877
Charlesworth, E. (1872), 'On Perforated Stones from the Suffolk Crag', Eastern Daily Press, April 6th
Charlesworth, E. (1872), 'Exhibition and description of some remarkable objects found in the Suffolk Crag Formation simulating human workmanship', Pall Mall Gazette, April 10th
Charlesworth, E. (1872), 'Perforated Sharks' Teeth found in the Red Crag of Suffolk', Pall Mall Gazette, April 10th
East Anglia Daily Times, 2nd June, 1880
East Anglia Daily Times, 5th June, 1880

Folkestone Chronicle, 29th October 1870

Folkestone Chronicle, 5th November 1870

Frank Leslie's Illustrated Newspaper ,June 30th 1877

'Ipswich Firm's remarkable Development – From "one-man" concerns to world-wide-organisation,' S.C.R.O. Newspaper Cutting File S 668.6 Fison's

Henslow, J.S. (1845), *Bury Post*,

Henslow, S.J. (1848), 'On Fossil Phosphates,' *Gardeners' Chronicle*, p.180

Henslow, S.J. (1848), 'On the Phosphate Nodules of Felixstowe in Suffolk,' *Gardeners' Chronicle*, p.764

Ipswich Journal, 30th August 1889

Lawrence, W. 'The Last Felixstowe Coproliter,' *Suffolk Chronicle and Mercury*, February 17th 1950, p.5

Leighton Buzzard Observer, 17th January 1871

Mark Lane Express, 27th April 1874

Midland Counties Herald, Feb.20th 1862

Norwich Argus, 'How Chemical Manures are manufactured', undated article in Suffolk County Record Office, Bury St Edmunds

Ogden, W. (1983), 'Suffolk shell solves museum mystery' *East Anglian Daily Times*, 21st October

Suffolk Chronicle, J.S. Henslow's article on the 'Phosphate Nodules of the Red Crag', 28th December, 1850

Suffolk Chronicle, W.D. Clarke's article 'Ipswich Museum Expedition to the Crag Diggings', January 15th 1851

Suffolk Chronicle, 26th November 1898

Suffolk Chronicle & Mercury, 'Down at the Falkenham "Dog" – Memories of the Coproliting Days,' 24th March 1950

Taylor, J,E. 'The Story of Felixstowe Cliff', *East Anglia Daily Times*, 23rd July 1891

The Illustrated London News, 26th August 1871

The Times, 8th July 1851, page 8

The Times. 29th July 1858, page 10

The Times, 14th December 1870, page 11

The Times, 6 April 1874, page 9

The Times, 5th June 1880, page 6

Tye, W. 'Coproliting in the Deben Peninsula,' pt.1, *Suffolk Chronicle and Mercury* 23rd December 1949

Tye, W. 'Coproliting in the Deben Peninsula,' pt.2, *Suffolk Chronicle and Mercury* 30th December 1949

Tye, W. 'Coproliting in the Deben Peninsula,' pt.3, *Suffolk Chronicle and Mercury*, 6th January 1950

Documents in Record Offices, Museums and various Archives

Abbot's Hall Museum, Suff. Photo Surv. Waldringfield photographs
Correspondence, Allied School, Felixstowe, 11th Nov. 1855
Bedfordshire County Record Office, Peel's Estate Papers, Sandy
Cambridgeshire County Record Office (CCRO) 1861 – 1891 census returns
CCRO. Borough of Camb. Minutes July 30th 1857
Ipswich Museum, anonymous note in Coprolite file
Cambridge Folk Museum, Porter, E. Notes on her conversation with C. A. Swann
Cambridge Folk Museum, Enid Porter's notebooks 15/64-65
Cambridge Railway Station, notes 15-D-2
CCRO. Lecture notes of Rev. L. Jenyns, Bottisham
CCRO. Rev. Conybeare's diaries, March 9th 1875
CCRO. Bidwell 43 p.181
CCRO. Little Eversden Parish Vestry Minutes;
CCRO. Cambridge Session Orders 1869-1874 pp.26,69-70,91,118-121,133-8,187-195,235-244
CCRO. Guardians of Cambridge Annals. Annual Minutes 9th December 1868
CCRO. Francis Bill Books A-N 1863 pp.347,362
Cambridge University Library. Add.7652 II Q
Charleston Museum, South Carolina, unidentified publication in Major E.W. Willis's scrapbook, Marine and River Phosphate Mining Co

Fertiliser Manufacturers Association, (FMA.) Peterborough, Railway Rates 1888-94; Commercial matters 1890-98; Ann. Rpt. 1916-17 p.76, App. pp.xi-xv

Ipswich Museum, Markham, R. Notes on Edward Charlesworth, 1813-1893

Museum of East Anglian Life, Stowmarket, Norsk Hydro file,

Rothamsted Library Archives, A1, Lawes to Henslow 13th June 1845

St. John's College, Cambridge, Muniments 162.7/4

Suffolk County Record Office (SCRO), Boyton Terrier, 1879

SCRO. CB412:4125 Box 2

SCRO. FC47.A1/1

SCRO. FC54 A2/1 p52

SCRO. GB412:4125, Box 2, Minute Book 21/9/1867 - 6/8/1941

SCRO. HA 38/2/76-90

SCRO. HA 65/2/46-48

SCRO. HA 119 50/3/209

SCRO. HA 119 50/3/2 Walton Papers

SCRO. HA 119 50/3/209

SCRO. HB 10/9/60/48

SCRO. HB 416/F.2 pp.13, 31, 63, 81, 91, 127, 153

SCRO. HC 434.8728.227-9, 269, 310a

SCRO. Ipswich Dock Commission report 1871

SCRO. HD 328/1 Waldringfield

SCRO. 1851 – 1891 census returns; 1871 Vol. I, p.353

SCRO. "Humble Gumble," (Hervey Goodwin), (1854) 'Letters from Felixstowe'

Suffolk County Sites and Monuments Records. 03026, 03054, 03678

Valence House Museum, Dagenham, Lawes Chemical Manure Co. Minute Book, ,1872-79, 16th November 1880; 21st June, 29th August, 1881, 1882

Account book in possession of Mr. C.A.P. Waller, Bury St. Edmunds

Parish Book in possession of Rev. Trevor Waller, Waldringfield Rectory, Woodbridge

Hopkins, S. Original MS in possession of Deacon of Bassingbourn Congregational Church, pp.210ff., Xerox copies in Cambs. Collection and CUL.

Local Directories and Handbooks

East Anglia Handbook, 1872-74, 1878-1879 pp.3ff
Harrods County Directory, Suffolk, 1858, 1873, 1877, 1883
Kelly's Post Office Directory, Suffolk, 1858, 1873, 1874, 1877, 1883, 1885, 1892
Kelly's Post Office Directory, Norfolk, 1879, 1883, 1892
Slater's Directory, Suffolk, 1850
White's History, Gazetteer and Directory of Suffolk, 1850, 1855, 1874

Ordnance Survey Maps

1st Edition 25" Suffolk
(1881), 68.16, 75.2, 75.12, 75.15, 83.3, 83.15 89.1,
(1889), 90.1,90.2,
(1890), 69SW,
(1891), 69NW, 76SE, 77NW, 83NW

Websites
http://www.ast.cam.ac.uk/~ipswich/Observatory/Tomline.htm
http://www.bbc.co.uk/suffolk/nature/walk_thru_time/05.shtml
http://www.eng-
h.gov.uk/archcom/projects/summarys/html97_8/2059.htm
http://www.eveningstar.co.uk/Content/columns/kindred/htm/040906
water.asp
http://www.gruts.com/darwin/articles/2000/henslow/index.php
http://www.ruralhistory.org/nof/victorianfarming
http://www.schooneryacht.com/resume.html
http://www.snapevillage.org.uk/indexfr.html?framed/aboutsnape_info
.html~info
http://www.stowman.fsnet.co.uk/prentice_family.htm

http://www.yara.com/en/about/yara_centennial/heritage/fisons_inter
.html
http://www.yara.com/en/about/yara_centennial/heritage/fisons_inter
.html
http://www.waldringfield.info/1850-1950.htm)
http://en.wikipedia.org/wiki/John_Bennet_Lawes

,

www.ingramcontent.com/pod-product-compliance
Lightning Source LLC
Chambersburg PA
CBHW071411090426
42737CB00011B/1429